THE HILLWALKER'S
GUIDE TO MOUNTAINEERING
ESSENTIAL SKILLS FOR BRITAIN'S CLASSIC ROUTES

ABOUT THE AUTHORS

This book has been co-written by two authors who bring the distinctive and complementary perspectives of expert and enthusiast to the subject of making a safe and satisfying transition from hillwalking to mountaineering.

Stuart Johnston MIC

Stuart Johnston is one of Britain's foremost mountaineering guides, instructors and trainers, running winter and summer courses for all levels of mountain enthusiast, from beginner to aspiring leader or climbing professional. A member of the Association of Mountaineering Instructors, and a holder of the UK's highest qualification in the field – the Mountain Instructor's Certificate – Stuart is also a consultant adviser on outdoor health and safety, and a qualified instructor on Wilderness EMT (Emergency Medical Technician) courses.

Stuart runs a successful climbing, adventure and training business from his base in Perth, Scotland, delivering courses throughout Britain and overseas for individuals, groups, clubs, businesses, schools and other organisations. He is co-author of the best-selling *Mountain Skills Training Handbook*, and an associate member of staff at Glenmore Lodge, Scotland's National Outdoor Training Centre in the Cairngorms.

Stuart Johnston Mountaineering can be contacted at www.climbmts.co.uk

Terry Adby

Terry Adby is a freelance writer with an interest in outdoor, adventure, environmental and travel themes. His writing has appeared in *The Daily Telegraph, Scotland on Sunday, The Telegraph Magazine, Trail, On the Hill, High Mountain Sports, Climbing, Focus, Quicksilver* and *Spain* magazine, plus numerous specialist and business publications. A member of the Outdoor Writers' Guild, Terry is a hillwalking mountaineer who has walked, scrambled and trekked in locations including Britain, the Himalaya and the Pyrenees. When summer or winter climbing, usually in Scotland, he gets by with a little help from his friends.

Terry lives and works in York, from where he has also run an independent public relations and marketing consultancy business since 1993. He can be contacted at www.terryadby.com

THE HILLWALKER'S GUIDE TO MOUNTAINEERING

ESSENTIAL SKILLS FOR BRITAIN'S CLASSIC ROUTES

by
Terry Adby and Stuart Johnston

2 POLICE SQUARE, MILNTHORPE, CUMBRIA, LA7 7PY
www.cicerone.co.uk

British Library Cataloguing-in-Publication Data. A catalogue record for this book is available from the British Library.

ACKNOWLEDGEMENTS

We would like to acknowledge the help and support of those people and organisations who contributed in one way or another to the production of *The Hillwalker's Guide to Mountaineering*.

A number of people – friends, colleagues and professionals – have given generously of their time and knowledge.

Christel Langeveld made a more patient and easier-on-the-eye(!) photographic model than the authors could ever have done for the purpose of illustrating the technical sections. Simon Steer, a qualified Wilderness Emergency Medical Technician, drafted the mountain first aid section, and what is included here is largely his work. Duncan MacDonald and Christel (again) made excellent first aiders and 'casualties' for the camera. Duncan also helped with some of the technical shots.

Bruce Goodlad UIAGM, a highly regarded and experienced Alpine guide, acted as technical editor on our draft, and made a number of important contributions and observations.

Naomi Tuck allowed us to use her work as the basis for many of the navigation illustrations. Simon Melia from Capel Curig was a great help with the Ogwen Valley routes. Jeremy Ashcroft produced the line illustrations of the routes we have included, which are artworks in their own right.

When compiling the route descriptions we were both struck by how often it was possible for one or both of us to have completed a route without getting a decent photograph of it! We are grateful to John Cleare, Gary Latter, Kirk Watson, and Tom Bailey (courtesy of *Trail* magazine), whose pictures helped dig us out of this particular hole. All uncredited photographs were taken by the authors.

Mountain Spirit, the Aviemore outdoor and telemark shop, generously supplied Haglofs clothing and other gear for photography, which made it look like we always keep things looking nice and shiny. We would also particularly like to thank DMM, Grivel, Salomon, Leki, Mountain Equipment, Silva, Petzl, Thermarest, Anquet Maps, X-Socks, and their UK distributors for their assistance.

Jonathan Williams at Cicerone provided an enthusiastic and immediate response to our original proposal for this guide. The Cicerone team have been not only helpful and instrumental in making our manuscript, photos and illustrations look like a book, but also, in respect of deadlines, patient! We would also like to thank Sue Viccars for her skill and attention to detail in editing our manuscript.

This list would be incomplete without thanking everyone (well, almost!) with whom we have ever shared a day on the hills, either individually or together. While it may not always seem so at the time, almost any day spent in the mountains is both a satisfying experience and, at some level, an educational one. When we go to the hills in company both can be enhanced.

Finally, this book could never have been written without the support of our long-suffering families who (most of the time, anyway!) just left us to get on with it, putting up with essential 'writing, research and photography' absences, evenings and weekends spent staring at computer screens, and interminable telephone conversations about 'the book'. By definition it is dedicated to them.

Terry Adby and Stuart Johnston, September 2003

Front cover: On the Cuillin Ridge traverse, descending the south ridge of Sgurr à Ghreadaidh
Back Cover: On the Cneifon Arête, Glyderau, Snowdonia

CONTENTS

The Cuillin Ridge on Skye: where 'walking' becomes mountaineering

WARNING

Mountaineering can be a dangerous activity carrying a risk of personal injury or death. It should be undertaken only by those with a full understanding of the risks and with the training and experience to evaluate them. Mountaineers should be appropriately equipped for the routes undertaken. Whilst every care and effort has been taken in the preparation of this book, the user should be aware that conditions can be highly variable and can change quickly. Holds may become loose or fall off, rockfall can affect the character of a route, and, in winter, snow and avalanche conditions must be carefully considered. These can materially affect the seriousness of a climb, tour or expedition.

Therefore, except for any liability which cannot be excluded by law, neither Cicerone nor the authors accept liability for damage of any nature (including damage to property, personal injury or death) arising directly or indirectly from the information in this book.

PART ONE
FROM HILLWALKING TO MOUNTAINEERING

WHEN IS A WALK NOT A WALK?

There was a time when climbing meant climbing, and hillwalking meant walking, and everyone knew where they stood in the mountains – either on steep ground, or off it. But as walking, climbing, and outdoor activities generally have grown in popularity, something significant has changed – the meaning of 'walk'. The dictionary definition may charmingly recall the days when it meant putting one foot in front of the other. But much of what you'll find on the 'climbing and walking' shelves of your local shop – or in any month's offering from the UK's outdoor press – suggests something more.

So, to which 'walks' does the modern hillwalker aspire? Well, the easier stuff includes, say, the slanting traverse of Jack's Rake across the sheer face of Pavey Ark in Langdale – a grade 1 scramble, once classed as an 'Easy' rock climb. Few writers will suggest you need a rope or advanced climbing skills on this ground. On the other hand, few walkers will feel totally at their ease here. Which is not to say they don't enjoy it – on the contrary, they love it!

Other routes that have a habit of popping up in 'best walks' books are more serious still. Curved Ridge, for instance, on Buachaille Etive Mor, offers technical and demanding ground for anyone but an accomplished rock-jock. And just down the road in Glen Coe the Aonach Eagach lures you in like a slumbering dragon with miles of tricky scrambling along its spiny dorsal, lots of exposure, big drops and a long way from help. If this is walking, why aren't you up there with your grandmother on a Sunday afternoon?

These and other similarly challenging routes are the objectives that today's ambitious hillwalkers aspire to in their thousands. But are they really 'walks'? The term 'scrambling' is used of course, but even this – particularly to the less experienced mountain-goer – can sometimes seem like a slightly cosy description that glosses over the true seriousness of the situation. The vagaries of grading this semi-technical ground are not always very helpful either. Learning what scrambling grades mean by experience is all very well – as long as you survive the experience.

The fact is that to be negotiated confidently, enjoyably and – most important of all – safely, mountain journeys such as these demand a combination of skills and equipment that are essential to safe travel in the hills when a variety of ground, including steep terrain, is to be negotiated. In other words, the *ambitions* of the hillwalker require the *skills* of the mountaineer.

The aim of this book is to teach and illustrate this essential mountaineering skill-set, and to describe a selection of classic British mountaineering routes where the techniques and equipment involved can, with time and the right approach, be successfully applied in summer conditions.

Winter Mountaineering

This is a much bigger subject and, under full winter conditions, any of the routes covered will require a much higher level of technical climbing ability than lies within the scope of this book. Nevertheless, it's odds-on that most hillwalkers who will enjoy the challenges discussed will want a piece of the winter mountains too, and so we include a chapter on essential winter walking skills.

This book is not a comprehensive manual; on the contrary, it is intended to keep things short, practical and to the point. The skills you will find here are taught with a view to tackling some of Britain's classic mountaineering terrain, and in describing sections of routes where they can be applied we have paid most attention to the climbing or technical passages, as these are the sections where the challenge to the budding mountaineer is most keenly focused.

Overall, the skills taught are intended to be an economical selection of practical and relatively easy-to-acquire techniques that can be directly applied. Inevitably, these include 'single-pitch' climbing skills, but in our opinion most ambitious hillwalkers aspire to be – in fact, by definition, are – mountaineers, rather than rock climbers. They aspire not so much to a day at a roadside crag or a full-on encounter with a massive rock wall, as to committing and rewarding mountain journeys that combine mountaineering skills such as scrambling, bivouacking, navigation and ropework. We hope this book will help some of their aspirations to be met.

WHERE DO YOU START?

The most popular 'walks' in Britain involve one, or a number of, classic 'crux' challenges, that teeter on the brink of being too scary, exposed or technical for many of the people who attempt them. Most who do, however, somehow manage to drag themselves up, over or along them. These are typically grade 1 scrambles in very popular areas – routes like Striding Edge, Sharp Edge or the aforementioned Jack's Rake in the Lake District, or Crib Goch, Bristly Ridge and Tryfan North Ridge in Snowdonia. The relatively low accident rates on these routes sometimes belie the trepidation they engender in the large number of marginally experienced hill-goers who undertake them each year. It also suggests that most wait, sensibly, for good conditions – in the wet

or wind they are all a distinctly more challenging proposition. But the point is that most people manage them, usually rope-free, enjoy them – and want more! More routes, more challenges and more mountaineering experiences.

If you recognise yourself in all this it's hardly surprising. Most fit and active hillwalkers can enjoy a grade 1 scramble, albeit aspects of the experience may give them cause to recall Noel Williams' bleak warning that 'unroped scrambling in exposed situations is potentially the most dangerous of all mountaineering activities' (see Further Reading). Even if they've never heard those words, the thought has probably occurred to them. It's hard to deny that the element of 'frisson' is – if only retrospectively on some occasions – part of the fun.

Beyond the level of grade 1 scrambling, things quickly get much more serious, and it is on mountaineering routes involving such sections – whether on the Cuillin Ridge or St Sunday Crag in the Lakes – that many people find either they are at (or beyond) the limit of their current abilities, or that they are taking unacceptable risks. This is when they, or perhaps a member of their party, need to master a new set of skills and techniques to fulfil their aspirations, and this is the skill-set described in this book.

The selection of classic routes that we go on to describe here vary enormously in degree of difficulty and seriousness – for many Tower Ridge on Ben Nevis, for instance, will be a distant goal of which they can, as yet, only dream. Nevertheless, the specialist skills of the mountaineer can start to be applied at a much lower level than this. We have largely concentrated on routes that involve terrain where the crux is categorised at grade 2 and above, the one possible exception being a direct ascent of Tryfan's famous North Ridge. Of course in less than perfect conditions, climbing-related skills are likely to be called for on many British grade 1 scrambling routes. In any case, it should not be forgotten that successfully negotiating the mountaineering journeys featured here involves much more than merely overcoming the technical sections.

THE GRADE DEBATE

Few systems are perfect, and the British system for grading scrambles and climbs certainly isn't. Grading is perhaps more of an art than a science, and as such there's a large element of subjectivity in it. Until you get to a route you never really know what you are going to find. Its grade is just a starting point, usually quite a useful one. However, the advice given in this book should help you deal with what you do find when you get there.

Grade Definitions

The definitions of scrambling grades below are taken from one of Britain's most popular early scrambling guides, Brian Evans' *Scrambles in the Lake District*, first published in 1982 (Cicerone Press): they are certainly as good as any.

Grade 1 is a straightforward scramble, with little or no route finding difficulty. The described route takes the most interesting line, which can usually be varied or even avoided at will. Generally, the exposure is not great, but even so, great care must be taken to avoid a slip.

Grade 2 will contain longer and more difficult stretches of scrambling, where a rope may be found useful for safety in the occasional exposed passages. Although individual sections of the scramble can usually be avoided, these sections may be inescapable once the scramble is underway. Some skill in route finding is required to follow the described line.

Grade 3 is a more serious proposition, only to be undertaken by competent parties. A rope is advisable for safety on occasional exposed passages, and for some pitches which demand easy rock climbing. A steady leader is required, with the ability to judge how the rest of the party are coping with the situation, and a rope should be used wherever the safety of an individual is in doubt.

Grade 3(S) denotes a particularly serious outing, perhaps containing a very exposed passage on poor rock or vegetation, which would be especially serious for a solo mountaineer. Recommended only for experienced and competent climbers.

A 'grade 3(S) Moderate' denotes a grade 3(S) with a significant section of Moderate grade rock climbing, and 'grade 3(S) Difficult' denotes one with at least one crux section at Difficult standard. Adding one, two or three stars indicates the overall interest and quality of the route.

Climbing Scramblers

The hillwalking mountaineer clearly has an interest in where scrambling ends and rock climbing begins, though it's not a simple division. As the scrambling descriptions above indicate, high-level scrambling includes sections (usually short) of graded rock-climbing terrain – 'Easy', 'Moderate' and even 'Difficult' – which, while still at the lower end of a system of rock-climbing grades that soon disappears off the scale for the scrambler, can feel like – and be – very serious ground. When we refer to 'climbers' in this book we are generally talking about hillwalking mountaineers operating on this sort of ground.

Misty and moody on the Clach Glas–Blaven traverse – but what's the grade?

Scrambling grades are not scientifically precise. Nor will they in any way sum up all the problems and difficulties you are likely to meet during a full day's mountaineering. Nevertheless, interpreting them and their significance is crucial to assessing important aspects of the level of challenge you will face when planning an outing.

Grades can be either summer or winter grades (the latter being generally far more serious and beyond the scope of this book). Summer grades assume good conditions, and anything less will almost inevitably increase the degree of difficulty or seriousness. The step from grade 1 scrambling to grade 2 can be big, and to grade 3 huge. Yet similarly some terrain can be transformed in grade by little more than, say, a rain shower or a stiff breeze.

Between routes categorised in the same grade there can also be distinctly different levels of difficulty, or nature of challenge. Striding Edge, for instance, generally gets a grade 1 for the terrain, but is basically a walk (a fantastic one, admittedly) on a narrow path on or below the crest, with exposure in the form of steep-sided slopes, and a bad step which is not too tricky. It's a superb position, but in terms of difficulty cannot be compared to the full-on grade 1 scrambling experience offered by, say, Bristly Ridge in the Glyderau or Llech Ddu in the Carneddau.

Differing Opinions

Grades can even be inconsistent on the same route. Research for this book alone has shown Glen Coe's Aonach Eagach to merit a grade 2 scramble, a grade 3 scramble, and a Moderate 3(S) rock climb – all assuming summer conditions. Two of our other chosen grade 3 routes are described elsewhere as being in one case of Moderate difficulty, and in another, Severe. There's nothing sinister in this – and we certainly do not have the definitive answer. The grades we have given our chosen routes are our opinion, nothing more.

It all proves the point that precise grading is largely a question of conditions and personal judgement. When it comes to actually tackling the route there's only one opinion that matters about how difficult it is, and that's your own. Regardless of what your route description says, you must be able to cope with what you find – whether that means completing the route safely, or withdrawing without incident (people have always reserved the right to run away when faced with danger – think of it as a noble art rather than a wimp out, because the ability to make the decision to retreat, and then to do so safely, is a survival skill you should always carry on the mountain).

DRAWING THE LINE

Scrambling grades may be largely subjective, but we need to a draw a line between aspects of the mountaineering activity covered in this book, and full-on rock climbing. If climbers crave the 'in-your-face' struggle with vertical rock and personal demons, and ambitious hillwalkers go for an expansive mountain journey at a less death-defying angle for the sheer sensation of 'being there', where's the middle ground? Most people will know intuitively where it falls for them, and it's probably some level of scrambling terrain. But for anyone wanting to take on the lessons of this book, the challenge is to shift that ground forward a bit. How far depends on your personal ambitions, but we have deliberately avoided routes that involve more than single-pitch climbing. None of the crux passages featured here is a multi-pitch climbing route. They all form part of mountain journeys that require the general mountaineering skills also described here, along with a degree of climbing knowledge, and the ability to apply both to a challenging objective.

So what is mountaineering? There's an ongoing debate in the outdoor community about where the different categories of mountain activity meet and merge. When does scrambling become climbing? When does hillwalking become mountaineering? A simple answer is 'who cares?', and we'll go with that. The important thing is not the name you give your chosen activity but that, when operating in the mountains, you know you have the skills, temperament and equipment to handle it.

Almost every mountain walker is a mountaineer by its broadest definition – 'a person who climbs mountains' – but when you get into the realms of steep terrain, serious exposure, sustained scrambling and technical equipment, many of the skills needed to perform safely are core mountaineering skills. You are not just playing at it. You might not be challenging Doug Scott for a place in the hall of fame, but many of the concerns you have, and techniques and equipment you use to address them, will be much the same.

A Mountain Apprenticeship

Exploring hills and mountains is a simple pastime which you can't help feeling should come naturally. But the fact is that – as with any craft – once you've decided to raise your game a bit, acquiring the skills to match your ambition takes time, practice, dedication and experience. The problem is that when we're on the learning curve in a mountain environment the stakes are always high, and events can outstrip experience in seconds. The Scottish writer Jim Crumley has written eloquently of the need for a mountaineering 'apprenticeship', a gradual process of learning about and understanding 'the greater scale and the greater forces' of the hills and their environment over a long period. 'You have to know how good you are; you have to know how bad the mountains can be,' he writes. The

problem is we don't all have the benefit of an outdoor-packed upbringing. Many people only discover the hills in their adult life, and then they want to get on with it. But limited experience and pressures of time can easily result in dangerous situations. Regardless of age and circumstances, a self-imposed 'apprenticeship' is important, if only because the consequences of rushing into things in the mountains are all too obvious.

As you develop your mountaineering ability you should try to practise new skills thoroughly in risk-free situations, and consolidate steadily. Do as many routes as you can at each grade. In the early days of climbing it was standard practice to do all the main routes in a particular grade before stepping up to the next level of difficulty. Nowadays it's all too easy to get 'fast-tracked' onto terrain you're not really equipped to handle. But if you raise your level of commitment gradually, you'll enjoy your climbing more and be a better mountaineer for it. As Crumley says, 'You have to know how your best matches up to the mountain's worst…There will be other days. The mountain will wait for you.'

A Modern Approach

It's appealing to believe the essential experience of being in the mountains now is the same as it was 50 or 100 years ago. That may be true, but at the same time mountaineering activities are constantly evolving in terms of equipment, knowledge and techniques. At the extreme end of the scale these advances have helped roll back the frontiers of what is humanly possible. But on a more down-to-earth level they can benefit everyone, no matter what their ability or ambition. This book concentrates on what works (!) but, as with other sports and pastimes, being bang up-to-date on effective techniques – 'current best practice', to use the jargon – can be a huge benefit to the modern

Fulfilling your mountaineering ambitions means combining adventure with the steady accumulation of learning, practice and experience

A leap of faith on the An Caisteal Gap, Skye? A mountaineering objective will always be challenging, but should also be realistic for you and your team

mountaineer, provided you know how to apply that knowledge.

A Broad Base

Many of the ideas and recommendations in this book are based on – or informed by – what is currently taught to students on recognised British climbing and mountaineering courses, and also on the experience of working and walking with outdoor enthusiasts and practitioners throughout the British mountains.

Inspiration, Ambition and Reality

Britain's mountains may be small, but they are perfectly formed, superbly situated, incredibly varied and offer big adventures for the ambitious. Much of the fun of hillwalking lies in the possibility, and then discovery, of what lies over the next horizon. As experience and confidence in the mountains develop, so ambitions and objectives grow. Almost without realising it, hillwalkers are soon into the realms of mountaineering. Whether or not they are equipped to be there – either in terms of skills or gear – is another matter.

Inspiring and ambitious objectives like the Aonach Eagach, Curved Ridge, Cneifion Arête or even the diminutive but tricky Broad Stand on Scafell, feature somewhere on the horizon of virtually all adventurous British hillwalkers. They provide excitement, challenge, enjoyment, possibly fear and, once completed, a deep sense of satisfaction. But they are also mountain journeys that demand an approach and a skill-set beyond those of the mere walker.

From navigation to route finding on difficult terrain, to climbing and ropework, success hinges not just on enthusiasm and delight in the surroundings, but on competency and confidence in a range of specific technical abilities. It's all very well to know that a grade 3 scramble may involve rock climbing to Difficult standard, but to complete one that does offers a real and warranted sense of achievement.

Tackling your own mountaineering objectives in search of adventure means facing a personal challenge. Chris Bonington has said that adventure begins when you step outside your comfort zone. That doesn't have to mean risking your neck too much; if you're not really confident you have the skills and equipment to deal with the situation you put yourself in, you probably shouldn't be there. It's a fine line, requiring careful judgement as your skills develop.

Belaying a scrambler on typical British mountaineering terrain

PART TWO
THE SKILLS FOR THE HILLS

Planning and Preparation

There's a part of most hill-goers that yearns to just wander out into the wilderness and get lost. The problem is if you try it that's what tends to happen, and things go downhill from there. The truth is most of us are squeezing our precious days on the hill in between the deadlines and detritus of modern life, and – whether it's an hour, a day or a week – we want to make the most of it, and get back safely.

The key to making the most of your time on the hill is to plan your days and prepare for your objectives. Why plan? It gives you a framework within which to think about the many important decisions you will inevitably face in choosing to spend a day having fun in a potentially dangerous place. The less you plan, the more dangerous the mountains are. Those decisions will include where you are going and what you are going to do, how long you are going to allow, what you will need to wear and carry, who you are going with, and what you might do if something goes wrong. Good planning will enable you to prepare well, both physically and mentally – particularly important if you have set a challenging objective – and in terms of equipment, provisions, transport and everything else you will need to succeed. Plans can change, of course, but experience shows that if you've thought things through and prepared well you will improve every aspect of your performance on the hill, and your level of achievement too.

Perhaps the biggest benefit of planning is in safety, not least because you cannot understand the risks you are facing unless you have first assessed them. Knowing where you are going and what obstacles you are likely to encounter – from weather to terrain – helps to ensure you will succeed, survive, and avoid the embarrassment of an unnecessary call-out of the local Mountain Rescue team. You will almost certainly enjoy yourself more, too.

Basic Checklist for Planning any Day's Mountaineering in the British Hills

- Read a reliable route description, and plot the route on a good, up-to-date map

- Monitor the weather and assess how it will affect your plans

- Get a reliable mountain forecast as late as you can before going – yesterday's forecast for tomorrow is not good enough

- Gather any footwear, clothing and provisions that you will need

- Prepare any other equipment that you will need, including technical gear

- Think about body fuel – what food will you take, will you start well hydrated, and will you need to carry all your water, or are there sources en route you can use?

- Consider the members of your party – is the route suitable for all of them? Has your team got the skills to get everyone through the route safely?

- Think about how long the route will take. Work it out in sections, and determine your likely start and finish times. Be aware of your escape routes in the event of things going wrong. Plan the whole route, not just the way to the top (most accidents happen on the way down).

- Work out how you will get there and how long the journey will take. If the route demands an early start make sure you factor in enough travel time.

- Tell someone where you are going, and your expected times of departure and return.

Driving all your preparation should be the goal of self-reliance. You should be able to predict and handle the challenges you are likely to meet, and not go out on the hill *expecting* someone to bail you out if you get into problems. Anyone can get into difficulties, but planning to be self-reliant means being confident that the mountaineering objective you have set is within the capabilities of everyone involved, and planning accordingly.

Going it Alone
Should you ever go alone? The 'golden rule' that says 'No' is countered by the knowledge that to be alone in a mountain environment can be not only one of the most intense of experiences, but also one of the most educational. For most people safe mountaineering of the sort discussed here requires a team of at least two; and although we would definitely not recommend 'solo-ing' steep terrain as a pastime, it is undoubtedly true that no mountain-goer is ever as keenly aware of the need for self-reliance as when he or she ventures out into the hills unaccompanied.

Access

Before setting out in the British mountains you should always try to establish any legitimate restrictions or conditions on access. The bodies representing Britain's hillwalkers and mountaineers have worked to establish good relations with landowners in recent years, and it is in everyone's interests that these are maintained (see Responsible Access, page 166). One important development in Scotland has been the Scottish Hillphones System, an innovative telephone system that allows hillwalkers to find out on a daily basis where deer stalkers will be operating in Scotland during the stalking seasons. The telephone message system is operated by sporting estates throughout Scotland. The scheme was set up in 1996 by Scottish Natural Heritage (SNH) and the Mountaineering Council of Scotland (MCofS) to enable stalking and hillwalking to take place on the same mountains at the same time, reducing potential conflict between hill users. By 2003 it covered 12 areas and a quarter of Scotland's Munros, as well as many other hills under 3,000ft (914m), taking around 4,000 calls a year. It has helped to improve cooperation between hill users and foster a responsible attitude to land access.

The system operates by participating estates leaving a daily answerphone message informing walkers about which areas will be affected by stalking. Hillphones leaflets with the relevant telephone numbers and stalking dates are distributed to tourist information centres, outdoor shops, activity centres, hotels, B&Bs, bunkhouses and campsites, and the scheme is publicised in mountaineering magazines and the mainstream press. More information can also be obtained from the Mountaineering Council of Scotland (www.mountaineering-scotland.org.uk). The organisers hope that ultimately all mountaineers will call Hillphones in the same way as they would check the weather before they set out, and we would certainly endorse this.

Looking north from Beinn Fhada towards Gleann Gaorsaic, Kintail. The right to explore such areas of outstanding natural beauty comes with responsibilities.

You'll find a pair of boots useful!

Mountaineering Kit: the Essentials

Speed and Lightweight Travel

The lightweight principle proven and established by Alpine-style mountaineers in the world's biggest mountain ranges is just as applicable to a day out in the British mountains – especially when the weather is not on your side. The lighter you travel the further, and faster, you will be able to go for less effort – and the better you will feel. There are people who take a macho pride in carrying the heaviest possible pack, and have no truck with the reality that less, when it comes to an enjoyable day out, is infinitely more. What these losers don't realise is that travelling light is not just a question of principle. A heavy pack full of unnecessary equipment is a burden you and your team can do without – a group should pack as a group, and avoid unnecessary duplication of team kit. Things start to go wrong in the mountains when people get tired and demoralised. A lightweight pack is an issue of safety as much as anything else.

A Cautionary Tale

A guide and his client were crossing the Cuillin Ridge. The weather was scorching, the going hard, and the client – as it turned out – overheating and dehydrating. Once diagnosed, stripped bare and receiving recuperative medical treatment, the still-confused client was surprised to see his guide taking a keen interest in the contents of his rucksack; in fact, emptying it at speed. 'What the hell are you carrying all this stuff for?' Because you told me to!' 'I said you *might* need it. Not to bring the whole lot.' 'Ah...well...you can never be too sure...'. The client and guide were the authors, and ultimately the trip was successful. But in the prevailing conditions the 'better safe than sorry' approach to rucksack packing almost contributed not just to failure, but to evacuation from the mountain on medical grounds.

So What Should you Carry?

Everyone has their own list of 'essential' items for the hills, but you don't need to carry all of them every time you go out. It's possible that approach will get you nowhere fast. The advent of ultra lightweight and compact gear has made it easier to carry more stuff onto the hills without it compromising your trip – but that doesn't mean you have to! Choosing the right gear for each trip is a question of preparation, judgement and experience.

This section looks at some of the essential gear that mountaineers should always carry, and why it is important to carry it and know how to use it. There will always be a limit to the amount of gear you can and should take with you, but having the right safety equipment to hand, for instance, is imperative in the case of an accident or mishap. Travelling light in the mountains should mean travelling faster and easier, without compromising safety. This section is about assessing your real gear needs, and getting the balance right. (The same principle should be applied to technical climbing gear – see page 71.)

Clothing and the Layer System

It is dangerous to get wet in the hills, worse still to get wet and cold. It's not unusual for even a summer day in Britain's mountains to encompass at least three seasons, sometimes more. Your clothing arrangement needs to be able to cope with these changes (and that's before anything goes awry). One of the biggest dangers of an unplanned night out, for example, is the cold conditions on high mountain summits at any time of year – in these circumstances becoming hypothermic is a real threat, more so if an injury is involved. The front line of defence against such problems is the layer system.

The Layer System

This system consists of layers of garments that form barriers of protection against the elements. Applied properly it should keep you dry and comfortable at any time of year and in all conditions. In the mountains it is easy to get intermittently both too hot and too cold, often depending on whether you are 'working' or resting. Belaying and climbing, for instance, represent the two extremes which can exist side by side. The layer system makes it easier to control your body's thermal regulation. When you get too hot, you can take a layer or two off; when you get too cold, or conditions either change or threaten to, you can put more layers on.

Layer 1 – the Base Layer

You should begin with the base layer – the one next to your skin. Modern-day fabrics are designed to wick away perspiration, drawing moisture and sweat away from your skin. This layer is essential for comfort and should have a good wicking performance. A specialist garment made of a thin wool mix fabric is ideal. Cotton garments should be avoided as they retain moisture, rather than wicking it away. Not only is this uncomfortable, but it can also increase the rapid cooling caused by wind chill. In hot weather conditions many people are happy to wear a good base layer on its own, as it will provide thermal regulation, not mere warmth.

Layer 1: base layer

How you cover your legs is largely a matter of personal preference. In summer Powerstretch pants are good for all sorts of mountaineering, but equally lightweight trekking trousers, or even shorts, may be your preference. Whether you choose thermal bottoms will depend on personal preference and conditions, although in winter a 'long johns' base layer can go a long way to helping keep your overall body temperature, and therefore your performance, up.

Layer 2: mid layer

Layer 2 – the Mid Layer

On top of your base layer a slightly heavier Thinsulate, wool or fleece garment is good. There are plenty of options for mid layers nowadays, but warm, comfortable and not-too-bulky is the best combination. A wind-stopper fabric is slightly heavier but very effective in maintaining core warmth in wind-chill conditions. A high neck cuff with a zip can be useful for additional flexibility in temperature regulation. For leg wear in cold weather a fleece pant is worthwhile.

At least one spare mid layer should generally be carried as it is this layer that is used to warm up – for instance, when stopping for a break – or to cool off, on a steep uphill section. As this suggests, the mid layer can actually be a combination of garments.

Layer 3 – Waterproof and Windproof Shell

This should be jacket and trousers in a good-quality, breathable fabric. If you are able to afford the luxury of two jackets it is worth selecting an ultra-light option such as a Dri-Lite jacket for summer wear when good conditions are forecast, and a full-weight mountaineering jacket for other times.

Layer 3: windproof and waterproof shell

Hands and Feet

The body's extremities must not be forgotten. Fleece and waterproof gloves are an important combination, as you want your hands to stay warm and dry, but also functioning. Gloves can easily get lost in windy conditions and spares should be carried. When hands and feet get cold you can lose the ability to look after yourself properly and perform even simple tasks such as working a jacket zip, taking a bearing, tying a knot or placing a piece of protective equipment. In time this heat loss can also contribute to lowering the body's temperature, encouraging the onset of hypothermia and increasing the risk of an accident. If you want dexterity too, go for warm, waterproof gloves. Mitts are warm, but clumsy.

Protecting your feet in cold weather is also important. For wet weather and snow using a waterproof boot is essential. A boot gaiter will also help keep the water out. Also avoid wearing cotton socks (and other garments) as they will hold moisture and cool you down. Instead, choose a robust 'climate regulating' sock – lightweight for summer, heavier for winter. Modern specialist socks are not designed to be worn in combination. Some have density and cushioning zones designed so that the feet never lose contact with your shoes, helping to increase foot comfort – socks that wick moisture away from the skin are ideal – and help prevent pressure points. To guarantee foot comfort, socks should always fit snugly – to ensure this you may consider buying a smaller size than normal.

Headwear

Similarly, a lot of body heat is lost from the head so keeping it warm is of prime importance, especially when it is likely to get wet *and* cold. Apart from a good-quality hat, you can also wear a fleecy neck gaiter in combination with your headwear. This will maintain protection to the base of the skull and neck. A spare hat is always worth considering.

Top Tips for Keeping Warm

- Control your thermal regulation and prevent overheating by removing/adding clothing or opening/closing vents and zips.

- Wear a warm hat in cold conditions and use your hood. In winter wear double-lens ski goggles when walking into driving snow.

- Keep the wind out. The cold wind will quickly take heat away – your water-proof/windproof garment will prevent this. Not everyone likes to wear their shell garment just to keep the wind out, but wind-blocking mid layers are now available.

- Stay dry on your inner layers. Wet clothes transfer heat much faster than dry, so it's essential to use good wicking next-to-skin layers and breathable shell garments in wet conditions.

- Remember it is easier to stay warm than to get warm.

- Don't sit directly on cold or wet ground – use something like a sit-mat or a ruck-sack to insulate you from it.

- Always eat plenty and hydrate well. Food is energy, and energy converts to body heat.

- Find shelter when stopping for a rest or to eat, particularly in bad weather, and consider carrying a bothy bag, which will keep the cold away whilst resting. As a rule, when you stop 'working', wrap up.

- If you get cold put on your spare warm top. Sometimes it is best to have a size larger than usual so you can fit it over the other layers easily. A spare Thinsulate and fleece-lined top will help you to keep out the cold and stay dry.

Contents of your Rucksack
Rucksack Liner
All rucksacks leak, so a waterproof liner is essential to keep your rucksack contents dry. Rucksack liners come in robust plastic-bag form or coated neoprene dry-bag style.

It is also worthwhile packing your contents into separate waterproof bags ('dry bags') inside the rucksack liner.

To keep your kit dry a rucksack liner or dry bag is essential

An 'off the shelf' first aid kit for use in the mountains

LIFESYSTEMS
MOUNTAIN
FIRST AID

First Aid Kit
A first aid kit is necessary for common soft tissue injuries, especially foot blisters. A standard first aid kit will suffice, although it's a good idea to include some extra items:

- Hypostop, a dextrose gel administered for hypoglycaemia
- Hydration salts, such as Dyoralite
- Compeed, for blister prevention
- Duck tape (also known as gaff or gaffer tape) for strapping an ankle and general fix-it.

It's wise to use a purpose-made waterproof first aid bag rather than a plastic box (and also to think seriously about doing a basic course on first aid in a mountain environment).

The simple survival bag really can be a life-saver – if you know how to use it

Survival Bag

This is an absolutely essential piece of safety gear, but one that is often misunderstood and misused. Many people opt for the silver-foil bag but this has a number of disadvantages, not least the fact that used on its own it will radiate heat away from the body – the opposite effect from the one wanted, and potentially dangerous. Foil bags also tend to delaminate into a see-through bag after a couple of years' storage, especially if they get damp, and the material is very thin and breaks easily. From most points of view a plastic survival bag is better: the plastic is generally robust, and will not deteriorate. In an emergency you can make a stretcher from it. If you have one of each using the two together – the foil *inside* the plastic – can be very effective.

Bothy Shelter

You might think that bothies are made of bricks and slates – but nowadays you can carry one in your rucksack! Bothy shelters are made of ripstock nylon, and when removed from their stuff bag (and filled with people) form a dome shape. A bothy shelter isn't just emergency kit: they come into their own in nasty weather, such as a passing storm, and in that sense can prevent problems occurring in the first place. To use a bothy bag select a suitable site for a rest and pull the dome over your head – everyone inside then sits down together, the occupants' heads holding the roof in place. The bothies are centrally heated by the occupants' body warmth – you will

Carrying a bothy in your bag provides instant shelter when you need it

Taking refuge
in a bothy shelter

notice a difference almost immediately. A bothy shelter may not be an essential piece of equipment, but given that they are very light and pack down reasonably small, they are worth carrying. They come in 2, 4, 8 and 12 person sizes. Combined with your survival bag a bothy shelter is the ideal answer to an unplanned night out on the mountain.

Head Torch

Carrying a head torch is essential. You may not plan to come off the mountain in darkness, but you might have to if you underestimate your route, go wrong, or have a mishap that delays you. In winter daylight hours are short, especially in Scotland, and if you do get caught out in the darkness, it helps if you can see your map and compass – a head torch will also leave your hands free to use them – and the terrain you are walking on. A torch is also very good for signalling should you need to attract the attention of a search and rescue party.

Which Head Torch?

There are lots to choose from. The diminutive Petzl Tikka is excellent – compact, light and robust. It gives a diffuse light; others give a more direct beam. Go for a small, lightweight option if you are carrying the torch 'just in case'. Always remember to carry spare batteries and bulb (unless you are using the new LCD lights – as used by the Tikka – where spare bulbs are not necessary).

Mobile Phones

There is still some lingering snobbery about phones on the hills and their possible intrusion into the wilderness experience. But as long they are used responsibly – when you need genuine assistance from the rescue services, or have found someone who does – they are arguably an essential emergency item, and without question a potential lifesaver. Telephoning will be much faster than walking out in these circumstances – assuming you have coverage, which is still by no means guaranteed in mountain locations (one reason why you should not rely solely on your phone being able to bail you out). You don't need to have the phone switched on while you are out – only use it for emergencies. Preserve the battery life, and keep it dry by storing it in a waterproof bag.

Map and Compass

It's the fundamental rule of any mountain excursion: always carry a map and compass, and don't just *know* how to use them – *actually* use them, even when the weather seems completely benign. Part of the challenge and enjoyment of hillwalking and mountaineering is being able to navigate your way from point to point. But should the weather close in, being able to navigate your way safely off the mountain is of paramount importance. Remember to protect your map in a waterproof map case (not the big ramblers' ones, but the more practical 'leaf' variety pioneered by Ortlieb). The most robust mountain compass on the market is the Silva Type 4 compass, which also has luminous markings on the main working parts for ease of night-time navigation.

Guidebook

A guidebook – specifically a scrambling guidebook for the type of 'crux' mountaineering sections featured later – is essential for route finding. If you are planning to do any classic mountaineering route in Britain (on any terrain except the more extreme climbing grades) it's odds-on not only that someone has been there before you, but that there is a guidebook covering the area and route. You should not only research the route using the guides available, but also take the relevant guide with you – certainly on a first visit – to help you find and then negotiate the route. Not only is it informative to see how the description compares to what you experience on the ground, having the guide may also save you time and prevent you wondering at every stage if you are where you are supposed to be, and where you should be going next. In practice you will find many routes are harder without the help of a guidebook. In particular, route finding will be more difficult, and you will be more likely to stray onto the wrong ground.

Remember...

Any guidebook information is a reflection of the author's opinions and preferences, and such books should be used as a tool, not followed slavishly. Be fully prepared to disagree with their assessments – very often you won't be alone!

Plastic Whistle

A whistle should always be carried for use in emergencies only. It weighs only a few grams and is small and compact. If you have to use it to attract attention, use the international distress signal. Anything else may lead passers-by to think you've lost your dog, your marbles, or something else that doesn't concern them. You must attract attention in the right way.

International Distress Signal

- 6 long blasts within 1 minute, with a clear pause of 10 seconds between each blast

- Repeat the above after 1 minute

- You can also use flashlight (6 flashes) – or even shout, if you are able to

- It is absolutely critical that you pause for 1 minute, then continue

- Do not stop signalling until you are totally sure your position has been noted

Spare clothing

How much spare clothing you take, and what, depends on the prevailing weather conditions and the type of outing you are planning. It is always best to have at least one spare mid layer, spare gloves and a spare hat, especially if the weather is likely to be cold. If you have to spend an unplanned night out such spare clothing will be important for your physical well-being and morale. It doesn't have to be bulky or heavy – invest a bit extra in good-quality, lightweight items.

Hydration and Body Fuel

Food and drink are the fuel you need to keep going in the mountains, but it's not always easy to get the right balance and type. Your priority should be to start the day well fed and well hydrated… and to continue it like that. If you are dehydrated and hungry at the end of a long day your physical and psychological performance will be affected, and you are far more likely to make a mistake or have an accident. Take as much energy food and fluid as you reasonably can, and use it – don't wait until you are thirsty and hungry. Some people find they have little appetite while walking, but will still probably be using twice the energy

they normally do. Eating little and often suits some people, others prefer a 'proper' lunch – but the important thing is to carry (and consume) enough calories, in an accessible form. This may not be the same for everyone, and certainly does not have to be 'power bars'. Dried fruit, for instance, packs energy into a tasty, accessible and easily digestible form.

When it comes to hydration, by the time you feel thirsty you will already be getting dehydrated. It's a well established fact that as little as a 2% drop in hydration can

Whatever system you use it's essential to keep well hydrated when you are mountaineering

significantly affect both physical and psychological performance. Fluids with isotonic content without doubt improve your performance over plain water, and carrying isotonic powders, to be mixed with mountain water (providing you are sure of the source) is a good way of staying hydrated without having to carry litres of fluid. A hydration system such as a CamelBak bag and straw can be effective when walking as it enables you to sip fluid whenever you need it; you don't have to stop and get a bottle out every time you want a drink (a good excuse not to bother!). It also keeps water cool. One potential drawback is not knowing how much you have consumed, but it's always better to consume fluid than save it 'for later' – by which time you may be dehydrated. Drinking plenty of water (and not too much alcohol) in the days before a trip will also ensure you start well hydrated.

Top Tips
- Plan your hydration stops and, when taking a sit-down break, check how much water you have consumed. On balance, most people drink too little on the hill, and the chances are you will need to drink more often. Good hydration will help provide you with energy, coordination and concentration.

- In colder weather a small flask is obviously excellent for hot drinks, such as orange or blackcurrant. Hot tea and coffee provide the same morale-boosting effect, but being diuretics will not aid hydration.

- For food, whether you take sandwiches, dried fruit, chocolate, bananas or anything else, the basic rule is to take nutritious, calorie-packed things that you like.

Trekking Poles

While many hillwalkers will feel that trekking (or walking) poles are not an essential item, for a growing number they certainly are. Their value has been recognised by mountaineering professionals for many years, and whether or not you are an *aficionado* the benefits of using them are indisputable. It's not long since the average British mountaingoer considered trekking poles to be the preserve of the elderly, the professional or the poser. But in recent years there has been an explosion in their use as the increasingly 'savvy' UK hillwalker has come to understand, largely through experience, some simple facts about using poles:

Trekking poles can be a real boost, but you should know when to put them away, depending on the terrain and conditions

- walking up and downhill is easier and less tiring
- stamina and fitness levels are increased
- strain on legs is reduced
- users have a better and more upright walking posture
- users cover ground more quickly
- a day out is made more enjoyable
- in an emergency poles can be used to improvise a stretcher to evacuate a casualty, or even to splint a limb.

Aiding progress up and down slopes is probably the main attraction of trekking poles. They are fast becoming essential pieces of kit and should be selected – and respected – like any other piece of mountain equipment. Equally, you should know why you are using them, where they do and don't work, and when to put them away.

So why use them? Trekking poles have many benefits for all types of users, but there is clear research-based evidence that they offer two major benefits: one associated with weight transfer, and the other with coordinating balance. Anyone who has used poles will know that much less effort is required on steep uphill sections, due to the momentum gained from the combination of the transfer of weight from legs to arms, and also the use of the arms' muscle power to assist the propulsion of the body in the uphill fight against gravity. To achieve the most efficient use, pole length should be such that your arms remain at right angles when gripping the handles.

The real benefit of this comes across the course of the day, and in combating the accumulated fatigue of uphill walking. On a big mountaineering day this is hugely beneficial, helping to preserve your energy for the climbing sections of the route when it is really required.

Weight transfer from the lower to upper body also takes place when poles are used to descend steep terrain. Up to 14% of a walker's body weight can be transferred if double poles are used to descend steep ground. Again, the length of the poles must be considered for this transfer to work efficiently, and on a steep downhill section around three quarters of the walker's height is recommended.

Using poles when going downhill reduces impact within the knee, which increases comfort and energy conservation and prevents long-term injury. The most common sort of injury symptom associated with hillwalking is knee pain, which comes on when making long, steep descents. Using poles can help to relieve the stress on tired legs on downhill stretches and, as with uphill use, promotes better posture and breathing.

Help with Balance

The other great benefit of using trekking poles is that you are, in effect, turned into a quadruped. With four points of contact, balance is much improved, especially on uneven terrain such as scree slopes. Poles are also useful when crossing rivers, and when walking on soft ground (including snow, when used with 'buckets' on the ends) due to the more even distribution of the body's weight.

This is not intended to be a comprehensive explanation of the use of trekking poles; there is plenty of information available from manufacturers. Nevertheless we are happy to declare that poles are, without question, hugely beneficial to the mountaineer. Detailed information on their use is available from manufacturers' websites, such as www.leki.de.

Top Tips

- Telescopic poles will extend in length to cater for walkers of all heights, and so are very dynamic.

- Use poles from the walk in to the walk out, or when you feel the need for them.

- Consider using poles when ascending and descending steep terrain.

- At the end of a mountain walk your legs will be tired, so using poles on the descent will be of great benefit.

- Mountain rescue techniques – particularly when evacuating a casualty – rely on the length, strength and light weight of trekking poles. In such situations poles can be a life-saver.

- When packing poles in your rucksack, either pack them down the compression straps of your pack, on the outside, or split the sections of poles and pop them inside. This makes scrambling much safer, and will help to prevent poles from catching on rocks when ascending or descending steep terrain.

- Poles offer an excellent barrel for storing a quantity of gaff tape, which can be used for anything from first aid to temporary garment repair.

A handy place to store some multi-purpose gaff tape

Even trekking poles have their limitations and can, if used inappropriately, be potentially hazardous. When should we not use poles, or change our approach?

- When scrambling on steep ground – either descending or ascending where hands on rock will be better positioned for balance – poles should be packed away, otherwise they will be unwieldy and dangerous.

- When walking through a boulder field or loose ground, or simply downhill, be sure to take your hands out from the wrist straps. The pole tip can sometimes jam between rocks and launch you forward. If you fall you are likely to break your wrist.

- Never substitute your ice axe for a trekking pole in a situation where you might have to arrest a slide. In winter use your ice axe on steep terrain, always basing your decision upon what happens if you slip. Your best chance of survival in this situation is to have your ice axe in hand, not a trekking pole. Self-arrest using a trekking pole is inefficient and dangerous.

- In winter some people opt for a combination of ice axe and trekking pole on easy-angled snow slopes. In this case you should ensure that the ice axe is always located in the uphill hand, and you should not use the pole wrist strap for the downhill hand. Generally, however, it is best *not* to combine ice axe and pole use – pack the poles away when faced with a steep snow slope and use the ice axe.

Bivouacking

Planned or Unplanned?

A well-organised bivi site

A very well-organised bivi site!

Bivouacking is a means of staying in the mountains overnight without a tent. It may be a planned or unplanned 'stopover', the highlight of your trip, or a survival tactic in the face of adverse conditions or events. 'Bivvying' high on a ridge or summit plateau on a summer night can be one of the most memorable and enjoyable mountaineering experiences. In contrast, an emergency unplanned bivouac can be one of the most unpleasant experiences that anyone can have in a high mountain environment – especially in poor weather and without the necessary equipment for a comfortable stay.

An Unplanned Bivouac

The important thing as you hunker down for an unplanned night out (where there is no realistic alternative) is to be confident that you can look after yourself, keeping sufficiently warm, dry and 'body fuelled' to get through the night in good shape and do whatever you need to do when morning comes – whether that means continuing your onward journey, or waiting for help to arrive.

Common Reasons for Unplanned Bivouacking Include:

- Underestimating the time needed to complete your route.

- Discovering, whilst on the route, that you are unpractised in the technical skills required to move smoothly and efficiently, and so you get delayed.

- Your navigational ability being not quite as good as you thought (or hoped!) when caught in poor visibility and deteriorating weather conditions. In such cases progress is slowed down and/or parties get lost. This is the most common human error of mountain-goers all over the world.

- Your risk assessment has completely underestimated the hazards and difficulties of the terrain on the approach and/or on the route itself. This could be anything from rising river waters cutting off your return, to slippery rock on a smooth ridge traverse making progress slow.

- Becoming injured and having no option but to wait for rescue.

- Simply not being able to get off the mountain in daylight.

Equipment for an Unplanned 'Bivi'

There's a difference between *unplanned* and *unprepared*, and carrying the equipment for an unplanned bivi means you have prepared well. Anyone preparing a mountaineering trip should carry lightweight, basic survival gear, and statistics show that people who get caught out unexpectedly but who carry these basics will normally survive in most weather conditions. The flip side of the same statistics show that people who do not carry the basic survival gear are, at the very least, far less likely to return from their trip without being rescued (that's if they are lucky, of course).

Recommended Basic Emergency Items to Carry on High Mountain Trips

- Polythene survival bag and foil blanket
- Spare mid layer top
- Spare hat and gloves
- Head torch with spare batteries
- 4-person bothy bag
- Spare food/drink

If you are forced to bivi out using no more than this kit to supplement the gear you are already wearing, you need to consider very carefully the three basic survival requirements: shelter, warmth and food/hydration. Try to find a dry, sheltered spot, out of the wind and rain, such as the lee side of a hill or an in-cut at the base of an outcrop of rock, or small cave. If you can't get out of the rain but you carry an emergency bothy bag then you will have automatic shelter.

Top Tips

- Insulate your body from the cold surface by using a small sit-mat or the foam spine/frame of your rucksack. Carrying a small section of bubble wrap just enough for your bottom to fit on, also provides an excellent insulator.

- Put your spare gear on – it won't keep you warm when it's in your bag.

- Wrap yourself up in insulation using your foil blanket inside your plastic emergency bivi bag, then put your feet into your rucksack.

- If you have a mobile phone and you have reception then use it to call a personal contact or the emergency services to let them know your location and condition.

- Have a prepared 6-figure grid reference ready, and a description of your surroundings.

- Unless you are very hungry and thirsty consume your food and drink steadily. Your body will need the energy to keep warm, but eking it out will help your morale.

Remember

An unplanned bivouac is usually cold, unpleasant and best avoided. But you should always be prepared for one.

Planned Bivouacs

In contrast to the unexpected experience of an unplanned bivouac, a planned bivouac can form an integral part of a big trip. It's the ultimate adventure to combine a mountaineering outing that involves scrambling and bivouacking in one of Britain's classic destinations, such as the Cuillin Ridge on the Isle of Skye. Getting it right is very satisfying – it

A planned bivi means carrying all you need for a comfortable night

might include warm and dry shelter when necessary, but if you plan to bivouac when a dry forecast is expected you can easily sleep out in the open on a mountain top or ledge offering fine views and a spectacular location for breakfast.

Sleeping Kit

A Gortex bivi bag with, for summer conditions, a 2–3 season sleeping bag, is ideal. To insulate you from the ground, a three quarter Thermarest is suitable, and it (or, alternatively, a cut-down Karrimat covering hip to shoulder) should be inserted inside the Gortex bag. These items should all be as light and compact as possible. It might cost more, but if you are planning on doing a fair bit of bivouacking it will be a worthwhile investment. There are some larger, hooped Gortex bivouac designs on the market that you may prefer over the standard bivi bag. It's worth considering whether you really need one, and whether you are happy to carry the extra weight.

Cooking Kit

For summer conditions a very small stove such as the diminutive MSR Pocket Rocket is all you need, with a small canister of gas. This is one of the most efficient and lightest pressure-control stoves on the market. One small cooking pot is the minimum, two pots a luxury. Try to avoid aluminium – go for stainless steel or non-stick types.

Food

Part of a good bivi experience is decent grub – a proper meal. Try your bivi food before you venture up into the hills for the night. You need something that can be heated and prepared very quickly, but is also delicious and nutritious. Don't take food that you do not enjoy. Eat it with a large plastic spoon, which is easy to clean.

Hydration

On long hot days it is essential to replace salts and minerals lost through dehydration, and even more so if you are staying out for a night and perhaps another day. Don't let thirst be your guide. Hydrate regularly, ideally from natural sources. Factor locations with a water supply into your route planning. If you don't you will need to carry a lot of water for an overnight bivi, probably in extra water carriers, and that can take the edge off the whole experience!

There are many very good hydration systems on the market – including those from CamelBak and Platypus – that you can carry on your back and drink from while on the move. If you want to go super-light and super-cheap though, empty wine-box bladders can be adapted for use (but don't empty them by downing the contents the night before the bivi!). They hold at least 2 litres of liquid, and all you need to do is cut the plastic bladder rim down at least 1cm. The tap will come off and go on easily without the bladder leaking. One drawback is that there is no straw so you cannot drink from it while on the move.

A plastic mug or a plastic water bottle with a wide lid that can be used for drinking and eating is always useful.

Less is more: sleeping mat, head torch and stove – lightweight and compact kit selection can make a real difference to the enjoyment and success of your trip

Selecting a Site

When Planning your Bivouac, Select a Site that has all the Key Features:
- Shelter from the wind, especially for cooking
- Water source nearby
- Flat area to sleep on
- Great views
- Off the beaten track
- Shelter, for wet conditions – however good your equipment is.

On a long trip it can be worth having a reserve location or two in mind, in order to allow some flexibility to your itinerary.

Top Tips
- Check the gas canister is working before you depart.
- Pack away all items in waterproof dry bags.
- Assess the likely weather high up, especially air temperatures and wind conditions.
- Take some form of communication with you.
- Always let a responsible person know where you have gone and when you expect to return.
- Plan and prepare to enjoy the experience.

What Size Rucksack do you Need?

As with all mountaineering activity, the smallest rucksack you can get away with is ideal. A pack of around 40 to 50 litres capacity, with side compression straps, should be big enough if you are have the right kit and pack well. If you have a large pack – say, 60 to 70 litres – you will simply take too much gear, and probably have a less enjoyable trip as a result. Take the smallest, lightest kit you can get away with. If only light showers are forecast, take light waterproofs.

Packing your Rucksack

Many people struggle to find enough space in a smaller rucksack even to carry the most essential items for a trip – but it can be done! Avoid bulky contents; unpack gear from stuff sacks, 'stuff' items in the rucksack and pack flat, ensuring the whole volume of the sack is used. Making proper use of the compression straps on a good climbing rucksack also helps.

Navigation might not have the sex appeal of abseiling or ice-axe arrest, but in our view it is the top-priority mountain skill, and one that should always be taken seriously. Why? Well, not least because navigational errors are one of the most common root causes of mountain accidents, the first point in a chain of events leading inexorably to a more obvious mishap. Navigating may well be simple in essence, but in practice it's a difficult skill (or range of skills) to acquire. Some people may prefer to follow the lead of others. But what if you want to walk on your own, or you become lost, separated or even injured? Similarly, in perfect weather it can be tempting just to follow your nose with a quick glance at the map here or there to check you are on track – we've all done it. But what if the weather closes in unexpectedly and you're still miles from the car? Navigation is an enjoyable skill that everyone who goes to the hills should try to master.

Navigation can also be very frustrating when you are faced with foul weather situations. It may seem a better idea simply to avoid bad weather, but guaranteed good weather in most British mountain ranges is rare. In any case, it is far more satisfying to navigate your way through the inclement stuff when you are confident of your skills and ability. There are a number of comprehensive books on mountain navigation, but this section concentrates on outlining the key techniques that all mountaineers need to master. Practising them in realistic situations will not only help you develop a feel for navigation, but will also boost your confidence in using them when you need to.

Getting Started

The starting point for successful mountain navigation is always to be aware of your surroundings, and to check continually throughout the day that your route is going according to plan. The more people there are with navigation skills in your team, the stronger the group navigation will be, particularly in a challenging situation, when it's essential to skill share and support one another. You need the right equipment to navigate effectively, but equipment alone cannot make you a good navigator. You have to get out there and gain mileage using your map and compass. The more you prac-

Navigation essentials: map, map case, compass, pace and timing card, watch and head torch

tise, in all conditions, the better your judgement will become when faced with tricky route-finding decisions on big mountains in poor visibility.

> **Think**
>
> When travelling in to the mountains in good visibility navigation is easy, but can you navigate *back out* of the wilderness in poor visibility and unsupported?

Essential Equipment

Choosing the right navigation equipment is very important, and you will need to consider both performance and practicality. The most important single factor by far is that, whatever you buy, you learn how to use it correctly.

Know how to navigate when it really matters

Compass

The main features that make a compass suitable for all situations are:

1. Long base plate with measurement markings 0mm to 100mm down one side
2. Romer scale on the base plate
3. Luminous markings on the base plate, compass housing and travel arrow
4. Magnifying glass
5. Stiff compass housing
6. Lanyard
7. Bearing markings on compass housing in degrees and not millimetres.
8. Magnetic north arrow
9. Grid north arrow
10. 'Read bearing from here' marker

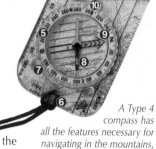

A Type 4 compass has all the features necessary for navigating in the mountains, whatever the conditions

One of the most robust mountain compasses on the market is the Silva Type 4, which contains all these features.

Map Case

Whether you use a poly bag or a purpose-designed plastic-and-material one such as the Ortlieb models, you will definitely need a map case. If your map gets wet, from rain or from dropping it into a stream or puddle, it will disintegrate and be useless. Clear, sealable poly bags are good and cheap, but they can puncture easily and probably won't last more than one trip. A purpose-designed case will enable you to fold your maps, carry and refer to them easily, and will keep them dry in all weathers. The Ortlieb map cases are most robust, and can be folded easily without cracking and leaking. They come in a number of different sizes, including the 'standard' 27cm square map case. However, for mountaineering something smaller is useful, and Ortlieb's A5 document bag is ideal, easy to tuck into and retrieve from a pocket. You can fold the map to view on two sides, and usually get the whole route displayed.

Maps

For any route you will need a copy of the recommended map. OS and Harveys are the obvious choices for most UK mountain regions. Cutting maps down, and removing their covers, can be a good way to reduce weight and bulk (providing you only get rid of the bits you know for certain you are unlikely to need) and will also make the map easier to handle and fold. You can also now buy and download maps from CD-rom, print to scale, and then laminate them. One early problem with this system was that in downloading and printing the scale could change significantly, but the best services – Anquet Maps is the market leader at the time of writing – have overcome this, with reliable maps (provided under licence from the OS and Harveys) that print out at a known scale onto an A4 sheet. The CD-rom products are specifically designed for walkers and mountaineers. On screen you can quickly scroll and zoom around the maps, which have such useful tools as a 'find place' feature to locate villages, hills, rivers and so on. Height data is also included, so you can see height profiles and estimate time of walking – using Naismith's formula (see page 47) – before you even set foot on the hill. If you're really getting into the technology you can even plan routes and save them to a GPS unit, and exchange routes with others, or download pre-made routes from the web.

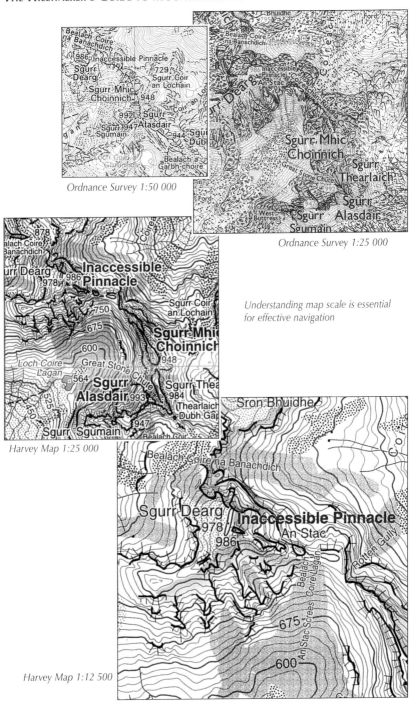

Ordnance Survey 1:50 000

Ordnance Survey 1:25 000

Understanding map scale is essential for effective navigation

Harvey Map 1:25 000

Harvey Map 1:12 500

Map Scale and Measuring Distance

What map scale should you use? The most common map scales used for travelling in the British mountains are 1:50 000 and 1:25 000, with 1:12 500 also gaining popularity where available. The important thing about scale is that, once you understand it, you can measure distance accurately. This is important for route planning, and also for micro-navigation, where you break down long journeys from, say, kilometres into manageable chunks of hundreds of metres. Once we know the distance travelled, and to be travelled, we can work out factors such as speed of travel and estimated time of arrival.

The 1:50 000 and 1:25 000 scale maps are often preferred for mountain navigation. However, when scrambling in complex terrain it can be easier to use either a 1:25 000, or a 1:12 500 map (though the latter are less readily available). The feature detail can be easier to interpret on some styles of maps than others. Ideally, you need sufficient detail, but not too much of it – sometimes in precipitous mountain areas a 1:25 000 scale map may be almost unreadable in places.

Choosing a Map

Choose a map with a scale that makes sense for your outing, taking account of the fact that some scales will make navigation easier than others on different terrains. It's worth comparing how different maps deal with the same terrain. Refer to the following guidelines when working out which scale is most suitable for your particular route:

1:50 000 scale maps provide the greatest land-mass spread (that is, cover a larger area in less detail) with terrain features detailed down to 50 square metres: 1cm = 500m; 1mm = 50m; 2mm = 100m. Benefits include:

- Uncomplicated contour definition

- Fewer features marked *may* help you to focus on the important ones and not get distracted

- Larger land-mass area covered

1:25 000 scale maps provide a smaller selection of land-mass spread, with terrain features detailed down to 25 square metres: 2cm = 500m; 1mm = 25m; 4mm = 100m. Benefits include:

- Enhanced feature detail in less complicated land masses, for example more streams, and smaller lochs or lakes, will be highlighted (in very complicated land masses – such as parts of the Cuillin Ridge – this level of detail can be confusing).

Where available, *the Harvey's 1:12 500 scale maps,* such as on Skye's Cuillin hills, will provide really good contour information especially in steep, precipitous mountains.

Contour Lines

A contour is a line joining places of equal height above sea level, and is shown in brown on OS maps, and in brown or grey on Harvey's maps (grey representing predominantly rocky ground). Black lines are cliff symbols that represent steep-sided mountains, and contours are mixed in with cliff symbols to indicate the nature of the terrain. When interpreted correctly, contour lines enable the shape, angle and height of any mountain to be clearly identified.

Map Setting

Map setting is not hard, but is the single most important skill to be learned before moving on to other aspects of navigation, because it makes life so much easier. The contours and features on the map are orientated to the actual features on the ground. Having set the map the navigator should always hold the map in an orientated position as he walks in the chosen direction of travel. By doing this the navigator will be able to follow the terrain easily as ground and map relate to one another. Once the map is orientated it should not be turned or moved from its position. It is the navigator who should change position by moving *around* the map.

Without map setting it is very easy to set off in the wrong direction, often as a result of blind assumption and intuition. In navigation the value of the latter is vastly overrated! Correct use of map, compass, tools and techniques is the best way to navigate accurately.

There are two ways to set your map:

Map setting by observation means orientating the map to match what you see around you

Using observation, orientate the map features to the actual features on the ground matching paths, mountain tops and so on. This only works in good visibility.

Drop your compass on to your map and orientate map grid north to magnetic north on the compass (see page 39). You can use this technique in good and in poor visibility, such as at night-time.

Map setting by compass is essential in poor visibility

Contour Interpretation

Contour interpretation is the art of translating information on height, shape and angle of terrain from a map and relating it to the ground, whilst travelling along a route. This is a vital aspect of map reading and navigation: without it you cannot determine how high you are on a mountain, its mass or bulk, or whether you are walking into dangers such as very steep ground and cliffs.

Good contour interpretation will allow you to travel safely through the mountains, and with practice you will be able to clearly identify obvious land features, helping you establish your position, and move safely, in all weathers.

Height The actual height of contours will be given on the map and is normally printed through the contour lines at every 50m. The vertical distance between them, also shown in the map key, is 10m, as highlighted on a 1:50 000 scale map (every fifth line will be a thicker one – an index contour line – indicating a 50m increase or decrease in height).

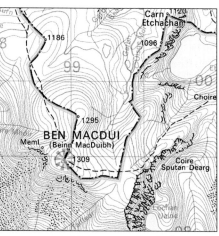

OS 1:50 000 scale map showing the summit of Ben Macdui

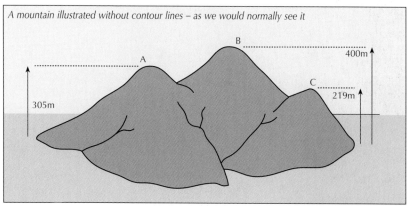

A mountain illustrated without contour lines – as we would normally see it

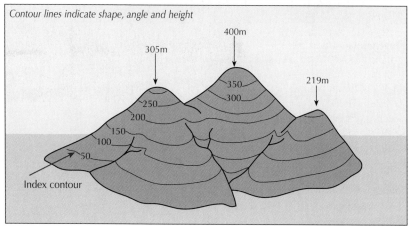

Contour lines indicate shape, angle and height

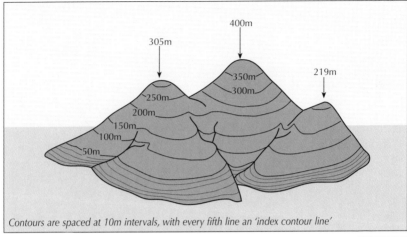

Contours are spaced at 10m intervals, with every fifth line an 'index contour line'

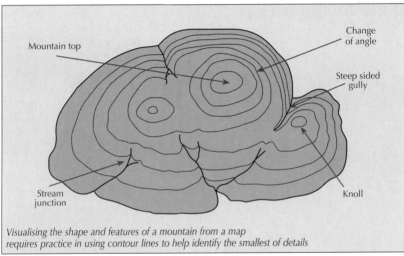

Visualising the shape and features of a mountain from a map requires practice in using contour lines to help identify the smallest of details

Shape Contour shape provides you with the overall shape of the terrain, and features of the land mass from, say, a knoll (small hilltop) to a large mountain summit.

Angle The distance between the contours indicates the steepness of the terrain – the closer together the contour lines, the steeper the terrain. Where it gets very steep, thick black lines are used to highlight precipitous cliffs.

Angle of terrain is represented by the spacing of contour lines

Steep terrain & cliffs

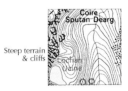

Taking a Compass Bearing from the Map

This is the first thing to be done when working out where you next want to be on your route. See page 39 for the diagram of a compass.

Taking a compass bearing can be practised using a simple lined piece of paper, as indicated in the illustration

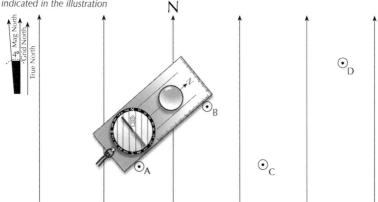

How to Take a Bearing from the Map

Identify where you are on the map and where you would like to travel to. Although you may have some way to go, keep the distances over which you take a bearing short. Simply break the journey down into manageable chunks.

Use the edge of your compass, or one of the coloured lines on the compass base plate. Place it so that the edge or line runs between position A (where you are now) and position B (where you want to go next), passing through both points. Be careful to ensure the direction of travel arrow, located on the base plate, points towards position B. Without moving the compass from this position on the map, turn the compass housing so the grid north arrow and the lines in the compass housing point to grid north on the map, running parallel to the map grid lines.

Taking the compass off the map you will now be able to read what is known as a grid bearing at the 'read bearing from here' marker. But to make this accurate for use 'on the ground' you need to add to it what is known as the 'magnetic variation', to arrive at an accurate magnetic bearing. The magnetic variation is the difference between grid north and magnetic north, which in the northern hemisphere is 4° in 2003. The current magnetic variation is indicated at the top of most maps of mountain terrain. It changes over time, which is one of the reasons it's important to have a recently published map.

Having added the magnetic variation, you have now completed a compass bearing. This method is known as 'grid to mag' (we have added the magnetic variation to our grid bearing). An easy way to remember this is the saying 'grid to mag, add'. An alternative method is 'mag to grid' ('mag to grid, get rid' – when you subtract the magnetic variation from your reading), which is most useful when practising relocation (see page 48).

Walking on a Compass Bearing

This is the skill of travelling precisely in the direction that your compass indicates you need to go, over whatever distance you need to travel, on the way to your next destination. Following a bearing in poor visibility or darkness is one of the hardest mountaineering skills to master, but it is a skill that can be learnt with practice.

Top Tips

- Ensure you connect the compass to your jacket using the compass lanyard – it makes the compass accessible and will prevent you losing it if you drop it.

When you are preparing to walk on a bearing hold your compass in front of you to line up your next feature with the direction of travel arrow – but don't hold it out in front of you whilst walking

- Once you have taken your bearing, place the compass in the palm of your hand, and extend your arm directly in front of you so it is positioned in the middle of your body. Ensure the direction of travel arrow is pointing away from your body.

- Turn your body round so that the magnetic needle lines up with the grid north arrow located in the compass housing.

- Look down the 'line of sight' using the direction of travel arrow – it is the direction of travel arrow that you follow. Be sure to hold the compass still and level.

- Sight a small feature or object in front of you, a short way off and directly in your line of sight (ie on your bearing). Walk to that point.

- While you are walking the compass should *not* be held out in front of you. You already have your eyes fixed on a position that you know is a point on your bearing, and the maximum length of each leg will therefore be limited only by visibility.

- Repeat the procedure until the required objective is reached or your estimated pacing (see below) is complete.

Common Errors

- Walking with the compass held out in front of you in the line of travel. As you walk the magnetic needle will move from side to side and your eyes will not be focused on the target feature, but on the compass and your feet. You *will* walk off bearing.

- Not studying the terrain to be encountered before setting off; knowing the shape, angle and nature of the ground in front of you provides excellent reference points.

Pacing, Timing and Relocation
Pacing

Pacing is an essential poor-weather navigation technique, and is based on knowing exactly how many double paces it will take *you* to walk 100m on the flat.

Measure 100m on the ground, either by using a long measuring tape or by finding two features on a map that are exactly 100m apart, on a straight line. This should be done on flat ground – a road or track is fine. Walk from your chosen point A to point B, at a normal, comfortable, relaxed pace. Do not over-stride. Count every second step, for

Speed Kph m Distance	2	3	4	5	6
50	1min 30secs	1min	45secs	36secs	30 secs
100	3mins	2mins	1min 30secs	1min 12secs	1min
200	6mins	4mins	3mins	2mins 24secs	2mins
500	15mins	10mins	7mins 30secs	6mins	5mins
1000	30mins	20mins	15mins	12mins	10mins

Use a pacing and timing card as an aide-memoire when navigating in the mountains

instance every time your left foot lands on the ground. The number of steps you count is your pacing figure for 100m.

The number of double steps that you take to walk 100m will change drastically when walking uphill or through uneven terrain, such as a boulder field, so it is best not to pace on steep terrain. However, it is worthwhile practising pacing up gentle inclines and travelling downhill to establish how your pacing will be affected. Walking through soft deep snow or marshy ground on the flat, or carrying a heavy load, will also have an effect, as will fatigue – most people will take more paces at the end of the day than at the start.

Nevertheless, pacing can be a highly effective tool for poor-weather navigation, helping you to establish with good accuracy how far you have travelled and therefore, where you are.

Timing
Timing is another way of calculating distance and the speed at which you are travelling. The best and most widely known formula used is Naismith's rule. Originally expressed as 3 miles per hour plus 30 minutes per 1,000ft of ascent, this approach can be applied flexibly to allow for different walking speeds and ascent/descent rates.

Naismith's rule is very accurate, and also allows for variation if at any time during – or, particularly, nearing the end of – your journey, your pace slows as a result of weary legs. Correct application of the formula allows you to work out how fast you have been walking or intend to walk.

Having made a calculation for either ascent or descent you should always monitor the accuracy of your prediction, and factor any variation into subsequent calculations.

Working out Timing Using Naismith's Rule
To work out timing for ascent, simply take the estimated flat rate speed – 4kmph is the norm, but is by no means universal – from A to B. Count the number of contour lines between position A and position B, and add one minute to your time for each contour line (ie. 1 minute for every 10 metres of ascent). For example, you have measured 500m from position A to B at 4kph. This will take 7.5 minutes. Let's say there are 9 contour lines between position A and B. Add the 9 + 7.5 and the total time for the ascent should be 16.5 minutes.

To work out timing for descent, take the flat rate time (unless the ground is very steep or tricky, when adding up to half a minute per contour line may be more accurate).

Remember

When both pacing and timing, you still need to map read, as you may have walked faster or slower than you calculate. Pacing and timing are simply an aid to confirming accuracy.

Relocation

This technique comes into its own when you need to determine your position on the hill in poor visibility, or at night. The most efficient relocation technique is based on working out slope aspect – that is, calculating in which direction the slope you are on is facing – to determine your position on the hill. It can be used any time you are lost or are unsure about your direction of travel.

Imagine you are descending a slope, but unsure of your precise location.

The arrow indicates your direction of travel from the spot height 1295. Your intended route was initially due west, back to the path. The black arrow is your direction of travel, highlighted by stopping and taking a bearing to ascertain the aspect of the slope you are on.

- Stop, and take a bearing down your current line of travel, and subtract the magnetic variation to arrive at a grid bearing. This method of taking a bearing is known as 'mag to grid'.
- Position the compass baseplate on the map in the area you have been walking, map setting to achieve the correct orientation.
- Now taking care to ensure that the grid-north arrow in the compass housing is parallel with the grid north lines on the map, move your compass across the map in the rough area you think you are (maintaining parallel lines with compass and map).
- As you do this, the direction of travel arrow on the compass will be indicating your current line of travel. Where the lines on the baseplate of the compass cross the slope at exactly 90° will indicate your approximate position. You have now established slope aspect, or, in other words, in which direction the slope on which you are walking is facing.

You can now map read and look for features on the ground that relate to that area to confirm where you are. You may decide to carry on descending if safe to do so. Alternatively you may have discovered that you have been walking in the wrong direction. Now that you have established your position you can route plan to get to where you would like to go. Map reading is a key part of relocation.

The 'mag to grid' method of taking a compass bearing – that is, taking a bearing directly to a feature on the ground without using the map, and then positioning the compass on the map – can also be used to confirm a feature that you wish to positively identify. As often as not this can just be for fun – say, picking out mountain tops.

Grid References

A grid reference is the best way to describe a precise location on a map. It is extremely important to know how to take and calculate a grid reference of your exact position at any time, whether to report an accident to the rescue services, or simply to be sure of where you are.

Most map keys will explain how to take a grid reference. However, being practised before you get on the hill is important.

Calculating a Grid Reference

- First quote eastings, the vertical grid lines. Locate the first vertical grid line to the left of your location and read the large figures labelling the line either at the top or bottom margin of the map, or on the line itself. Let's say this is 98. Now estimate the distance (or use your compass for greater precision) in units of tenths of a square from the gridline to your location – say 3.

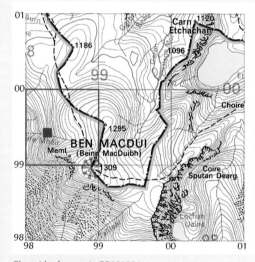

- Now quote the northings, locating the first horizontal grid line below your location and read the large figures labelling it, either in the left or right margin of the map, or on the line itself – say 99. Then estimate in tenths from the grid line to your location – let's say 4.

The grid reference is GR983994

- Your grid reference will read GR983994.

- To be completely accurate it is good practice to prefix the sheet reference number, as this is unique to your map and – assuming the grid reference is correct – provides a unique location: Sheet 36 GR983994.

Map Symbols

Map symbols are the 'language' of maps and, a bit like the Highway Code, have to be learnt. It is all too easy to glance at the most obvious symbols and consider them to be self-explanatory. While features are often represented 'logically', this is not always as helpful as it seems. Knowing what the symbols mean is essential for efficient and accurate map reading. Make a habit of comparing what you see on the ground with how it is recorded on the map whenever you are out, and you'll soon learn them.

Symbols are especially useful when planning your journey: being able to say, for instance, when and where you will encounter terrain that is steep, dangerous, loose, marshy or forested, or whether you have a right of way, or are entering land that is covered by access arrangements, is an advantage.

Route descriptions, such as those found in this book, will often refer to known land features to help you find your way. Practise studying map symbols and relating them to actual features, and be aware that map symbols will vary between different map scales and mapmakers.

Words

Don't forget that the words used on a map are also a way to help identify features, and that in Britain mountain nomenclature varies from one region to another. Britain has many types of mountain, with different names for the typical shapes and features. For instance, a col in England is a bealach (or even bhealach) in Scotland; lochs or lochans in Scotland may be llyns in Wales, and lakes or tarns in England. Learning these names and recognising the geographical variations makes life much easier when planning and following a route and predicting the likely terrain.

Using Map Features to Navigate

One of the objectives of route planning is to choose either the desired or the most efficient route between two points, and the purpose of navigation, combined with route-finding skills, is to turn that plan into a reality. Navigation is both a science and a creative process, and there are various ways in which we use the map and the terrain it represents to arrive at our objective.

Attack Points

'Attack points' are used when you wish to navigate to a less-than-obvious feature on your route, possibly from a long distance away. This system involves bisecting the navigation leg into two distinct legs. You first travel to an easily identifiable attack point – a large or obvious feature close to your final target, and from which it can be easily reached – such as a stream junction, a knoll, or a plantation. Having reached your 'unmissable' attack point, you then head for your target feature, which should be nearby. By aiming for a large feature as a point of reference first, you will have greatly reduced the margin of error and increased your chance of arriving safely at your (less obvious) target destination, because you should only have a short distance to cover before you get there. The use of attack points is of great benefit in poor visibility.

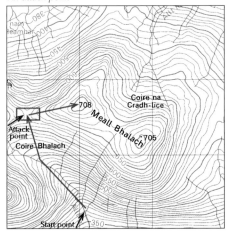
An attack point

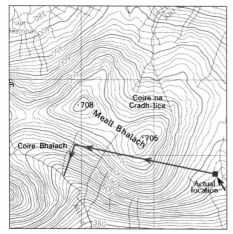

Aiming off: in this example the navigator has aimed downstream from the stream source. When the navigator reaches this point, he will turn downhill, following the stream to the stream junction. Aiming off is commonly used when travelling in poor visibility.

Aiming Off

This is another extremely useful technique in all weather conditions, but especially in poor visibility when you are trying to arrive at a specific feature (possibly an attack point), such as a stream junction. If you aim directly for the junction from a distance away it's quite possible that when you get where it 'should be', it will not be there. Having arrived at the stream, how would you know whether you were above or below the feature that you were aiming for?

Aiming off means deliberately giving yourself a safe margin, say, to arrive at the stream at a point you know is above the junction that you wish to reach. When you reach the stream you will then know that the junction is downstream. In other words you walk to the stream, turn and walk downstream to arrive at your feature. This technique is 'playing smart' with the terrain, and will avoid potential worry and confusion when locating your target.

Remember

Attack points and aiming off are by no means the only techniques available when using map features to navigate, but they are the most popular and the most important.

Dog Leg

A dog leg is used when the navigator is required to avoid a large, dangerous feature. As the diagram illustrates, the navigator will take a bearing and follow a set distance past the danger. Then the navigator will take a new bearing to rejoin the planned route.

Boxing

The classic example of boxing is when you have been following a corrie edge in poor visibility. You come across, say, a huge precipitous gully which cuts back into the cliff by some way, across the line of travel. It can be avoided by applying the following procedure:

Dog legging in action

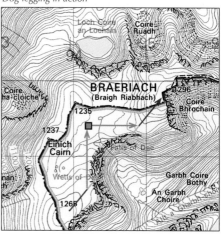

- Maintaining your original bearing on your compass, stop and turn your body through 90° to align your compass needle at 90° from your original bearing.
- Follow the compass direction of travel arrow for a set distance that you are confident clears you of the line of the danger.
- Stop: turn your body to realign your compass on your original bearing, and pace for a set distance until you are past the obstacle.
- Now do 'step one' in reverse – turn your body and compass through 90° degrees in the opposite direction, and pace the distance required to rejoin your original line of travel. When you get there, turn through 90° again, and follow your original compass bearing.

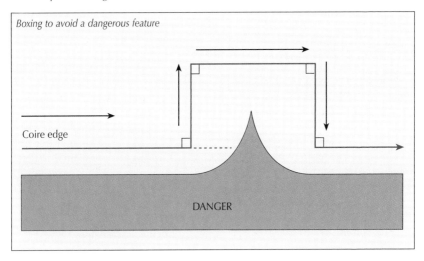

Boxing to avoid a dangerous feature

Coire edge

DANGER

The Use of GPS (Global Positioning System)

Given its growing profile and use it is appropriate to spend some time discussing GPSs. We do not intend to concentrate on how to use a GPS (that information is readily available elsewhere) but rather to discuss some of the pros and cons concerning its use in a mountain environment.

A GPS device is a hand-held receiver of transmissions from satellites orbiting earth. This impressive technology can provide accurate information about your position on the ground, with the GPS capable of calculating your exact location, displayed as a map grid reference. For a GPS to work it needs at least three satellites to 'talk to it', but all being well it can be accurate from 100 square metres down to 6 square metres.

There is no question that a GPS can be a very useful tool in the mountains, and has its place. But the question many people ask

The GPS has a place in the mountains, but you have to know how to use it with map and compass; it is no substitute

when they think about buying one is, 'Will I also need a map and compass?' The answer is, most definitely, 'Yes'. Map and compass remain the indispensable navigation aids in the mountains. Used properly both are much more useful, and important, for planning and successfully undertaking a mountaineering route than a GPS, and that is unlikely to change for a very long time.

What Main Benefits does the Handheld GPS Offer to the Mountain Navigator?

- A grid reference of your actual position

- The facility to return to a position you have visited earlier

- Whilst on the mountain, entering a position of a specific grid reference you would like to visit, to which the GPS compass will indicate a direction

- You can enter waypoints prior to a journey to use as a navigation aid during your trip

What are the Main Concerns?

- An exposed mountainside is no place to start programming in your intended route. This should be done at home as part of your preparation.

- You need to be completely *au fait* with the functions of your GPS before you rely on it. For instance, to use the track back facility to return to a position you visited earlier you have to know to keep it switched on all the time.

- Your position may not be in a clear line of sight with overhead satellites, if you are in a deep valley for example

- Signal reflection – large areas of rock can reflect the signal, causing it to travel further and cause an error in calculating your position

- User error is always a possibility, particularly if fatigued or stressed. Perhaps the most significant and common error occurs when taking grid references from the map to input to the GPS. If you then accurately follow the incorrect reference, that is where you will end up!

- Loss of battery power is not unlikely in cold conditions

- A digital compass is harder to follow than a manual one

- Where do you get your detailed information about the surrounding terrain?

- A GPS can't (yet) map read. Map-based micro-navigation skills are critical to safe travel in a mountain environment, especially in poor visibility.

- For those travelling outside the UK, in very remote areas of the world, there might not be enough satellites available

A GPS is an excellent navigation aid, but whether it is an essential piece of equipment is largely a matter of personal judgement. In our opinion, in the British mountains at least, it is not. Certainly it should never be used on its own in a wilderness environment. If you do use a GPS use it wisely and be aware of its potential shortcomings.

Remember

The GPS is here to stay. The technology is phenomenal and no doubt will get better and better. But regardless of whether you carry a GPS or not, you will always need your compass to navigate effectively. It requires no batteries and it has pinpoint accuracy, when used correctly with an up-to-date map.

Route Finding

However you navigate your way around the mountains one of the most important skills is the art of route finding: picking the specific line on the ground by which the navigational points along your route will be joined up. Put more simply, the way that you choose to walk, scramble or climb over the terrain. Route finding is a navigational skill in its own right, and requires the combination of interpretation of the terrain and judgement. On difficult terrain this is particularly relevant. If on a scrambling route, for instance, you appear to be encountering terrain that is well above the grade of the route, but other clues suggest it is the right way, your judgement as to whether it is the correct line or not is critical. The tendency to say, 'It says so in the guidebook, so it must be right' should be avoided. Similarly when it comes to assessing the need for a river crossing. You have to make all your own decisions in the mountains, and many of them concern route finding.

Route-Finding Tips

- Study your map and guidebook information prior to your trip, and refer to both when you are out.

- On the approach to the route look for features that indicate where you are and where you are going.

- When you can see your objective take time to study any route diagram that you are carrying and match up any features on the ground.

- If unsure about your route identification, pull back to a point where you are sure of your location and work your way back in again.

- Don't set off across risky terrain if you are not sure where the route is going.

- Experience will help, but learn to understand scale.

- Remember that things will always look and feel different on the ground to what you expected.

- Don't let anxiety cloud the right route-finding decision – keep calm.

At least one British weather forecaster has been known to miss the odd hurricane or two. It just goes to show: the weather is a complex subject that few people – even those who make a living out of it – will ever master completely. Fortunately British mountaineers don't need to be ace meteorologists. What they do need is to acquire and apply some basic knowledge of how prevailing weather systems will interact with mountainous terrain, and how that will affect their plans on a particular day on a particular route.

There are plenty of good books and sources of information on weather, including specifically mountain weather. It is a subject that is too important to miss out altogether, but too huge to deal with comprehensively. We will therefore concentrate on a practical approach to interpreting weather information, on how to apply this to your preparation and planning, and on the skill of monitoring developments as your day on the hill progresses.

One Way Out...

Interestingly some hillwalkers choose to avoid the weather altogether! It is not unheard of for experienced applicants undergoing training for the Mountain Leader Training United Kingdom's (MLTUK) Mountain Leader Award to initially struggle to muster the descriptions of at least 40 personal 'quality mountain days' that are required in their log book. For the purposes of the MLA, a quality mountain day involves some unpredictability in the conditions.

Understandably, many hill-goers choose to venture out mainly on copper-bottomed sunshine days, avoiding the hard stuff. But part of the fun (and the challenge) of the British mountains is dealing with the vagaries of their weather. The most dramatic mountain days – the ones you really wouldn't have missed – often involve a mixture of conditions; and, in any case, settled weather in the hills is rarely guaranteed for more than a few hours. True competence means being able to handle the hills whatever conditions they throw at you – which is not (by any means!) the same as saying you should be able to attempt any route, whatever the weather.

Understanding Weather Information

It is important for all mountain-goers to try and understand how the weather can or will affect an outing, in summer or wintertime. Planning and preparation for any outdoor activity is most often thought out around the weather. Information gleaned in advance will influence where you go, the route you take, how high you go, what equipment you will need, how long your journey will take, and what skills and knowledge it will require.

The weather information for hillwalkers and climbers provided by the Met Office and other weather sources is generally excellent in its detail and structure. However, what we must always remember is that the weather forecast is merely an informed prediction, not a complete and accurate picture for the next 12- or 24-hour period. A forecast at the time of release is generally very accurate for at least six hours. Many forecasts *can* be accurate for longer periods of time, but are less likely to be so. The mountaineer has to learn to interpret the trends and features of forecast weather to understand how prevailing conditions are likely to affect plans – a process that is best begun several days before a major trip, and that should be continued during its course.

Weather or not? Knowledge of clouds, and other clues, will help you work out the oncoming conditions

Isobars

Weather is fuelled by air pressure. The lines shown on a weather map are called isobars – these join points of equal atmospheric pressure, the meteorological equivalent of contour lines. Weather charts showing isobars are extremely useful as they identify features such as:

- *Anticyclones (highs)* A body of moving air of higher pressure than the surrounding air, in which the pressure decreases away from the centre, causing winds to circulate around the centre in a clockwise direction in the northern hemisphere, including Britain
- *Ridges* Areas of high pressure, often an elongated extension of an anticyclone, bringing generally settled weather
- *Troughs* The low pressure equivalent of a ridge, generally bringing unsettled weather.

Such features move in a fairly predictable way, and so it is also possible to predict the weather.

Wind Speed and Direction

Isobars also highlight wind speed and direction, through the spacing and orientation of the lines. A quick way to determine the likely wind speed at altitude (say, the top of a mountain of 3,000–4,000ft/914–1,220m) is to count the number of isobar lines spread across the UK. Multiply the number at 10mph per line and you will have a reasonable approximation of the wind speed on the high tops.

> **Remember**
> The closer the isobars the stronger the wind

'Wind direction' refers to the direction from which the wind comes. A south westerly, for example, is blowing *from* south west to north east. In the mountains this knowledge can be critically important – for instance, in assessing avalanche risk or the safety of being on a knife-edged arête. When it comes to planning your day, wind direction should be a major consideration.

In the UK, wind speed is measured in knots (nautical miles per hour) and forecast winds are given in miles per hour: 1 knot = 1.15mph.

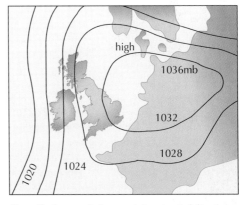

Curved isobars can indicate variations in wind direction

But in addition to basic wind speed, gusts – a sudden variation of the mean wind speed – can be a significant problem in the mountains. Typically a gust can be up to 60% higher than the main wind speed.

The impact of wind on the mountaineer is influenced by the combination of wind strength and direction, which combine in the very common mountain weather phenomenon of orographic uplift. This is where the air rising over the hills and the mountain tops causes air turbulence – air currents formed by wind blown across rough ground. Wind speed increases with altitude as the air rolls up the land mass and over the mountain tops, often three times faster than the speed at the foot of the mountain.

Information about the wind gives an indication of the type of weather likely to be experienced. A marked or significant change in wind direction will also influence a change in the

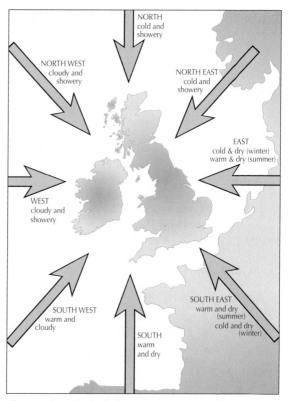

This map shows the kind of weather that can generally be anticipated as a result of different wind directions

weather. For instance, northerly winds will tend to bring cold air from the polar regions to the British Isles, and southerly winds will bring warmer air from the tropics. As air approaches the British Isles across the sea it will be moist, getting drier as it tracks across land.

Lows and Highs (Cyclones and Anticyclones)

In a *low (cyclone or depression)* air is rising and as it does so it cools. Cold air can hold less moisture than warm air, so as the air rises the water vapour it contains condenses to form clouds and perhaps precipitation. Consequently the weather in a low will be cloudy, wet and windy – the wind will blow in an anticlockwise direction around the low. There are usually fronts associated with a low-pressure system.

In a *high (anticyclone)* winds will tend to be light and will blow in a clockwise direction – the air is now descending and inhibits the formation of cloud. The light winds and clear skies lead to settled weather sometimes, and overnight fog and frost – an important consideration not only on the mountain, but also on your journey to and from it.

If an anticyclone persists over Northern Europe in winter much of the British Isles is likely to be affected by very cold easterly winds from Siberia. However, in the summer an anticyclone in the vicinity of the British Isles often brings fine warm weather.

The generally changeable weather in the British Isles is caused by the succession of lows, with their associated fronts and anticyclones, running across the country from the Atlantic Ocean.

Fronts

A boundary between two air masses is called a front. In the latitude of the British Isles a front is usually a battleground between warm, moist air from the tropics and cold, relatively dry air from the polar regions. On a weather chart the round (warm front) or pointed (cold front) symbols point in the direction of the front's movement. Fronts are associated with low-pressure systems and move with the wind, travelling from west to east.

At a front the cold air undercuts the dense warm air. This causes the warm air to rise over the wedge of cold air. As the air rises there is cooling and condensation leading to the formation of clouds – when the clouds thicken up it begins to rain.

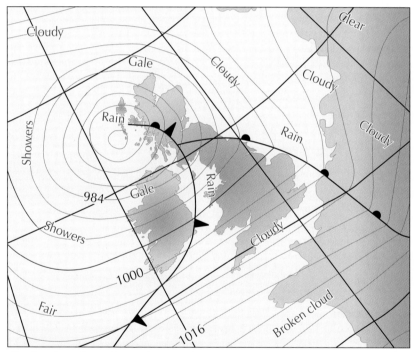

This chart shows the weather in relation to a depression and its associated warm, cold and occluded fronts

Distinguishing Between Warm, Cold and Occluded Fronts

- *A warm front advancing will replace the cold air*

   When the front approaches there will be thickening cloud and eventually it begins to rain. When the warm front passes the air changes from being fairly cold and cloudy to warm and overcast.

- *A cold front advancing will replace the warm air*

As the cold front passes the weather changes from mild and overcast to cold and bright, possibly with showers. The passing of the front is marked by a narrow band of rain and a change in wind direction

- *An occluded front can be thought of as being the result of a warm and cold front meeting*

Ahead of the occlusion the weather is similar to that ahead of a warm front, whereas behind the occlusion the weather is similar to that behind a cold front

Clouds

Clouds consist of droplets of water (ice or snow) in suspension. You cannot see the droplets, but you can certainly feel them, say in fog, where you get slightly damp. The warmer the air the greater the capacity to carry moisture. If the temperature falls, or too much moisture is fed into the clouds, it will shed in the form of rain, hail or snow (precipitation). One of the most useful indicators as to the likelihood of rain, and its extent and duration, is cloud type. Identifying different cloud types and what they mean can pay real dividends in forecasting mountain weather.

Cloud Types

Basic Cloud Types

- *Cirrus* Feathery, either white or transparent, but can obscure the sun.

- *Stratus* Like a fog, and can be associated with drizzle – often occurs in a warm front.

- *Nimbus* Thick cloud with dark, grey underbelly likely to produce heavy rain.

- *Cumulus* Puffy and sometimes harmless, but can develop into huge masses bearing showers, rain and thunderstorms. Typical for the back side of a low which has passed overhead. In storm conditions nimbus and cumulus can rise up to 10–15,000m and more; definitely conditions to avoid if possible.

Having identified a basic cloud type, altitude is another key factor in working out what will happen.

High Cloud (6,000m and Upwards)

- *Cirrus* Very white feathery clouds (mares' tails), but can develop in to huge masses consisting of ice particles. Usually indicate wind aloft. If it thickens indicates weather deterioration with the approach of a low. Observe the barometer. Depending on the intensity of the approaching front, weather will deteriorate within 12–24 hours.

- *Cirrocumulus* Mackerel sky. Rows of small, white, puffy clouds, very high up, sometimes forming banks. Thicker than cirrus, it is harmless, although can foretell changeable weather.

- *Cirrostratus* Thin high milky film, through which the sun can be seen, sometimes with a halo or 'brocken spectre'. Harmless until the cloud thickens, often indicates approaching low-pressure system, arriving within 12–24 hours.

Medium Cloud (2,000–6,000m)

- *Altocumulus* Larger and thicker version of cirrocumulus occurring in areas of high pressure or on edges of warm zones. If clouds develop vertically in early hours or up to mid-morning, it foretells thunderstorms which will normally occur during the afternoon. Before thunderstorms cloud will have disappeared.

- *Altostratus* Sheet-like grey cloud covering entire horizon, like a layer of medium-level fog, through which sun may sometimes still be seen without a halo.

Low Cloud (up to 2,000m)

- *Nimbostratus* Mass of low, grey, rain-bearing cloud – normally following alto-stratus with the passing of a front. Steady rain will set in.

- *Stratus* Soft, grey, fog-like layer of cloud as low as 300 or even 150m. If dense, stratus can drizzle and poor visibility will be found between warm and cold fronts.

- *Stratocumulus* Dense, lumpy, grey cloud at 700–1,500m. As it intensifies to form a solid grey layer across the sky, you can expect it to rain within one or two hours.

- *Cumulus* Typical fair weather cloud, forms as separate white puffs. Develops during the morning but leaves large areas of blue sky. Forms due to rising warm air over land and will disappear towards the evening.

- *Cumulonimbus* Much larger towering and more dramatic cloud than cumulus. Can rise to great heights with huge tops developing into irregular mountain-like peaks – is associated with heavy rain and thundery squalls. The higher the cloud peaks the stronger the squalls.

Sources of Weather Information

Using a range of forecasts in the build up to and during a mountain trip is a very good way of getting enough information to draw your own conclusions about what the weather will do. Sources include national and local television (which don't always tell the same story), radio, telephone and fax services, and the internet, including the Met Office website (www.met-office.gov.uk). Outdoor shops, National Park offices and other establishments with an interest in the climbing and walking world will often post the day's forecast in a prominent place; you should always get the latest mountain weather forecast for the area before setting out.

Remember

For winter it is essential to check out avalanche information services such as the Scottish Avalanche Information Service (www.sais.gov.co.uk).

Scrambling or Rock Climbing?

Any great mountaineering route involves tackling steep ground, and so inevitably an element of climbing is called for, whether on snow, ice or rock. In the context of this book that climbing would generally be on summer rock and would be categorised as scrambling, but it's important to be clear that scrambling *is* a form of rock climbing. This is particularly relevant when you consider the ability level of the participant and what they are taking on. Let's take as an example the Cneifion Arête in the Glyderau, Snowdonia. If you are an accomplished rock climber you might think of the arête as a scramble, but to the mountaineering hillwalker this route, particularly on its lower third, could never be any less than a rock climb. It looks like one, feels like one, and the skills you need to deal with it safely are, without any shadow of doubt, those of the rock climber. That means we are concerned with mountaineers being able to deal with climbing passages, but probably without 'becoming' rock climbers.

What exactly constitutes 'steep ground' is relative – different people have different tolerances – but the fact is nearly all mountain-goers are drawn to the most pleasing lines on a mountain, and they are often steep! Some believe the ability to move up and down rock cannot be taught, and it's true some people do have a far greater natural aptitude than others. Nevertheless, regular practice can make a huge difference. The coaching of techniques, and a level of awareness about ways to rock climb safely and efficiently – some do's and don'ts – can also improve performance, and perhaps most importantly confidence, when it comes to tackling testing passages of high-level scrambling. On a technically straightforward climb, confidence can have a huge influence on success or failure, and lack of confidence is most keenly felt in an exposed situation.

Exposure

Defining Exposure

Almost any description of a scrambling route will talk about exposure – 'a sense of', 'limited', 'significant', 'massive', and so on – but it takes quite a lot of experience (some of which we would not want to repeat in a hurry) to work out exactly what these descriptions mean for ourselves, and the answer to one simple yet important question: 'Will I be scared witless?'

Anyone can 'go for it' dangling over a couple of feet drop onto a climbing mat. What 'exposure' means, in simple terms, is that you are aware that if you slip you are going to fall and get hurt – or worse. But exposed positions can also be amongst the most exhilarating places to be on a mountain, and while the feeling can spook some people, for others the adrenaline rush they experience is the essence of why they go out in the hills. Yes – they actually enjoy it. Many others enjoy it much more in retrospect, but however you view it, it's all part of the kick you get from being out there. Until you are put in an exposed position, you don't really know how you will react.

For these reasons exposure is a relative concept. Technically easy ground in an exposed position can become impossible to negotiate for someone gripped by the fear of falling off. If they are that frightened they've got at least one very good reason to be so. To handle the kind of exposure involved in many of the routes referred to in this book safely

Learning and practising how to move on rock will make you a better, safer scrambler

requires physical preparation, mental belief and technical competence. Ultimately it's a question of developing confidence in yourself, your ability, your equipment and your climbing partners.

The first line of defence against the effects (and possible consequences) of exposure is a cool head and good technique, swiftly followed by a rope, harness and placed protection. Roped or unroped, if you do get 'gripped' by exposure, there are two things you must do to see you through the section. Calm down – try to relax mentally and physically – and concentrate on your technique. In most cases if you visualise yourself above that climbing mat you will realise that, technically, the terrain you are tackling is well within your capability.

Scrambling Technique

This section looks at a number of scrambling/rock-climbing techniques and manoeuvres that, if practised and applied, will help you to move safely up and down steep and rocky terrain involved in high-level scrambling, a level which may involve the odd move up to Difficult standard. This is not a comprehensive range of climbing techniques – there are many good books that provide those – but if you need to 'fist–jam', for instance, you have strayed off the kind of ground that we are dealing with here.

Practice Makes Perfect

Scrambling is one of the most satisfying forms of travel on a mountain, but to enjoy it to the full – and safely – you should practise and consolidate some of the basic technical moves and positions that overcoming scrambling terrain will inevitably involve. Your approach should always be steady, balanced and economical.

Confident and competent scrambling is about understanding the skills and techniques which are best employed when progressing on rock with your hands out of your pockets. As soon as a walker uses the combination of hands and feet to assist with balance and movement on rock it becomes scrambling. At the top end of the grades scrambling involves making exposed moves in very exposed situations – the rock may be steep, and in such cases it is normally only the size and security of the holds that enable this to still be classed as scrambling; albeit it must also be considered as low-grade rock climbing. A slip or fall in such a position on a top-end scramble, without the use of ropes, will very probably be fatal.

It should never be forgotten that unroped scrambling is potentially one of the most dangerous of all mountaineering activities. In particular scrambling in wet conditions can be hazardous. Not only because certain rock types, or worn rock, can get very slippery, but also because water can run down sleeves and into other parts of clothing, which is both uncomfortable and off-putting. Whenever possible plan to scramble in dry weather, and to avoid strong winds on the route. Apart from anything else, it's more fun! In winter conditions scrambling moves become much harder, with routes automatically transformed into snow and ice grades requiring winter mountaineering and climbing skills beyond the scope of this book.

Wear the Right Equipment

When practising scrambling moves always wear a helmet, especially when on a mountain route. In order to scramble without falling off and to make comfortable progress a good scrambling boot is essential – a rigid sole with soft leather uppers is ideal. This will provide plenty of foot support when the weight of the body is compressed into the boot edge. Note that the feet provide the all-important friction when scrambling. If you start to use body parts such as bums, tums and knees, you will not have that security – so stay on your feet as much as you can.

Scrambling Moves

Edging

Edging is when the outside and inside edge of the boot is used to rest on a small rough section or lip of rock. The angle of the rock will probably be steep when using this technique.

Using a rigid-soled boot allows you to edge on small features in the rock

Smearing

The front of the sole of the boot lies flat against the rock with the heel slightly raised. This position allows the weight to compress over the toes, creating friction and excellent grip. Smearing works best on less steeply angled slabby rock surfaces.

Smearing involves lifting your heel and balancing your weight on to your toes to create friction

Boot Jam

The front of the boot is placed into a crack in the rock, using the stiff edges of the sole to hold the weight of the scrambler. This is a very common and useful technique. One slight drawback is that you do need to be able to pull your boot back out from the crack, so place it in position rather than deliberately pushing and squeezing it in.

Placing your boot into a crack can provide excellent support and rigidity. Place your boot carefully; never force it.

Flat foot friction is achieved by placing your feet flat on the rock, rather than by walking heel to toe

Flat Foot Friction

This is a good method to use when descending easy-angled rock-slab terrain and involves maintaining all your weight evenly across your feet, generating enough pressure to create good friction between the sole of your boot and the rock.

Toe Jam

Should the width of the crack be too small for the entire boot, use the toe. This is achieved by placing the toe into the crack vertically, and rotating the heel. Once the toe is placed rotate the heel towards the horizontal position and you will get tremendous grip. It's not the most comfortable hold, but it's very effective.

Place the toe of your boot into a crack by angling the boot to one side, then torque the heel in the opposite direction

Hand and Finger Holds

There are many different handholds, but the easiest ones to use are those that are horizontal and in-cut, where the angles are in your favour. When the holds are sloping outwards they are much less reassuring.

Maintaining a compact grip increases the strength of your hold

If the hold is big enough to take your whole hand then that is what you should use. For smaller holds get as many fingers on it as you can. Placing fingers on top of one another, or just simply keeping your fingers close together, will strengthen your handhold.

Placing your fingers into a crack and pushing your knuckles or thumbs outward enables you to expand a grip into a narrow hold

Body Position

The right body position is very important for scrambling; you should aim to find the best position for balance. The key point to remember is that weight should always be pushed into and over the feet. Remember that your legs are much stronger than your arms – so think feet, not arms.

You should always try to keep an upright posture, maintaining your arms in a straight position as much as possible. When climbers push and pull with bent arms they get tired and lose strength very easily. Climbing with bent arms will also stop you from using your legs properly, which in

A climber showing good balance, and not hugging the rock

turn will lead to you falling off backwards. A common mistake is to 'hug' the rock; you should maintain space between body and rock.

When we climb we must constantly adjust our body position to suit our foot and hand technique. Sometimes you may need to climb an awkward move sideways, because the holds might be sideways and that will be the best way to negotiate that particular move.

The Mantle Shelf Move

This technique is used on ledges. Simply place the hands on the top of the ledge and pull up as if you are climbing on top of a wall or getting out of a swimming pool. Keep the arms straight and place one foot onto the mantle shelf, maintaining straight arms.

A mantle shelf move

Literally, bridging a gap

Bridging

Bridging is a very straightforward technique. You spread the feet on either side of two opposing walls, in a corner or a chimney. Bridging can also allow you to have a rest, with one leg placed on the opposite wall, or with your arms on either one wall or on opposing walls.

Planning to Succeed

Success on a challenging scrambling route is about having both the right psychological and physical approach, and the former can have a huge impact on the latter. Anyone can 'flash' a scramble within their grade, especially when things are going well, but equally anyone can experience negative thoughts. This can lead to effects from desperation to backing down from the move or route. A classic physiological sign is uncontrollable leg shaking, and such responses are quite normal when you have thoughts of falling or failing on a route or move that is well within your ability. Once again, planning and preparation can help you to overcome the problem.

Top Tips

- Practise sound scrambling moves before attempting a route. This can easily be achieved by visiting some low-level rock slabs or boulders where you won't come to any harm should you slip.

- Always remember to use your eyes when moving, to look for the best body position that will lead to balance and control. The same goes for foot and handholds.

- Certain rock types will offer more or better friction than others, but all scramblers will encounter loose rock or dubious handholds at times. If you have to use such a hold, first pull in a downward direction to check for stability. Better still, find another hold.

- When scrambling on a knife-edged arête keep to one side: you will stay in balance much more easily.

- When down climbing, avoid facing outwards. Instead, turn and face into the rock from the moment you are required to scramble, until you reach a safe area.

- *Maintain three points of contact with the rock* and don't overstretch on any partic-ular move – *economy of movement* works best. Don't make a move if you are off balance or in doubt.

- Remember it's not just about physical ability but psychological control – so stay motivated, hydrated and practised.

- Try to maintain your composure at all times, and if you feel anxiety coming on make a conscious effort to slow down, calm down, and progress with a cool and rational head.

Technical Gear: Choosing it and Using it

When preparing to go mountaineering you must consider the essential technical equipment you will need to tackle your chosen route successfully and safely. Here we discuss some of the most important items and their uses, and make suggestions for selecting the right gear.

Helmet

You only have one head, so it is worth wearing a helmet to protect it. This includes when you are scrambling, or even walking on steep terrain if you feel there is sufficient risk. A helmet is essential for a number of reasons including, most importantly, protecting yourself from:

- falling debris while your climbing partner leads above you
- banging your head if you slip or slide accidentally as you ascend or descend steep ground.

Get your rack together: the well-prepared scrambler needs some technical gear

There are many different sorts of helmet, most of them lightweight. However, when selecting a helmet for general rock climbing and mountaineering you should look for something that is not only lightweight but also offers good all-round protection against impacts from all sides. Make sure the strap is convenient and easy to manipulate and adjust, especially when wearing a hat underneath. For comfort look for something with good ventilation that will help keep your head cool. Modern foam/shell constructions are a good choice.

Helmets come in a variety of shapes and sizes; weight, strength, fit, ventilation and comfort are all considerations when choosing one

Harness

A good, well-fitting harness doesn't just make you safer, it provides a tremendous feeling of security which can give a great boost to your confidence. Choose one with adjustable leg loops so that in colder conditions you will be able to fit your waterproofs and windproofs underneath it. Your harness should include the following features:

Make sure you get a harness that fits over your wet-weather gear

- overall sizing that will fit you when wearing waterproofs
- at least four gear loops
- leg loops linked to the front of the waist belt via belay loop/abseil loop
- light in weight.

Please note that the harness pictured above does not have a fixed belay/abseil loop. One that does is shown on page 95 – and this is the type to ask for when buying a harness. There are many harnesses available and it is worth trying a few on and even, as with all kit, testing them if possible.

Top Tips

- Manufacturer's recommendations for correct use of your chosen harness and its belt buckles must be followed at all times. Instructions are often displayed on the inside of the harness waist belt.

- When trying a harness on for fitting remember to wear your wind/waterproof gear to see whether it still fits properly – it's no good discovering that it doesn't fit when you're on the mountainside.

Getting your Rack Together
Karabiners

Consider carrying at least six HMS screwgate karabiners of the same size and design, and six small karabiners. HMS screwgate karabiners are large in size to allow the smooth functioning of friction knots such as the Italian hitch. They are also commonly used in conjunction with belay plates to enable smooth, slick

'Krabs': (right to left) HMS screwgate karabiner, small screwgate karabiner and snaplink karabiner

running of the rope. Small screwgate karabiners used here will grab and jam friction knots, especially with ropes from 10.2mm diameter upwards.

The smaller screwgate karabiners will be used for building anchors and protecting a personal abseil; have a few spare in case you lose one or two on the route. Snaplink kara-biners are used on extenders, to extend protection by forming 'runners'.

Prusik Loop

A prusik loop is used for protecting a personal abseil

A French prusik is the most common prusik knot used when protecting a personal abseil

A prusik loop is a length of 5 or 6mm dynamic cord that is joined together using a double fisherman's knot. The prusik loop is used predominantly for protecting a personal abseil and is rigged in a way that if you were to release your grip on an abseil rope the prusik allows you to stop, hands-free. There are other uses: for example, if you want to retrieve stuck gear from a route or if you need to self-rescue. See French prusik (page 83).

Belay Plate

Not all belay plates are the same and it's important to choose the best one for your purpose. Belay plates are designed for single-rope use, half-rope use or twin-rope use. They are also designed for use with ropes of different diameters.

So how do you choose a belay plate? For a start, don't be confused by the terminology. For routes involving adventurous scrambling you need a single (or 'full-weight') rope, but a double-rope belay plate! This means you will be able to retreat via an abseil from a crux section of a route and also retrieve your rope. It also means if you decide to progress to full-on rock climbing you will have the right belay plate for any double-rope multi-pitch climbing.

A selection of belay plates – it's important to get the right one for the thickness of rope you are using

Buy a belay plate that is designed for full-weight ropes as you will predominantly use this type of single rope, from 9.4mm and upwards. All these ropes will run smoothly through your plate. There is a broad range available on the market, and the Black Diamond ATC plate is exceptionally good value.

Extenders

Extenders (also known as 'quick-draws') allow the climber to extend the rope from placed protection in the rock. This is important: if you do not extend the link between placed protections and the rope, the vibration and angle of the rope movement will extract the placement from the rock for you – just when you don't want it to. Carrying at least four 15cm extenders on a route will

You should carry a selection of extenders

suffice. You should buy them with snaplink karabiners fixed at each end, with the gates facing the opposing sides of the extender.

8ft dyneema tape sling.
Tape slings are very lightweight and easy to tie knots in

Tape Slings

Tape slings are very useful when building anchors, or when an extra-long extender is required to extend the rope away from placed protection. Using a tape sling will straighten out any awkward angles in the rope that may potentially create rope drag (at the risk of pulling out carefully placed protection). We recommend taking two 8ft dyneema tape slings and one 16ft dyneema tape sling; these are lightweight and very easy to tie knots in.

Rocks on wires

A standard set of 'rocks on wires' will come in sizes from 1–10 and will be invaluable.

When leading a crux or exposed section of a route, for instance, you may establish protection using the rocks on wires, by placing them in parallel or horizontal cracks in the rock. You can then 'extend' the wire by using an extender, and clip your trailing lead

Always use a screwgate karabiner to carry your rocks on wires, just in case you need a spare

rope into it. If you were to fall off you would only fall as far as your last placed protection, and then the same distance again. For example, if you are 2m above your last piece of extended protection – or 'runner' – then you will fall 4m before you stop, assuming your attentive belayer holds on to the rope end using the belay plate, or another friction knot such as the Italian hitch (see page 80).

Rope
The rope to buy for scrambling is a single (also known as a full-weight) rope which, as the name implies, is designed to be used on its own.

Half ropes are designed to be used in pairs, running parallel, clipping into alternate placed protection. Twin ropes are designed to be used by clipping both parallel ropes into the same extender. The use of half ropes and twin ropes is generally restricted to advanced rock- and ice-climbing activity.

Rope length is important. The standard length is 50m for a single rope for scramblers, although some will opt for 60m; 50m will certainly suffice for the majority of scramble routes, and some people will use 40m. The decision should rest on the length of the crux pitch, and length of any abseils to be encountered. A 50m rope will give you up to 50m of pitched climbing, and 25m of abseiling, as you will double the rope for this procedure.

Top Tips
- When you buy the rope from the manufacturer it will be tightly packaged. To take out the kinks, hold one end, drop the rope on to the floor and completely unravel it, running it through your hands from end to end.

- 'Coil' the rope, as shown, using lap coils. This will help to prevent further kinking in the rope.

Step 1 – Place the rope ends on the ground.

Step 2 – Start taking lap coils into the hand.

Step 3 – Lap coiling your rope provides a finished tie-off that is easy to carry.

Gloves

It is worth investing in leather- or neoprene-palmed gloves, because some rock types can be flesh eating – the hungriest being the gabbro on Skye's Cuillin Ridge. Once your fingers have been relieved of their skin, belaying, abseiling, general rope handling and also climbing become painful and difficult, putting yourself and those relying on you at risk. The only cure for this is prevention. It is common practice to wear gloves when rope handling, but it is essential to choose a pair that offers dexterity, comfort and resilience. Some people favour a well-fitting pair of gardening gloves, as they are cheap, easy to replace and long lasting.

Scrambling Boots

The days when one pair of boots was purchased for all seasons and all routes are on the way out – which is good news in every respect except for your finances! The kind of routes discussed in this book are best done in a mountaineering boot that is specifically suited to scrambling, which will give you a real advantage and confidence boost. For reasons of both technical performance and comfort consider the following features when purchasing:

- lightweight alpine boot
- rigid sole for edging on rock
- sticky rands – strips of rubber moulded round the boot. Enables better friction when boot jamming and all-round protection of the boot upper.
- water repellent
- light synthetic uppers
- snug fit – but not so tight as to cut off the blood supply to your foot.

You are looking for something that will be designed for anything from British mountaineering routes to the *via ferratas* of northern Italy. Pay as much attention as you can to getting the fit right over the whole foot, and particularly the length. You should not buy any boot without testing it on a downhill angle and kicking the toe end down into the floor to ensure that your toes make no

Stiff-soled boots designed for general mountaineering on rock and snow, in wet and dry conditions

contact with the end of the boot. If they do, the boots are too short. Boots should fit closely, but should not clamp your foot, allowing some toe movement when standing still.

Rucksack

Your rucksack needs to be suitable for both walking and climbing, so think about comfort and practicality for both activities. When climbing, balance is of major importance, and the best option is really a climbing sack which combines the necessary capacity and a comfortable harness system. A climbing sack will be uncluttered with gadgets, extras and exterior pockets, but they are also lightweight and do have compression straps.

Ready to climb

Climbing sacks are single compartment packs, which are both more compact and keep your load more stable. Some will find the single compartment idea off-putting, but adapting to it is largely a question of being better organised; organising yourself and your gear is one of the keys to efficient mountaineering, and in this respect buying a sack that forces you to improve in that area is a helpful discipline. The ideal capacity is 40 to 50 litres.

Top Tips

- Buy a pack that fits your back length. If the pack sits below your hips after buckling up the waist belt and adjusting the upper shoulder straps, it is too long and will not be stable or comfortable when climbing.

- Buy a plastic rucksack liner to ensure that the contents do not get wet in persistent rain, or during a stream crossing. Rucksacks are not waterproof. You should also consider stuffing the contents into separate dry bags.

Know your Knots

Knot a Problem?

If one of the most appealing things about a day in the mountains is its simplicity, knots represent the kind of complexity many people are striving to get away from. A fear of knots is just as likely to put someone off technical climbing as a fear of heights, and for many tying them is perceived to be a complex procedure best avoided. But the idea that all knots are awkward and difficult is not true. Mastery of just a few of them and understanding their uses will help transform your potential and ability as a mountaineer.

You can buy a whole book on knots, but the basic set of knots described here are those that are used in most climbing situations, and the minimum a mountaineer should know to be safe and effective.

One of the beauties of knots is that you can practise tying them anywhere, from the comfort of your home to the base of a crag. What is not recommended, however, is learning knots for the first time on a route. Learn the knot, and its function, before you commit to a route.

Rewoven Figure-of-Eight

To tie a rewoven figure-of-eight it is important that you select around 1m length of rope

This is one of the most readily used knots in climbing and is the recommended knot to use when tying into a climbing harness. It is called a 'figure of eight' because of its number eight-type shape when completed. This knot is very strong and absorbs stress

Step 1 – Tie a single figure-of-eight knot. Thread the length of rope through your harness, starting at the top and running through your fixed belay/abseil loop assuming your harness has one. (The harness shown here does not – see page 95 for one that does.)

Step 3 – Follow and reproduce the line of the single figure-of-eight (you are 're-weaving' the knot), until eventually you have produced one figure-of-eight knot comprising a double thickness of rope. The tail end of the rope should exit the knot, pointing out down the main length of rope, away from the body. Remember to ensure that the tie-in loop is the same circumference as the fixed belay/abseil loop, as indicated on page 95.

Step 2 – Re-thread the tail end of the rope through the figure-of-eight knot.

very efficiently when loaded. It also allows for an uncluttered rope loop, so that when clipping a screwgate karabiner with a belay plate attached there is no constriction of movement within the loop.

Step 4 – To tie off the tail-end of the rope use a double fisherman's knot – simply wrap the tail end of the rope back around the main rope twice, towards the rethreaded figure-of-eight knot, and then push the remainder of the tail-end back through the twists, in the direction of the main rope as it leads away from the harness. Now manipulate the knot until it is tight.

Step 5 – The final knot, tied off with a double fisherman's.

Clove Hitch

The clove hitch is a very simple knot, and one of the most used in climbing. It's probably the second-most important knot, and a favourite with climbers and instructors for both summer and winter use. It is commonly used for tying in to anchors, and for building both single and equalised anchors. When tying this knot it is always best to use an HMS karabiner, which will allow the knot to adjust properly without jamming and sticking. With some practice you can learn to tie this knot using one hand, but it is easier with two.

Step 1 – Identify where in the rope you want the knot to be tied, and create two loops as shown.

Step 2 – Place one loop behind the other.

Step 3 – Clip in to your karabiner through both loops.

It is important to remember that the rope should be clipped into the karabiner and should sit at the base of the karabiner spine. This is the strongest and widest point of the karabiner. The clove hitch can easily be converted to the Italian hitch with practice, without having to take the rope completely out of the karabiner.

Italian Hitch

Step 1 – Clip your rope through the prepared karabiner, noting the orientation of the HMS screwgate karabiner.

Step 3 – Clip the rope back into the karabiner by holding the 'krab' flat and positioning it on top of the loop; then opening the karabiner and clipping the loop into the karabiner.

Step 2 – Take the rope from the front side of the karabiner and bring it forward to form a loop.

Step 4 – You now have completed an Italian hitch.

This is another commonly used knot and is extremely useful for belaying, abseiling and general rigging. If you accidentally drop your belay plate you can use the Italian hitch as an effective replacement.

Care must always be taken to ensure that the rope is correctly handled when belaying. When using the Italian hitch make sure the dead rope does not rub on the locking gate of the karabiner. If it does the gate could open, causing the control rope to unclip, resulting in complete loss of control of a loaded rope.

Locking off an Italian Hitch

'Locking off' means adjusting the knot to stop the rope from moving, perhaps because the ascending climber needs a rest, or has a boot stuck in a crack. Locking off a friction knot enables the climber to have the security of a tightened rope. For this procedure we recommend a slippery hitch knot, backed up by a half-hitch knot that will not only lock off the rope securely, but will also enable you to untie the rope when under load safely and continue to lower someone, or take in rope when belaying.

When an Italian hitch knot is tensioned by a climber on the rope you should hold and pinch the knot with one hand securely all the time, using the other hand to tie the slippery hitch (see below). Wearing gloves is advisable, as ever when belaying.

Preparing to lock off an Italian hitch when not under load

Step 1 – Make an Italian hitch knot.

Step 4 – Pull the loop tight until it butts against the Italian hitch. You have now completed a slippery hitch. It is important to have at least 60cm of rope bight.

Step 2 – Take a bight of dead rope – a loop – and take it behind the live rope.

Step 5 – Wrap the bight of rope round the live and dead rope and through the hitch loop created, then pull really tight.

Step 3 – Take the rope back through itself.

Step 6 – You have now backed-up your slippery hitch with a half-hitch. The rope is completely locked off.

When reversing the procedure under load you should never let the bight of rope slip from your hands after untying the half hitch. Simply pull the dead rope and the knot will completely release itself. A jerk in the rope may be experienced – continue to belay or lower the climber.

Overhand Knot

This knot is used for many different tasks, such as tying slings for equalising anchors, tying a stopper knot at the end of a rope, or for making a sling from a length of rope or tape.

An overhand knot tied on a single rope – one of the most useful and versatile knots in mountaineering

Two ropes joined together for abseiling by using an overhand knot

The overhand knot is also used for tying two rope lengths together for abseiling and retrieving ropes. It is important to ensure the rope tail ends extend at least 60cm beyond the knot. You should also manipulate the knot tight before use.

Step 1 – Pinch one end of both ropes in one hand
Step 2 – Slide your hands down the ropes to about 60cm from the ends
Step 3 – Holding the ropes together, make a small loop at this point and bring the two ends back through the loop
Step 4 – Manipulate the knot tight. You should still have at least 60cm of tail ends coming out from the knot.

Lark's Foot (Cow's Tail)

The lark's foot is a knot used on tape slings only, never on rope. Although it is not a 'must-know' knot, we are finding it increasingly useful. It is only used when a tape sling is threaded through the climbing harness and used as a safety line (or cow's tail as it is commonly known). This extension is wrapped round the climber's waist and clipped on to the harness for tidy storage. For abseiling, the cow's tail is already positioned for use (see Abseiling).

To create a lark's foot, thread a 8'/120cm tape sling through your harness, as if threading a rope through for tying in. Then take the long end of the sling (the other end) and thread it through the short loop of sling (now emerging from the tie-in loop). Pull the long end through and tighten it, and you have tied a lark's foot, creating a cow's tail.

Beware

The lark's foot is a very weak knot, and if used in an anchor system will dangerously reduce the strength of the sling you have used, especially tape slings.

A cow's tail – this is always formed by a sling threaded through the harness

A cow's tail secured around the waist and clipped to the harness

French Prusiks

The prusik provides a means of protecting a personal abseil.

Two common prusik knots are used in mountaineering: the Klemheist and the French. The latter is used most, its advantage being that it can be released under load. This is essential when abseiling or dealing with emergency situations.

Making a Prusik Loop

You cannot make a French prusik without first making a prusik loop from your prusik. To do this your prusik, which should ideally be made of 5mm or 6mm dynamic cord, needs to be joined together using two double fisherman's knots (the same knot used to back up your rewoven figure of eight when tying on).

Step 1 – Pick up your 1m length of 5 or 6mm dynamic cord

Step 2 – Take one end of the cord and place it across the other end, wrapping it around and back on itself at least twice

Step 3 – Push the cord end through the loops created, and manipulate the knot tight. Ensure that you have at least 2.5cm of cord end visible from the end of the loops.

Step 4 – Repeat the process with the other cord end. As you roll it back on itself it should roll towards the first knot.

Step 5 – Push it through the loops created. Now manipulate both knots tight.

To Make a French Prusik

Simply wrap your prusik loop round your rope. You will need at least three turns. Ensure that the knotted part of the prusik loop is at the bottom. Ensure the twists are evenly spread and that there is an even loop created at each end. Now clip your screwgate karabiner through the two end loops created.

Preparing a prusik to protect a personal abseil

A French prusik ready to use for protecting a personal abseil

Top Tips

• When joining the prusik cord together it is worth considering the length of the final loop. An ideal size for most situations is 35cm.

• Your prusik loop diameter should always be at least 3mm larger than your rope diameter.

• Should the prusik loop be too thick you risk a catastrophic failure.

Belaying

Belaying is a method by which one climber draws in and pays out rope to which their mountaineering partner is attached, and in so doing protects them as they ascend or descend. In the event of a fall or bad slip, the belayer can stop the climber from coming to grief by 'locking off' the rope.

When you are belaying the rope you are holding is either 'live' rope or 'dead' rope. Live rope is the section that links the ascending climber to the belay device. Dead rope is the section that falls to the ground on the other side of the belay device. The belayer must never let go of the dead rope, as 'locking' off this rope is the means by which a fall is arrested. By remembering the names 'live' and 'dead' it should be quite easy to remember which rope you can't afford to let go of! In order to belay another climber effectively it is also essential to first establish a safe and secure position from which to do so. This is called a stance.

Belay Techniques
In this section we discuss the appropriate belay techniques for scrambling – direct belays and semi-indirect belays. When scrambling on exposed routes the mountaineer will usually select direct belays as a first choice if possible, because they are fast and easy to rig. However, they are still technical, and a lot of judgement is required to ensure that the anchor and position are good. Direct belays may be efficient, but to be successful there must be no doubt as to the integrity of the anchor chosen.

Direct Belay
The most important aspect of a direct belay is that it should be able to support a very large force without any possibility of failing. The belayer may be either attached or unattached to the anchor – this depends largely on how exposed or serious the belaying position. On some occasions it is not appropriate for the belayer to be attached to the anchor as they need to be standing well away from any possible dangers, such as on a plateau at the top of a route. However, the belay must depend upon an uncompromised anchor ie. an immovable object. The decision as to whether the belayer is attached to the anchor or not must lie with the belayer.

Example 1 – Rope and Rock
You can belay directly from a large rock by simply wrapping your rope round the chosen anchor, creating friction between rope and rock. If the anchor is too big too much friction will be generated and the rope will not be able to move. It is crucial that the rock anchor chosen is the appropriate size, and that it will not fail when loaded.

Care must be taken when positioning the rope round the rock to ensure that it lies well down the back of the anchor, and that when pulled the rope does not rise above the rock. If the anchor is below the

Using a direct belay by running rope directly behind a rock spike

belayer's hips the belayer will need to sit down; the belayer's hips must always be below the height of the anchor to which they are attached. Equally important is that the belayer's hands are not raised above the height of the anchor. The dead rope should always be pulled in a downward direction. This will prevent the rope from rising over the top of the anchor when taking in. To take in or let out rope simply control the rope by using a hand-over-hand method.

Top Tips

- Always wear gloves when belaying, as rope friction can be painful and may also cause you to lose control of the rope.

- Ensure that your stance (your belay position) is comfortable, stable and strong. The rope may rise off the anchor as the climber approaches you, so it is important to communicate with the ascending climber.

- You should only use the direct belay for an ascending climber or when lowering off small, awkward steps.

Example 2 – Italian Hitch

The Italian hitch is one of the most used belay knots, but it should only be used to protect an ascending climber (ie. a second) from a stance above, or to lower a descending climber from a stance. (To protect an ascending lead climber from *below*, a belay plate should be used.) Certainly an Italian hitch should never be used from a direct belay to protect an ascending lead climber because if the belayer loses control of the rope the anchor is likely to lift out of position – you will no longer have an anchor!

You can use the Italian hitch from either single or equalised anchors (see page 97). All you need is one HMS screwgate karabiner and a tape sling, or a central point of load from an equalised anchor. It is important that the friction knot rests at the broad base of the karabiner spine. Karabiner orientation is very important in order to avoid the friction knot resting on the locking karabiner gate.

The next step is for the belayer to position himself or herself in a comfortable, stable but strong stance.

Step 1 – Begin by holding the dead rope in one hand close to the Italian hitch knot. The other hand should hold the live rope approximately 60cm from the Italian hitch.

Step 2 – Gripping both dead rope and live rope, simultaneously pull the live rope towards the Italian hitch, and pull downwards on the dead rope away from the Italian hitch.

Step 3 – Transfer the live-rope hand to the dead rope. Then move the dead-rope hand back up the dead rope close to the Italian hitch. Ensure that you do not let go of the dead rope at any time.

Step 4 – Take your live-rope hand back to the live rope approximately 60cm from the Italian hitch and proceed to take in rope by following Steps 1, 2 and 3 again. Continue to repeat the cycle.

Operating the Italian Hitch

- *To lock off* the Italian hitch simply bring the dead and live rope parallel and hold tight.

- *To take in rope* it is important to always have at least one hand on the dead rope at all times. It is possible to pull the rope in hand-over-hand style.

The main advantage of this belay technique is that it is fast when taking rope in. Not all scramblers will climb fast (and actually it is wise to take your time). Nevertheless, some scramblers will travel naturally fast, and all will move that little bit faster where the terrain allows them to do so.

Top Tips

- Always consider where your spare/dead rope will be stacked as it accumulates at the belay stance. Don't allow it to fall down the cliff as it may snag, and will be difficult to manage.

- Organise your belay stance so that the rope can be stacked neatly, without impeding the ascending or descending climber, at the stance.

- Always wear gloves when rope handling direct belays.

- Remember! You can easily convert the Italian hitch knot to a clove hitch when the climber arrives at the stance, or you can easily clip another HMS karabiner to the sling and tie a clove hitch knot. Either way, you will have your hands free until they are ready to belay again.

Semi-Indirect Belay

A semi-indirect belay is when a belay plate is used, with either a single rope or two ropes. The belay plate is connected to the tie-in loop, and the belayer will also be attached to the anchor.

A semi-indirect belay absorbs and distributes load through the belay plate and back to the anchor without creating discomfort for the belayer, as the load will pass through the tie-in loop, maintaining independence of the belayer from any load. The belayer must be tight on the anchor for the system to work correctly and safely.

Belay plate orientation is crucial to the smooth running of rope, especially for taking in rope and locking off the system. The dead rope should always flow at a 90° angle – sideways on – to the belayer. You should observe a perfect S for SAFE in the shape of the rope (see photograph) as it runs through the belay plate, as this creates maximum friction.

There should be no awkward twists in the rope, allowing it to run freely through the plate. The S-shape will allow a perfect 180° lock-off with any obstructions, but you do need room to brake on the stance you have chosen. To belay safely it is vital never to let the dead rope – or braking rope – drop. If it does, and the climber slips, you will not be able to stop the rope from running freely through your belay plate.

Close-up of belay plate rigged and orientated to protect a climber ascending to a belayer

The S-shape of the rope through the belay plate indicates that the belay will operate effectively if locked off

How to Belay Correctly Using a Belay Plate

Preparation

- You may be belaying from above or below. Ensure that your body position is side on to the ascending climber, and facing towards the stance position where the ascending climber will eventually stand or sit.

- Connect your belay device to the tie-in loop created when you tied into your harness using the rope. This rope loop now becomes your belay loop.

- *Note* When taking in rope for an ascending climber the belay device is connected to the bottom of the belay loop, and when a climber is belaying a lead climber they must clip the belay plate to the top of the belay loop. This orientation will avoid unnecessary twist and kinks appearing in the rope and belay device, causing difficult rope handling and rope jam.

- Check that the rope orientation runs through the belay device in a neat S-shape with no twists or kinks. This will allow the rope to flow smoothly.

- When locking off an ascending climber the dead rope will be positioned *uphill* and to the side of the belayer.

- When locking off for a lead climber the dead rope will be positioned *downhill* and to the side of the belayer.

- When the belayer is holding the weight of a climber the force will be greatly reduced as the rope passes through the belay plate and into the belayer's hands. It is critical at this stage for the belayer to be completely tight on the anchor attachment so that there is no shock loading on the anchor.

- This set-up avoids any unnecessary pressure being applied to the belayer's hips via loading of the rope.

Belaying with a Belay Plate: Taking in Rope

Step 1 – Pull the dead rope down towards the live rope to allow the rope to run smoothly through the belay device.

Step 3 – Transfer your live-rope hand to the dead rope and reposition your dead-rope hand close to the belay plate.

Step 2 – Pull back the dead rope at an angle of 180° to the live rope. To pay rope out, reverse the process – pull out the live rope whilst maintaining control of the dead rope.

Step 4 – Maintaining your hand position on the dead rope, reposition your live-rope hand back onto the live rope approximately 30cm in front of the belay plate.

Repeat – Steps 1, 2, 3 and 4

During transfer of hands it is absolutely critical to ensure that both are gripping on to the dead rope, before taking the live-rope hand off. *The belayer must never let the dead rope go completely.*

To lock the rope off, for example in the event of a fall, simply pull the dead rope back behind the belay plate and hold, creating an angle of around 180°. This prevents any more rope being pulled through the belay device.

Top Tips
- Always have gloves to hand for belaying.
- When taking rope in, clip the belay plate to the bottom of the tie-in loop.
- When paying rope out to a climber, clip the belay plate to the top of the tie-in loop.
- Establish good clear climbing calls before you set off.
- *Always be an attentive belayer.*

Belay Plate Orientation in a Multi-Pitch Situation

Some mountaineering routes may require you to protect a number of pitches consecutively. On these multi-pitch routes the belay plate needs to be reorientated according to whether you are protecting an ascending climber from above or from below.

To protect an ascending climber from below, the belay plate should be clipped to the top of the tie-in loop. To protect an ascending climber from above, the belay plate should be clipped to the bottom of the tie-in loop.

Protecting a Pitch

The whole purpose of belaying is to protect someone who is ascending or descending a section of ground where a fall would result in injury or death. 'Pitch' is a term used for describing a section of ground, usually rock, from one belay stance to the next. In terms of distance it may stretch from 10 to 50m, depending on how long your rope is, the nature of the terrain and the climbing, and on how the pitch-length highlights are described in the guidebook information.

Most guidebooks will provide pitch lengths in metres, and when we talk about 'pitching' a route we are talking about breaking it down into pitches that we will protect. When scrambling on potentially dangerous terrain you should plan to pitch the crux sections of a route, and any other parts where you, or your climbing partner, feels exposed, at risk or uncomfortable without placed protection.

Leader-Placed Protection

It is important for the lead climber to protect the pitch both for personal safety and for the ascending second. Also, some routes are awkward and the most natural line does not always run straight. In these cases one of the benefits of protecting both leader and second is that the risk of a dangerous pendulum-swing effect in the event of a fall will be greatly reduced.

Protection is provided by using a number of different bits of specialist climbing gear that go by such unlikely names as rocks on wires, hexcentrics, and camming devices, otherwise known as friends and extenders. It is wise to work out in advance what you need for a particular route, and not to be festooned with too much gear.

A rack and gloves suitable for top-end scrambling grades

A set of 1-to-10 Rocks-on-Wires

Rock-on-wire placed to protect a climber – front placement

Rock-on-wire placed to protect a climber – side placement

Hexcentric placed to protect a climber – front placement

Hexcentric placed to protect a climber – side placement

A rigid-stemmed camming device

Rigid-stemmed camming devices with fixed extenders

A camming device – or 'friend' – placed for protection

Protecting an Ascent

This is straightforward in principle, although how smoothly it goes in practice will depend on the difficulty of the climbing and availability of points of protection, as well as the ability and experience of the lead climber. In simple terms, the lead climber stops at points to place protection in the rock, to which he clips his rope via an extender before continuing. At the top of the pitch he sets up a belay for the second who, on making his ascent, removes and collects each piece of protective gear as he comes to it.

It is a good idea for the leader to place an early piece of protection on any route, and wherever necessary thereafter. On harder grades placing gear as frequently as is feasible – at least every 1.5m or so – is good practice, and the harder the grade for your ability the more you should place. You need to get the balance right, though, because whatever the lead puts in the second has to extract. This means that the second may require the rope to be tight from time to time to support the climber while he removes the gear.

An ascending climber with pieces of gear clipped, providing leader-placed protection

An extender orientated correctly for clipping gear into

Protecting a Traverse

In the classic scramble traverse scenario you will inevitably spend time on a knife-edged ridge with serious exposure beneath your feet. No two routes are identical, but the chances are that you will be able to protect this situation using rocks on wires or by placing 8ft tape slings on to rock spikes. You can also protect the traverse by the leader weaving the rope in and out of rock spikes as you progress, providing natural protection for both climbers.

Climbers negotiating a knife-edge ridge

Top Tips

- Before the lead climber sets off it is best to make sure the dead rope is stacked neatly on the ground next to the belayer, who should be tied on to an anchor.

- Ensure that the belayer is on the opposite side of the arête when the lead climber is traversing – this provides additional security.

- The belayer should try to stay as low as possible – hips always below the anchor – to prevent the placed protection from popping out. The belayer should ensure that – unlike when moving together – there is ample slack rope between belayer and climber, as a tensioned rope will potentially rip out any placed protection.

Protecting a Descending Climber

There will be many occasions where there are no suitable anchors for abseiling, or for lowering someone down off a direct anchor. However, you may have an anchor that would be appropriate for a semi-indirect lower. This is where the belayer attaches himself to an anchor, such as a low spike from the ground, and protects a descending climber through the belay plate.

The descending climber should take the rack of gear and place protection at regular intervals as he descends. On arrival at a safe location the descending climber rigs and anchors a belay.

The belayer at the top becomes a descending climber and as he descends the belayer at the bottom takes in the slack rope. As the second or last descending climber makes his way down he extracts the protection previously placed. This technique allows both climbers to down-climb fully protected.

A climber placing protection as she descends, belayed from above

A second descending, belayed from below, removing protection placed by the leader

Top Tips

- It is important to ensure that the last descending climber takes all the climbing protection with him.

- Ensure that the dead slack rope is stacked before the first climber descends, which means running it through on top of itself to ensure the lead rope runs from the top of the stack.

- Tidy rope management is good practice. Avoiding the rope becoming knotted and twisted is an important safety issue and will also save much time.

- As each piece of protection is extracted, clip the extender karabiner with the rock and wire attached on to your harness gear rack – this will halve the length of the extender and prevent it from catching on rock as you descend.

Tying in to Anchors

'Tying in' is the term mountaineers use to describe the process of tying the rope into their harness, that is, attaching themselves to the rope. A climber faced with a decision to set up a belay has first to decide what system is most appropriate, most efficient and, most importantly, safest. But no belay system will do its job if the climbers using it are not tied into it properly.

The knot we use for tying in is universal – the rewoven figure of eight, with a double fisherman's stopper knot (see page 78). The harness manufacturer's recommendations will dictate how you should thread the rope through the harness, and these should be followed at all times. We recommend a harness with a fixed abseil/belay loop linking the leg loops.

The Tie-in Loop

The tie-in loop is the loop you have created in the rope by tying into your harness. This loop will accommodate your belay device. Avoid attaching your belay device into your fixed belay/abseil loop on your harness, as this is inappropriate for scrambling/multi-pitched routes.

When climbing on 'top-end' grade scramble routes or low-grade rock routes you need an anchor and belay system that is simple, effective and quick to set up. Travelling with care but with speed is essential, especially on long, technically demanding routes where a slow party could get benighted at certain times of year. One of the most time-consuming activities on such routes is anchor and belay building. Taking the time necessary to set up

Tied into the harness using a rewoven figure of eight knot. The tie-in loop, in this case, becomes the belay loop.

a sound belay, of course, is no bad thing! But a big route is no place to be testing new skills for the first time. Small three-to-four pitch routes at an easy grade offer great fun and are the best place to put skills into practice, once you feel you're ready to progress from the kitchen table, the garden, the garage or some other benign environment where you have practised your knots and got the feel of your gear. When you do get 'out there' the anchors and belay attachments in this section are what you are likely to use on most scramble routes.

Selecting an Anchor

Before selecting an anchor it is important to check that it is completely sound. You can do this by shock loading it – pushing, tapping and even giving it a good kicking, in a variety of directions. Don't hold back – if it moves at all, leave it well alone. Always inspect the rock itself, in case it sounds hollow, which probably means it is cracked. If you have any doubts at all as to the integrity of the anchor you must seek an alternative.

Most routes like those in this book have established belay points highlighted in some route descriptions, which means that you will generally find suitable anchors. However, that is no guarantee as to the suitability of an anchor at the time you inspect it. Also, there probably won't be any gear placements, and although you may find the odd piece that some other climber failed to extract, you cannot rely on this (and in any case, these should always be tested thoroughly before use).

Unlike our continental counterparts we don't have bolts and multiple anchor chains on our mountain routes (happily), so always be prepared for a 'traditional' route (unbolted) and an authentic belay-finding experience!

Single Anchor Within Reach
A single anchor is a one-point attachment. Place a sling round or over the top of the anchor – once you are certain it is suitable – using a single clove hitch knot. 'Within reach' means you can adjust the length at any time between the belayer and the anchor.

A belayer attached to a single anchor within reach

A belayer attached to an out-of-reach anchor using a clove hitch attachment

Single Anchor Out of Reach
If your single anchor is out of reach – ie. you cannot easily readjust the rope length between climber and anchor – clip your rope into the HMS screwgate karabiner at the anchor, then position yourself exactly where you would like to stand or sit, and tie the rope off in to your belay loop as shown in the photos.

On an out-of-reach anchor you adjust your attachment rope from your tie-in loop, and there are two very quick ways of doing this. One is to attach an HMS screwgate to the loop and then attach a clove hitch knot to it. This method is very simple and easy to adjust.

Closer view of the out-of-reach anchor attachment using a clove hitch knot on a karabiner

The second method is to tie a figure of eight on the bight through the loop – this is much harder to adjust, but with practice it is very efficient.

An out-of-reach anchor should only be used when your attachment point to the rock above an ascending climber is a reasonable distance back from the edge, as it will help you to reduce rope drag and enable you to watch the ascending climber.

A belayer attached to an out-of-reach anchor using a figure of eight on the bight

Top Tips
- When belaying you must always make sure that your hips are lower than the anchor. This will ensure a downhill pull should the second climber slip – anything else risks compromising the belay.

- It will also help the belayer to maintain a position in line with both the ascending climber and the anchor.

- When belaying always ensure that you are in line with the ascending climber.

Warning

To avoid compromising your anchor you must always have the tie-on rope from belayer to anchor very tight to avoid 'loading' the system with a sudden shock (shock-loading) in the event of a fall. Always keep the belay rope to the same side as you tie in to your harness.

A good belay and good belaying require discipline. Belaying is, by definition, a very serious activity. Some belayers can give the unfortunate appearance of just hanging around until it's their turn to climb. Avoiding this casual attitude is literally a matter of life and death.

Equalised Anchors
Sometimes one point of attachment just isn't enough. This may be down to the quality of the rock being poor, but sometimes it's just good practice. For example, even if the placement of a rock on wire is very good, you will always still need to back it up to create a solid belay stance. It is common practice to back up all placed wires – two anchors are always better than one.

Using the sling as an equalised anchor is the most common method. You may choose to use the equalised anchor system from time to time for extra security on harder grade routes, or simply when the need arises.

Creating an Equalised Anchor
This is created when two points of the sling are attached, secured and clipped independently to the rock. They are then brought to a central point for attaching the belayer and ascending climber. Each individual point of attachment will share the load. An equalised anchor always has a central point of attachment, so that should one anchor fail the other does not get shock loaded.

Building a Belay Anchor

Example 1
Step 1 – Take the sling and clip it into the two prepared HMS karabiners at the anchors. If you are short of HMS karabiners you may replace one of these with a snaplink karabiner. If doing this always place your HMS on your strongest placed protection.
Step 2 – Pull downwards on the sling between the two karabiners to the point of equal tension and in the direction of loading.

Step 3 – Tie an overhand knot in the sling and clip an HMS karabiner into the small loop created. This is your attachment point for tying in. If you are taking a direct belay clip another HMS karabiner to the sling for this purpose.

An equalised anchor using an 8ft dyneema tape sling, with an overhand knot positioned in the middle of the sling. The HMS karabiner is attached to the two separate loops formed by initially tying the overhand knot in the sling.

A karabiner rigged through loops created by an overhand knot in the middle of the sling – this creates the belayer's attachment point

Example 2

Step 1 – Tie a loose overhand knot in the middle of the sling – you have created two independent loops. Clip each loop into the prepared anchors.

Step 2 – Clip an HMS karabiner into each loop and orientate the karabiner so that the wider part points to the ground.

Step 3 – Pull the karabiner downwards and decide on the direction of loading.

Step 4 – Finally adjust the overhand knot by shifting it either way. Tie onto the HMS. This system can also be used for a direct belay by clipping a second HMS karabiner to it.

Example 3

Step 1 – Find a large boulder/rock; if it is sound and does not move then simply loop your 16ft sling over the top. This type of belay is fast to set up and offers great security.

Step 2 – Decide where you need sit or stand. Clip an HMS karabiner into the sling and tie on to the karabiner. You can also clip a second HMS karabiner to the sling for a direct belay.

Remember you can easily tie an overhand knot in the 16ft sling to make it smaller, which may enable you to position yourself closer to the anchor and give you a better belay position.

Creating a single anchor by placing a 16ft sling round a large boulder

Example 4

For this set-up we have chosen to use the rope to tie directly on to the anchors, demonstrating a within reach tie-off. This has been arranged by simply using clove hitches.

Step 1 – Tie a clove hitch on to the first HMS karabiner, then leave some slack rope and tie a clove hitch onto the second HMS karabiner. You can clip a third HMS karabiner on to your tie-on loop and clove hitch the rope back on to this point.

Step 2 – Adjust the clove hitch for the desired tension and the system is complete. You can also tie back to the tie-on loop using a figure of eight on the bight, should no screwgate karabiner be to hand.

Creating a single anchor using a threaded sling

Creating a single anchor by placing an 8ft sling round a spike

Using the rope to create an equalised anchor within reach, using screwgates

Using the rope to create an equalised anchor out of reach, tied off using a figure of eight on the bight attached to the tie-in loop

Angles of Equalised Anchors

If you get the angles wrong on your anchor whilst loaded, it will fail. An ideal angle of safety is around 90°. This allows a safe configuration maintaining a two-way load on the anchor points. Should you exceed this angle and then a three-way load is applied, the system becomes highly dangerous. Two-way loads must be pulling parallel in the direction of expected loading – should an additional load be introduced, say a horizontal one between the two anchors, the system will also fail, with catastrophic consequences.

To avoid bad angles you just need to move further away from your anchor. Avoiding bad angles is a good reason to use out-of-reach anchors in the first place, when tying into the system using a rope.

Example 1

The angle is exceeding 120°. Although it is independent and equalised there is a three-way load. The anchors are being pulled across and down at the same time. Do not do this.

More than 120° – a dangerous angle on an equalised anchor

Example 2

This angle is around 120° – the absolute limit of safety for an equalised anchor angle.

120° – the maximum safe angle on an equalised anchor

Example 3

This angle is around 90° and is well within a safe operating angle.

90° – an ideal angle on an equalised anchor

Moving Together

Moving together is a technique used to secure one or two climbers tied together on the same rope. It enables them to move at a good pace on steep and perhaps exposed terrain, without compromising safety. It can be very dangerous if used incorrectly, and this does happen as the system is often misunderstood. The most common error people make is to move together on exposed terrain unprotected: if one should slip and slide the other will most definitely get pulled off, with dire consequences. However, when used appropriately moving together is an essential technique that will not only keep you safe but will also speed your progress.

> **Remember**
> When using this technique one thing should be understood above all else: moving together *never* means moving without protection, in situations where protection is essential to safety.

Shortening the Length of Rope

The distance of rope between mountaineers moving together will depend on whether they are climbing as a group of two or of three, which in turn relates to terrain, route length, and technical difficulties. Most difficulties on routes of the sort discussed in this book are relatively short in length and compact in nature, so when scrambling around 10m of rope between two climbers will suffice. If you note a particular section of exposure to be slightly longer just increase the length of rope from 10m to, say, 25m to accommodate the terrain.

There are a number of ways in which to deal with the spare rope – the length of the rope that does not run between the two climbers – but we would recommend chest coils.

Making Chest Coils

Before you take chest coils make sure you are wearing your rucksack. Bring the rope from your tie-in loop over your head and down towards your left hand, which should be located just opposite your harness belt. This will be a guide to coil size. With your right hand take the rope from the stacked rope and coil it round your head into your left hand, maintaining tension at all times. Make a slight twist in the rope as you take each coil, which prevents the rope from kinking and becoming awkward to handle. Continue to take in coils until the desired rope length between the climbers is achieved. When enough coils have been taken in, put your left arm through the loops created.

To lock off the coils take a bight of rope from the main rope – around 35cm in length – and pass this right underneath and back round the rope leading from your harness tie-in. Holding the bight with your right hand, pinch both bight and chest coil with your left hand and continue by passing the bight behind the chest coils. Bring it over the top and down through a small half hitch that has been created. Now clip the small loop into an HMS screwgate karabiner located on your tie-in loop. When taking off coils after you have been moving together, don't just drop them on the ground: take them one off at a time, as this will prevent the rope from getting in to a tangle.

Moving Together Between Exposed Pitches

There may be occasions where easy walking is encountered before the next section of exposed ground, so rather than untie from the rope simply continue to move together. You can also shorten the distance between two climbers who have already taken chest coils by hand coiling the rope – gathering it into loops to be carried in your hand. Moving together in this way should only be used where no danger is imminent.

Making Chest Coils

Step 1 – Place the rope around your head as shown.

Step 2 – Position a stabilising hand for loop coiling at waist height in front of your body. Continue to take loops over your head.

Step 3 – Once you have the desired length of rope looped, place your stabilising hand and arm through the loops you have created. The rope is now crossing your chest and back.

Step 4 – Take a bight of rope about 60cm in length from the live end that runs to the ground. Bring it between your body and tie in rope, bring it round the tie-in rope, passing it back up behind the main coil of rope. Then bring the bight of rope back round and down through the space next to your thumb.

Step 5 – Clip an HMS into the bight of rope end and clip this to your tie-in loop.

Step 6 – Pull the live rope and your tie in should be tensioned and secure.

Moving Together and Using Protection

Before the leader sets off the second may need to establish a belay to use, until the rope has been paid out completely to the leader. This will allow the leader to establish distance between himself and the second, placing protection as he progresses on the route. Once all the rope has been paid out the leader may decide to take a belay or continue to move ahead.

If the decision is to keep going, the second must now move with the leader.

There are now a number of different forms of protection possible, such as allowing the rope to weave in and out of natural rock spikes. These, if sufficiently solid and accessible, will provide excellent and easy-to-use protection. The other method of security is leader-placed protection (see page 91).

It is important always to have at least two points of protection whilst moving together. However, as one is extracted another is placed. The climbers must communicate so both may have to stop when necessary. The rope between both climbers must be managed so that there are no slack points produced by one climber moving faster than the other. When done properly, this system works well: should one climber slip and slide, a counter-balance effect takes over without any shock loading of either rope or climber.

Climbers need to constantly interpret the

Moving together: the first climber leading off

Two climbers moving together with protection placed between them

The lead climber stopping and taking a direct belay to bring in the slack rope of the second

terrain ahead in case they need to stop and create a belay. If a steep section is encountered a belay is always necessary. Moving together on a steep section of rock is highly dangerous and requires much experience and judgement to work smoothly and safely. When the leader does stop he must take in the slack rope from the second. This may be achieved by a direct belay, which will help to prevent rope snagging as the second progresses, or any violent shock loading or pulling of the lead climber should the second slip or slide on a slack rope.

Top Tips

- Communication is the key to moving together really well. You should always maintain chat, and never assume what your partner is thinking.

- A leader and second can, at any point when moving together, choose to create a direct belay quickly. This is particularly useful when one of them is moving at a different pace.

- If you run out of rope, take a belay or extend the rope length by dropping some chest coils.

- When the leader runs short of gear with which to place protection he must stop and take a belay to allow the second to catch up and replenish the leader with protection extracted.

- If there is no belay at the end of the route – say a ridge meeting a plateau – the leader should not stop but should keep walking to maintain a tight rope at all times. The second will eventually reach the plateau area of safety, but if they take a slip before doing so there should be enough friction in the rope to arrest the fall.

- All members of any climbing party should acquaint themselves with the well-established system of climbing calls used by British climbers (see opposite).

Climbing Calls

When you are climbing and belaying in a pair or team it is inevitable that at times there will be physical distance between the participants. A clear, simple means of communication is required to communicate your intentions and coordinate your actions. Before you engage in climbing activity together you and your partners should familiarise yourself with the well-established system of climbing calls used by British climbers. This is something you can practise anywhere – don't leave it to chance, as these calls are a vital part of your team's climbing 'kit'.

Climb when ready
Call from the belayer at the start of the route or from the belayer at the top of a route. Before calling, the belayer will have checked that the anchor is secure, the belay method appropriate and the belay rig correctly clipped and orientated, with all knots and karabiners securely fixed.

Climbing
Call from the leader at the start of the route to the belayer, or from the belayer/second who is about to climb to the top of the route.

OK
Call back from the belayer to acknowledge that they heard the 'climbing' call.

Runner on
The leader indicates that the first runner has been placed and clipped.

Slack
Belayer must provide slack rope to the leader as he might be trying to clip a runner, or the rope between climber and belayer has gone too tight for the climber to make progress. The belayer should maintain some slack rope to the ascending climber unless asked for tight rope.

Tight
This call may be shouted to the belayer by the climber, or by the second to the belayer, as they may be expecting to fall.

Safe
The leader shouts this when he has reached complete safety and there is no chance of falling off. It is common practice for the leader to be tied in to the anchor before calling 'Safe'.

You're off belay
From the belayer who is now the second, informing the belayer at the top of the climb that the ropes are free to take in.

That's me
Call from the second to indicate that all the slack rope has been taken in.

Climb when ready
As before.

Below
From either a leader or second ascending who has dislodged a rock or has dropped something. This is to warn the second or anyone else who might be below. On hearing this call your instinct is to look up, but never do this as whatever is falling is likely to hit you in the face.

Rope below
This is an essential courtesy call when throwing abseil rope ends down a route. You don't always see people who might be at the bottom of your route of descent. A climbing rope in the face from 20m up is unlikely to endear you to them, and they might be keen to discuss the fact with you at the bottom of your abseil route.

Abseiling

Abseiling: the standard route off Skye's Inaccessible Pinnacle

Contrary to popular opinion, abseiling is not a sport in itself but a technique used to retreat or advance on a mountain route. All mountaineers need to know how to abseil safely. Rock climbers often abseil when there is no alternative way off the mountain, or when they need to retrieve gear stuck on the crag, or even an injured climber. Abseiling is not a difficult skill to acquire, but if not carefully prepared and employed is one of the major causes of accidents. It must be approached with clarity, caution and care.

Preparing to Abseil

The following factors must always be considered:

- *anchor selection* – is the anchor strong enough? Do you need to back it up?
- *abseil length* – is your rope long enough to reach safe terrain or a safe stance?
- *rope retrieval* – once you have completed your abseil will you be able to pull your rope back through the anchor without it snagging?
- *abseil direction* – do your ropes flow in the direction you wish to take? ('direction of travel') or will you be abseiling or swinging over a sharp edge?
- *objective dangers* – will you be abseiling on loose rock, or into the path of falling rock?

If you are unsure of any of these crucial points you must reconsider whether you need to abseil, or whether there is a safer way of achieving your objective.

Anchor Selection

Abseiling without a secure anchor for your rope is extremely dangerous and should never be done. Selecting the right anchor is critical. You will often have to 'build' an anchor from scratch, creating or finding a secure anchor that is not compromised in any way.

'Natural protection' is where you select a secure piece of rock, say a spike, that is solid and strong – not one that just looks that way! Your preferred anchor might look strong but, as with a belay anchor, you must always check by shock loading it before deciding whether to use it or not. Kick the rock spike with your boot, or push it with your hands, in a range of directions. If it moves at all, do not use it.

You may also anchor an abseil by using a thread belay. A thread belay is created by threading a sling or rope behind a feature, such as a rock jammed in a crack.

You may need to sacrifice some equipment, like two rocks on wires and a tape sling, to create an effective abseil anchor. Whatever your criteria the decision should always be to choose the belay anchor that is safest and offers the best protection. It's well worth leaving behind some nice shiny gear when you consider what's at stake.

Example A

A poor example of an abseil anchor with the angle and friction created likely to cause jamming, making rope retrieval impossible.

Example B

A good example of an abseil anchor created by putting a piece of tat over a rock spike.

Angles are critically important in an abseil anchor. You also need to think about retrieval of rope, so extending your tape sling that you have opted to leave behind is a good idea. If in doubt as to whether you can retrieve your rope or not, always extend your 'tat' if possible.

Top Tips

- Always carry a piece of abseiling 'tat' (an odd piece of rope or a spare tape sling which you are prepared to sacrifice).

- Tat will be left behind on the anchor when you retrieve your ropes.

- Always wear gloves when abseiling to protect your skin from any friction rope burn. Gloves will also prevent you from losing control of the rope.

Rigging your Abseil Rope

Tie one end of your rope to the anchor in case you lose your rope down the cliff. Feed the other end of the rope through the tat until the middle of your rope is positioned at the tat. Now it is safe to untie the tied-off end of the rope and place the two ends together. Now you are almost ready to 'deliver' the rope down the cliff. Either:

- Lap coil the rope into your hand – start from the anchor end of the rope and allow 3–4m of slack. Grip the centre of the flakes and then throw the rope down the direction of the abseil route.
- In windy conditions, lap coil the rope and place it through a chest sling so that the middle of the coils rests on the sling.

When lap coiling the rope it is best to start from the tail ends of the rope by handling them together – this will allow the rope to run freely as you abseil with it down the route. Before you deliver the rope down the cliff don't forget to check whether there is anyone at the base of the abseil, and to call 'below' if you are in any doubt.

A climber at the abseil anchor preparing to deliver the rope down the abseil route

A climber at the abseil anchor with lap coils on a chest harness, set up to abseil in windy conditions

Tying Two Ropes Together

Anyone with experience of long multi-pitch climbing routes will know that having two ropes has many advantages, especially if you are climbing as a team of three. The main advantage of having two ropes for abseiling is that you now have the ability to abseil 50m rather than 25m. If you research your route before you go, you should also know whether this option is likely to be helpful.

Simply take the two ends of rope and tie one overhand knot 60cm down the tail ends – manipulate the knot tight. You can then easily thread the rope ends through the anchor first.

Two ropes joined together (with a double fisherman's knot), coming off an anchor

Knotting the Rope Ends

In certain circumstances it is good practice to knot the rope ends when abseiling, especially if your abseil is a multi-pitch descent or you are unsure as to whether the rope ends are safely on the ground at the bottom of the abseil. A knot in the end of the rope will avoid the possibility of you abseiling off it into mid-air at the bottom. Some climbers tie both ends of the rope together, but this is not recommended as it will result in twisting and kinking of the rope when you descend. On most occasions tying knots in the end of the rope is not necessary, and may lead the rope ends to become trapped in a crack on the rock face, especially if windy conditions may push the rope back into the cliff. Remember if you are protecting your abseil by using a French prusik there should be no reason to tie knots at the end of the rope.

Protecting a Personal Abseil

This is where the abseiler is in complete control of the descent. The method described here can be used in all situations for a planned or emergency abseil, but is particularly good for a multi-pitch abseil (where more than one abseil is needed to reach safety).

Equipment Required for an Abseil

- Cow's tail using an 8ft dyneema tape sling
- Belay plate (ATC) double-rope device
- Two HMS screwgate karabiners
- One prusik loop
- Gloves
- Rope – recommended length 50m

Step 1 – Once you have threaded your cow's tail through your harness, tie an overhand knot 25cm away from the lark's foot. You have now created two loops in your cow's tail.

Step 2 – Clip an HMS screwgate karabiner with belay plate into the small loop located between the lark's foot and the overhand knot.

Step 3 – Thread the ropes through the belay plate and clip into the HMS karabiner.

Step 4 – Clip another HMS screwgate karabiner into the harness belay/abseil loop.

Step 5 – Attach a French prusik to the dead rope (or brake rope) and then to the prepared HMS karabiner.

Step 6 – The prusik will be held in the controlling hand. By simply pulling down on the prusik the abseil rope will be able to flow freely through the prusik, enabling the abseiler to descend. At any time the abseiler can release the grip on the prusik, which will then bite on the rope and stop the descent.

Step 7 – Clip an HMS screwgate karabiner to the spare sling loop and attach it to a gear loop on the harness for storage.

Set up for protecting a personal abseil

An HMS karabiner clipped to one of the abseil ropes above the abseil is helpful to identify the pull rope when retrieving your rope after abseiling

Top Tips

- When rigging and preparing your abseil rope you can use your cow's tail to secure yourself whilst standing at the edge.

- Whilst you rig your abseil protection it is worthwhile staying clipped to your abseil anchor. Once you have attached your French prusik you can test whether it is biting/locking off by simply leaning off the edge. Remember you still have your cow's tail attached to the anchor in case the French prusik fails!

- If the prusik fails all you need to do is create another twist in the prusik and then try again.

- Once everything is working unclip your cow's tail from the abseil anchor and store it on a harness gear rack – now begin your abseil.

- Place an HMS screwgate karabiner on the rope you will need to pull through to remind you which one to pull through, as you may have had to join two ropes together. This will avoid any unnecessary rope jam.

Personal Safety

Remember to always make yourself safe – when standing near a cliff edge use your cow's tail.

Italian Hitch Abseil

For this you must use an HMS screwgate karabiner, especially if double ropes are to be used. It's a useful one to know in case you drop your belay plate.

Both ropes are clipped in to the HMS with the dead rope directed towards the spine of the HMS karabiner – this is to avoid any unnecessary rubbing of the gate mechanism, and therefore accidental opening of the gate whilst under load.

Abseil using an Italian hitch

Top Tips
- Placing a free-running karabiner between the two abseil ropes helps avoid twisting of the ropes above the abseil device, creating most of the twisting and kinking below the desending abseiler.

- Before unclipping from the Italian hitch abseil at the base of the route, unwind any kinks leading to the tail ends. You can now pull the rope through without any further twisting and kinking.

Counterbalance Abseil

This technique can be used in a variety of situations, but care must be taken when rigging an anchor and managing two abseilers. You might choose this method for any one of the following reasons: saving time, inexperienced abseiler, injured or tired climber. There are two ways in which a counterbalance technique can be deployed.

Example 1

Step 1 – Climber no 2, using an Italian hitch from a secure anchor, has lowered climber no 1 to the base of a steep wall.

Step 2 – Climber 1 stays tied into the rope and does not untie from the rope ends.

Step 3 – Climber 2, having threaded the rope through the anchor sling, now prepares to abseil down the other length of rope.

Step 4 – As no 2 abseils he will be counterweighted by no 1 until he reaches the base of the steep wall.

Step 5 – Both climbers untie together and pull the rope through from the abseil anchor.

Another type of anchor that can be used is a direct belay. After lowering the first climber on a direct belay (usually rope around a large rock) climber 2 continues to wrap the rope around the rock which now becomes the abseil anchor. Climber 2 then abseils, counterweighted by climber 1, who is tied into the rope ends as before.

Top Tips
- Care should be taken to ensure that the abseil rope will release from the abseil anchor when the rope is pulled from the bottom.

- When the first abseiler is lowered to safe ground he can test the rope by pulling on it. If it doesn't move the abseiler waiting at the top to descend is in a perfect position to sort out any jamming of ropes.

- When using the abseil rope directly wrapped around rock, care should be taken to always ensure that it will release, as immense friction between rope and rock is created. You may need to sacrifice a sling or a piece of fabric like a glove or gaiter to ensure that the rope runs smoothly.

- Always ensure your anchor is secure.

- Never abseil off old pitons; always back them up or use an alternative.

A counterbalance abseil (Example 1). In this example the first climber has been lowered to the base of the route where he remains tied into the rope. The second climber now abseils using the weight of the first climber as a counterbalance.

As in Example 2 Climbers preparing to abseil simultaneously, counterbalance style

Example 2

Step 1 – A secure anchor has been prepared; the abseil rope has been looped through the anchor, and the tail ends thrown to the base of the crag.

Step 2 – Climbers 1 and 2 now each take a length of rope and both fix their abseil devices to the rope.

Step 3 – Both climbers now move together down the abseil ropes – a classic counterbalance descent.

Top Tips

- When counterbalance abseiling you should always make sure that each of the tail ends of the ropes have been knotted, as this will prevent an abseiler accidentally coming off the end of the rope.

- Always ensure that both climbers abseil in tandem and arrive at a safe stance together – remaining counterbalanced all the way.

- This is a time-saving method of descent but is also suitable for supporting an inexperienced abseiler requiring reassurance and coaching. The inexperienced abseiler is always accompanied and not left at the top alone.

- Be prepared to leave a screwgate karabiner behind, or a snaplink karabiner – if you use the latter you can lock off the gate with finger tape.

- Keep your hands away from the friction device while abseiling, to avoid accidentally trapping your fingers in it.

BODY POSITION FOR ABSEILING

Step 1 – To begin your abseil you should have your feet wide apart, and lean slowly back from the edge of the cliff until your feet are flat on the rock.

Step 2 – Relax in the harness in a 'sitting' position, with legs slightly bent, with your hands controlling the rope in front of your body.

Step 3 – Begin to abseil (or rappel) down the cliff – walking backwards down the face at a natural pace, not bouncing energetically in 'action movie' style.

Step 4 – Take great care not to lean too far back as you risk inverting (turning upside down) which can be highly dangerous.

Water Hazards in the Mountains

In this section we draw attention to the likely water hazards that can be encountered when travelling in the mountain environment, and give advice on how to cope with them.

Picturesque – but water in the mountains is always a potential hazard

The Risks of River Crossings

The most common water hazard you are likely to face in the mountains is a stream or river that blocks your way. With this in mind you should always consider the weather conditions prior to and on the day of your outing and think about how they will affect you. If it's been raining in the mountains, whether briefly or for an extended period, water levels in streams and becks can rise quickly, changing the nature of the watercourse out of all recognition. Think about the likely condition of any rivers – particularly mature ones – that you plan to cross on your route.

Deciding whether or not to cross a river can be difficult, but your starting point must always be to think about the very considerable risks involved. It is all too easy when you can't see the river bed to twist an ankle, break a limb, get pitched over and carried downstream by a fast current. There's always the possibility of becoming hypothermic, or even the risk of drowning. That may sound pessimistic, but where river crossings are concerned it is all too true. Making a decision to cross a significant river is one of the most serious choices you can make in the mountains and should not be taken lightly. If at all possible, avoid it.

Planning and Preparation

Studying maps and weather information is absolutely vital when planning your trip. Having an up-to-date picture of how much rain has affected the mountains recently is essential. Avoid streams and rivers that may be too risky to cross without the use of a bridge. Having knowledge and experience does not necessarily mean that you will be able to cross a river safely. Avoiding the crossing altogether, especially in white-water conditions, is one of the best mountaineering decisions you can take.

Key Considerations

If you do have to cross flowing water – even in calm conditions – take extreme care, especially if you are alone. If you are in a small group, and you are confident the crossing can be achieved safely, consider the following:

Water temperature Water in the mountains is very cold. You will definitely get your lower limbs wet, so it is important to think about keeping your equipment as dry as possible and how you can warm yourself up when safety has been reached.

Depth of water This is always very difficult to work out. A stream will often be much deeper than anticipated – the deeper the water the wetter and colder you become.

Uneven or rough stream/river bed Always wear your boots when crossing a stream or river – the river bed will be rough and very uneven, and your ankles will need support to avoid injury. You should, however, take off your socks and keep them dry for later.

Current The power of water can be surprising. Even in the shallowest of rivers the current can be very strong, knocking you off your feet with great ease. If the water looks fast flowing seek a more suitable crossing point.

Avoid automatically choosing a section of river that narrows suddenly – the current will be at its strongest at such points.

Calm or white water All rivers have a current, regardless of how calm they may appear, so always take time to find the best crossing point. If the water looks tranquil and shallow, that's good: being able to see the river bed will help you work out conditions underfoot, and what you are stepping onto. You don't want to fall over unnecessarily.

When appropriate, use a trekking pole for support. Always check out the river activity and terrain below your intended crossing point. You may find that if you are swept downstream you could be taken over a waterfall or into rocks.

If the water is white, avoid crossing altogether and seek an alternative route – white water is very powerful and serious.

When Not to Cross

Always seek out the best crossing options and don't let ambition cloud your good judgement – temptations are always best controlled by logic. Bad places to cross will be:

- above waterfalls
- deep-sided gorges
- rivers in spate
- fast-flowing water.

The potential pitfalls of crossing a river in spate are many. Getting yourself and your team into a position where you have committed to a crossing, and then discovering that neither advancement nor retreat is possible, can happen all too easily. Make sure you have a clear route across before you enter the water, including how you will escape from the water on the opposite bank.

If the water is deep, remember: hypothermia is a big problem if you have been submerged in freezing water conditions. In such circumstances a plastic survival bag will not stop you from becoming seriously hypothermic.

Techniques for River Crossing

If you must cross a river there are a number of tried and tested techniques you can use to minimise the risks, and these should be practised in advance. Remember: keep your boots on!

It is also essential that you practise your chosen river-crossing technique on dry land before committing to the river. Floundering in the middle of a river is no place to suddenly realise you haven't got it right. If practice on dry land is not going to plan, an alternative would be appropriate, including aborting the plan to cross.

Using a Pole

Face upstream and step in a sideways motion to progress across the stream. This is the strongest position, with feet apart, and braced for a possible slip. Remember, an uneven stream bed can be an awkward and slippery surface to cope with. Always select carefully where you intend to enter and exit the stream.

Line Astern

Individual members of the group hold onto each other's shoulders – not the rucksack straps. The leader at the top is comfortably braced using a pole and the team behind are supporting one another. The leader creates an eddy of calm water for the team behind to move through. Movement should be directly across or diagonally upstream.

Group Wedge

This is a very strong technique whereby the more apprehensive group members can be protected by being placed in the middle of the wedge, with the strongest members on the outside. Movement should be across or diagonally upstream.

People Pivot

The group huddle together, facing inwards with arms around each other's shoulders, keeping their feet apart for balance. The huddle rotates as the river is crossed, maintaining constant balance. This allows rucksacks to be kept on the outside of the group and so prevents discomfort to other group members. At any given time, one person should always remain stationary for stability. Movement should be across or diagonally upstream.

Roped Crossing – Diagonal Technique

Linking people in a river with ropes can be very dangerous. Someone who falls, tied to a rope, and is then pulled from upstream, will go under. However, there is one technique we have chosen to highlight. You must think about whether you would be able to achieve a successful roped crossing in your particular situation, and the consequences should it go wrong. Now that a rope is involved a dry run is even more important. A roped crossing is really only a good option if there are enough members in your party to perform all the necessary tasks to make it safe and efficient.

Using the diagonal method means setting up the rope across the river, positioned in a diagonal pointing downstream to take advantage of any current that would assist the travel of the person crossing.

Roped Crossing

Step 1 – To set up a diagonal line you need to pendulum the first person across the river. Often there will not be any trees or boulders to tie the end of the rope onto for security, so group members should sit down near the river edge and hold on to the end of the rope (human anchor). When using the pendulum method the width of the river is a key concern and anything more than 8m will cause problems in communication and possible rope length.

Step 2 – The person crossing finds the middle of the rope and makes a large loop using an overhand knot. The loop should be big enough so that they can easily escape from it if necessary. If you are the person crossing, put it over your head and under your arms. If you are wearing a pack ensure that the rope does not sit between the pack and your back; this would hinder your exit from the loop in an emergency.

A human anchor provides roped support during a river crossing

Step 3 – The human anchor holds onto one end of the rope upstream from your intended crossing point. Ensure that you have at least 20m of rope between you and the human anchor. The rope will now be tensioned as you lean back on it as you cross the river.

Step 4 – The spare end of rope should be held by someone downstream of the crossing point, in case the person crossing falls. In this event the human anchor upstream should let go of the rope completely, so that the downstream anchor can, assisted by the current, draw the person in towards the bank.

Step 5 – Holding the anchored rope firmly, the person crossing balances their way over the river, leaning away from the anchor. Hold the rope at chest height; it will remain tensioned and will continue to offer balance and support as you cut steadily across the current of the river.

A pendulum technique is used to get the first person across the river. Once there, you can create a diagonal tensioned line with human anchors on both sides of the river

Step 6 – Once you have reached the other side of the river, undo the loop knot and begin to take in the spare rope from the person on the downstream side. The upstream human anchor remains in position and continues to hold the rope. Once the rope is tensioned you can anchor the end on the other side of the river by tying it on to something solid, or sitting down to form another human anchor.

Step 7 – Now the rest of the group will make their way diagonally across the river *one at a time*, setting off from the position of the first human anchor, standing on the downstream side of the rope and holding onto it as they move downstream and across, working with the current not against it, until they reach the other side. The last person can pendulum across the river using the same technique as the first person who crossed.

Rope anchored diagonally across the river with a walker traversing using it for support

The Winter Mountains

...the best of winter is the undiluted single malt of mountaineering. Like all the best malts, however, it is utterly uncompromising.

Jim Crumley

Summer hillwalking and winter mountaineering are worlds apart, with virtually every dimension of the environment transformed in the latter season. The risks – and, arguably, the attractions – are multiplied many times over in winter, when the mountains become both wonderland and danger zone.

Because the effect of winter conditions (which, in Scotland, can commonly occur at any time from October to May) is so great, the difference in hillwalking tactics, techniques, approaches and equipment is also significant. We do not intend to cover all these differences, as to move from outlining the skills for moderately graded summer routes to covering those required for technical winter routes in the course of an introductory practical guide is to understate the gulf between the two.

But one thing is clear. The appeal of the winter hills is so great that any ambitious hillwalker will want to get out there and experience them; if you fancy the Aonach Eagach in summer, you'll probably happily take a bit of the Cairngorms in winter too. This book would therefore not be complete without introducing the essential skills and techniques necessary for safe travel on British winter mountain terrain.

These skills and techniques are those traditionally associated with winter hillwalking, although (as with scrambling and rock climbing) the difference between this and winter mountaineering can be (literally!) a grey area. Whatever the distinction, all the evidence from Mountain Rescue teams shows that the majority of winter 'shouts' are to bail out ill-prepared hillwalkers. For the purposes of this book, winter hillwalking has been exceeded when roped techniques and other technical approaches – for instance, snow belays – start to be employed. If you want to go further, take an introductory course in winter mountaineering (you may also look at the wide range of winter survival techniques). For now, however, our concern is safe travel for winter hillwalkers.

How the Hills Change in Winter

It's worth considering exactly how winter conditions affect the hills. This subject merits a book in itself, but the brief answer is 'in just about every way'. The weather is generally harsher, usually colder, often less predictable. Daylight hours are shorter, and route finding and navigation in snow-covered terrain much more difficult. It can be much more difficult to judge times and distances, not least because conditions underfoot are transformed. Snow and ice can cover everything from paths to cairns to streams. You might be skating over it or sinking into it; surface conditions in the same spot can change in minutes as temperatures rise or fall, or snow or rain comes in. For the ill-prepared 'the white stuff' can penetrate boots, and get into clothing. If flat ground can become difficult to walk on without assistance, slopes can be impossible. Gentle inclines can be completely unforgiving in the event of a slip, and even the spring scrambler, especially in Scotland, may find ridges and gullies pasted in old, hard snow. Even a mere smattering of ice can cause real problems on a grade 1 scramble, or less. Given the right (or wrong) combination of slope aspect, angle and conditions, avalanche is also a real and constant threat. And so it goes on. But it is also this very transformation of the hills in winter garb that makes them exhilarating, challenging and uniquely beautiful.

Enjoying perfect Scottish winter conditions

Planning a Winter Day

As with any trip, the most important aspect of a successful winter outing is planning and preparation, and all the same rules apply. But bear in mind the limitations that winter conditions impose. You have less time, and will be moving more slowly. You will use more energy, so will need to carry and eat more. Hazards will be generally greater, and in some cases hidden. Many navigational features will be harder to spot, and a route suitable the rest of the year might well not be possible under snow. Route finding may, in any case, be difficult. In the event of an accident, rescue will almost certainly be more problematic, and possibly more urgent. There's a greater risk of getting caught out in the dark, which would provide a serious test of survival. Whatever your plan for a day in the winter mountains, your margin for error should probably be even greater than it is at other times, and should take very serious account of the levels of strength, fitness and ability within your party. On the plus side, you might well have to carry less gear as you will be wearing more of it for longer.

Clouds and cornices – a front advances as a walker negotiates hard packed snow and ice on the Cairngorm plateau

Winter Equipment and How to Use it

Winter Boots

In an average British winter the mountain terrain from around 2,700ft (824m) is likely to be covered in hard snow and ice, with areas of bare rock. These conditions are most consistent in Scotland, but are also quite normal elsewhere. Four-season boots are essential to operate safely and effectively. These will support your weight without bending the toes or flexing at the heel, and should be comfortable, lightweight, completely waterproof and have a rigid sole. For winter hillwalking, a leather boot is the best choice in terms of comfort and performance.

When you are buying boots think of them as a multi-purpose tool. Getting them right is every bit as important as choosing the right ice axe – perhaps more so. Winter boots should have a good square edge to a Vibram sole, and ideally a protective rubber rand around, if the boot is made of leather. The rand protects the boot from wear and tear when constantly kicking through hard snow and ice.

The flex test – more than 10% bend in a boot can make it unsuitable for winter walking

Flex Test

When considering whether your boot is OK for winter simply apply the flex test. Take the boot in your hand and place the toe on the ground with the heel pointing upwards, then compress and attempt to fold the boot. If you have more than a 10% flex the boot will not perform on hard snow and could lead to you slipping.

If your boot fails the flex test you should consider using different ones, because a stiff, hard-edged boot is essential for support on firm snow. If the boot lets you down when kicking across a hard snow patch you are likely to slip.

Boot/Crampon Compatability

You may also need to use crampons, but if your boots have too much flex the crampons will not stay in place. It's very unnerving when a crampon pops off unexpectedly, and it can also be very awkward to get them back on again. Good boot and crampon compatibility is essential for you to travel safely in the mountains.

> **Remember**
>
> If your boot is too bendy, your crampon will simply part company with it when the weight and force of a simple walking step is applied.

Crampons

Wearing crampons enables the winter hillwalker to walk easily on snow and ice, on terrain that would often be difficult, treacherous or impassable without them.

There are basically two different types of crampon: articulated or fully rigid. For winter walking and mountaineering an articulated pair is the best choice, and they even work quite well for low-grade technical climbing too. Rigid crampons are generally the preserve of technical winter climbers.

Either 10- or 12-point crampons are appropriate for winter walking; 8-point crampons are also available but, having no front points, are not much use on steep snow slopes. The 9-point crampon, a more recent innovation, does have front points and is worth considering.

When selecting which type of crampon, you may choose either a step-in crampon (binding style) or a plastic toe-and-heel bail. A step-in crampon can only be used on a mountain boot, but is fast and easy to fit. Plastic bails will fit any mountain boot

Crampons come with different spike and fitting arrangements: (left to right) a 12-point crampon with a binding fitting; 9-point crampon with a strap heel binding; 10-point crampon with plastic heel binding. All three sets have a plastic toe bail and front points.

but can be slow to strap on. They can also be used on a robust and reasonably stiff-soled walking boot. Whatever system you choose you should ensure that your boot is compatible. Even winter walking and mountaineering boots will have a very small bit of flex, and a good articulated crampon is designed to bend with your boot, without falling off.

Carrying Crampons

When not in use, crampons are just a cluster of annoying metal spikes assembled in an inconvenient manner injurious to health and property. It's wise to defeat their nastier habits by securing them in a special carrying bag – at the very least it could avoid some holes in your rucksack. Once in the crampon bag, carry your crampons inside your rucksack. Some people strap them to the outside of their pack, but this can unbalance your rucksack, and they might also fall off.

Fixing Crampons to Boots

Always put your crampons on as soon as you think you need them, or even earlier. Pop them on before ascending or descending a steep slope that looks icy, even if there are plenty of rocks showing through or, say, when walking on broad but exposed areas close to gentle, snow-covered slides into oblivion.

Do not sit down to put on your crampons as you may slide off accidentally. It is also, even at the best of times, very awkward to fix your crampon on to your boot while sitting down. The following simple technique will have your crampons on quickly and easily:

Step 1 – Find a small clear area of ground or hard snow. Remember you have a left and right crampon, each identified by the final tie-off buckle being located to the outside of your boot.

Step 2 – Standing up, place one crampon on the cleared spot and face the front points away from you.

Step 3 – Maintaining balance step your foot gently in to the crampon – commence the strapping and repeat the process for the other foot.

Top Tips

- Use a small upward incline on the ground when stepping into the crampon. It makes strapping and balancing much easier and faster.

- Crampon failure – it is worthwhile carrying some plastic ties, a strap, and a small threaded nut and bolt in the event that your crampon fails. An emergency repair will get you through your day unscathed.

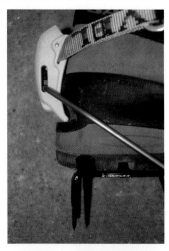

This crampon is fitting poorly on the heel of the boot, with too much of the heel extending beyond the base of the crampon. It should be readjusted

A well-fitting crampon, side...   *front...*   *and back*

Walking with Crampons

Preparing to Flat Foot

Flat footing enables you to place all vertical spikes into the hard snow at the same time (not including your front points). It is commonly used for walking on flat or easy-angled descending terrain. When flat footing your feet should be shoulder width apart.

Flat Footing

Flat footing. Walking downhill and keeping all spikes in the snow.

Front Pointing

This is a technique used for both ascending and descending. You must keep your boots at a right angle to the slope, and using your knee as a hinge, swing your front points into the snow, progressing with short steps.

American Technique

This is a combination of flat footing with a flexed ankle on the downhill boot, and front pointing with the uphill boot. It is important to keep a good distance between boots to prevent catching the crampons and tripping over. American technique can be used for ascending or descending.

Fitted Anti-Balling Plates

Anti-balling plates fitted to crampons are extremely useful in preventing large balls of snow forming on the base of your crampon, causing them to lose grip. This can happen when the snowpack is warmer and there is more moisture around.

The Ice Axe

An ice axe has a number of uses for the winter hillwalker, but if crampons are like the ice-chains that help your car grip the winter road, then an ice axe is your emergency braking system. You do not need to be on very steep ground to enjoy the security it provides.

Choosing an Ice Axe

There are walking, mountaineering or technical climbing axes, and the first two are both suitable for winter hillwalking. It's important to get the right axe for the task. Size is important, but small can definitely be beautiful. You need to select an axe that suits the terrain you plan to visit. Traditionally ice axes were manufactured very long – up to 80cm – but today axes are shorter. A good all-round ice axe is around 50–60cm long, which you can use for both walking and mountaineering quite comfortably. Axe lengths from 60–75cm are more common for walking on non-serious terrain where steep slopes will not be encountered. Shorter axes are preferable on steeper ground because if you find yourself in a 'step, slip, slide and stop' situation a 50–60cm axe length is most efficient when it comes to self-arrest.

A shorter axe is also more efficient for the other main winter hillwalking function of step cutting (and also for more advanced winter mountaineering use such as building axe belays).

Longer axes can be unwieldy when used for these purposes. Also, when stored on a rucksack on your back a long axe is more difficult to manage and access quickly.

A wrist loop should always be carried with your axe. The length of the loop should be no longer than the length of your ice-axe shaft. A detachable wrist loop (or leash) can easily be stored in your pocket for when practising ice-axe arrest. The question of where else you may choose to deploy or dispense with a wrist loop is the source of much debate in the mountaineering community. In a controlled, steep ascent or descent on snow it is generally advisable to use it. On less step gradients and awkward zigzags, you may wish to balance the inconvenience of continuously changing hands, with the prospect of losing your axe!

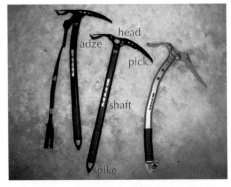

(Left to right) mountaineering, walking and technical axe

Carrying an Ice Axe

You are unlikely to use an ice axe throughout a whole mountaineering journey, so it will need to be stored for some of the time you are out. Easy accessibility is a priority should you need to get the axe out quickly. There are two methods commonly used, shown here.

Ice axes can inflict nasty injuries and need to be carried carefully; one option is on the side of the rucksack, secured by tightened compression straps. An ice axe should, however, always be easily accessible.

An ice axe can also be carried between back and rucksack....

....especially convenient if it is likely to be needed at short notice

If there's a chance that you will need your ice axe, it should already be in your hand

Often the best place for an ice axe is in your hand. When walking on snow-covered slopes there is absolutely no point in having it in your rucksack when your position is such that a slip could be hazardous.

> **Remember**
>
> The simple slip causes more accidents in the hills than anything else, so be prepared.

Helmet

If you are planning to journey on steep terrain in winter conditions it is advisable to wear a helmet. We are not suggesting that you should necessarily wear one from the moment you set out, but you should certainly have one available. A steep, icy, snow slope, a tricky rock step, unexpected terrain or loose rock can all justify the decision.

On many winter mountain walks steep terrain is encountered, which can be rocky, icy or snowy – often a combination of all three. Traversing, ascending or descending these slopes can take a long time, and require intense concentration. In these circumstances a slip is more than possible, and is one of the commonest causes of winter hillwalking accidents involving head injuries. Having a helmet available to put on and take off as required can easily prevent this.

Using an Ice Axe: Self-Arrest

Self-arrest is the term used to describe the most basic function of the ice axe: stopping yourself from (or when) sliding down a snow slope.

Practising Self-Arrest

Like all mountaineering skills self-arrest should be learnt and practised in a safe, controlled situation. Selecting a good practice site is vital; a concave slope will offer a safer angled run-out. You should also take into consideration whether the slope is avalanche prone, has hazards such as protruding rocks, and what is above and below – a yawning abyss below, for instance, would not be great! Hard icy snow can be another danger, causing you to slide too fast and to hurt yourself or damage your clothing. Once satisfied you have a safe run-out prepare your clothing for sliding, making sure zips are secured, pockets contain no objects liable to cause damage, and that your layers are fully battened down to prevent snow reaching parts of the body you would prefer it not to. It's best to wear old waterproofs, as sliding on snow can damage and degrade your good gear. Always were a helmet, but *never wear crampons when practising self-arrest* – you may catch the front points causing a potential major leg injury, not to mention a spin out of control. Wearing a rucksack can add to the realism of the practice, but initially prac-tising both the slide and self-arrest without one is most useful to perfect your stopping technique unrestricted.

Step 1 – Self-Belay

This is the first technique you should practise as, more often than not, it will prevent you taking a slide in the first place. Simply traverse along your practice slope and slip onto the ground. At this point maintain your grip on the head of the axe with your uphill hand and push the axe vertically down into the snow as much as you can. At the same time, with your other hand, hold onto the bottom of the shaft where it is closer to the snow surface. This will prevent any levering of the axe when attempting to stop yourself.

Step 2 – Self-Arrest Brake Position

The picture illustrates the correct position of the ice axe prior to braking. The axe is held at an angle of 45° across the chest. Both hands are correctly positioned holding onto the axe. One hand holds on to the head of the axe and the other covers the often very sharp spike located at the end of the axe shaft. It is worth noting that the axe is held very close to the chest, with the adze resting on the inside step between the shoulder and chest.

The ice axe should be held firmly across the chest for self-arrest (or ice-axe braking)

Step 3 – The brake position

The picture illustrates the brake position on the snow. Make sure that your head is facing away from the head of the axe whilst braking; this will prevent the axe whacking your jaw should it suddenly spring out of the snow. Also ensure that your feet are apart and off the snow, which will improve your stability. If your feet touch the ground at speed you can easily slide and spin out of control. Lifting your stomach off the ground whilst sliding and braking will apply forward weight to your shoulders and increase your chance of stopping.

Practising the brake position. By lifting your stomach off the snow you will position more weight forward and over the head of your ice axe, securing it even more into position

Practise self-arrest by sliding on your front and stopping before you start going too fast. Simply get into the brake position and lift your chest back with the axe firmly located – pick up some speed and then brake.

Step 4 – Relocating the ice axe

Often when sliding you may lose control of your ice axe, so practise relocation of your axe in the braking position. Lie front down in the brake position, then extend your arms holding on to the axe. Once you have picked up some speed locate your axe across your chest by lifting your chest back slightly and then place your weight onto the axe for braking – remember to lift your stomach.

Step 5 – Rolling on to the axe

It's unlikely that in a real situation you'll find yourself heading down a snow slope with your body conveniently positioned for self-arrest. You'll probably have to get into the braking position, so you should practise this. The first thing to practise is rolling on to the axe to take up the self-arrest position, as in the photograph. The starting position is sitting down, facing down the slope. When sliding on your bottom you now need to roll round into the brake position.

Always roll to the side that the head of the ice axe is located, as that is the shortest way to the snow. As you roll round begin to lift your feet so that they never touch the ground. You have now rolled into the brake position.

To practise getting into your ice-axe braking position, start sitting up...

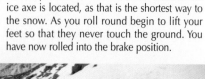

...then roll into the braking position, immediately lifting your feet off the snow

Step 6 – Head first on your front

This position can be scary, so be doubly sure you have a good safe practice area. The idea is to set off down the slope head first. Simply extend your arms out, holding on to the ice axe as you fall face first in a controlled manner, onto the snow. Once you have picked up speed, pointing the pick uphill you can scrape at the snow, and gravity will take your feet back round into the brake position. It can happen very quickly. Once your body has pivoted you will probably require relocation for an effective brake. In other words the axe will make one contact with the snow to turn you around, and then a second contact to brake.

If you prefer to practise from a static position use a friend to hold your feet before you slide off. Remember the technique is to place your axe out by your side to create a natural body pivot using gravity. Then relocate the axe to self-arrest.

Descending head first on your front. Ensure that your feet stay off the snow and your head looks towards the head of the ice axe, positioned to the side

Step 7 – Head first on your back

Again, you may find yourself in an unnerving position. Follow the photograph and place the ice axe in the snow opposite your waist – this involves a push, using your strength to get the axe into position. Gravity will then pull your legs round and into the brake position. Relocate the axe before self-arrest.

cont.

Top Tips

- Practise ice-axe braking on the left and right side.

- Maintain good foot clearance from the surface of the slope.

- Always wear a helmet.

- Take any valuable and breakable items, such as a compass, out of your pockets before practising ice-axe arrest.

- Always select a safe location to practise self-arrest, avoiding avalanche-prone terrain and hazards such as rocks.

Descending head first on your back. Again, ensure that you look towards the head of the ice axe positioned to the side, also rolling your upper body towards the head of the axe. This will bring your body round into the braking position.

If the slope is not too hard you can still stop a slide, even if you drop your ice axe, by positioning yourself in a spider-like fashion with boot and arms apart (hopefully while wearing gloves)

Walking on Snow

When practising walking on snow for the first time, or refresher training, you should consider all the hazards of the slope you intend to practise on, and do the same slope assessment as for self-arrest.

If walking on a snow slope the ice axe should always be held in the uphill hand, where it is best positioned for balance, preventing a fall, and for getting it into the brake position to arrest a fall if you do start to slide. It should be grasped round the head at the top of the shaft, and as you traverse the adze should be facing forward and the pick behind, with the shaft of the axe being positioned parallel to the body. The pick of the axe should always be pointing to the back of the hillwalker because if you need to self-arrest the pick – when drawn to the chest – will point towards the ground, not into your chest.

The Boot as a Tool

The statistics continue to prove that slipping and sliding out of control is the number one cause of winter accidents. Your boots are the front-line tool against this happening, but even the best winter walking boot will only be as effective as the techniques you employ. Learning to use your boots well will enhance your balance and coordination and could, along with good judgement, be a life-saver. It will certainly make you a safer winter mountaineer. Here we describe some of the step techniques that winter boots are designed to assist.

Slice Step

Ascent – This is probably the most used technique for walking on a snow slope. It simply involves a swing action from the lower leg, followed by a cutting action using the uphill boot sole edge. This creates a step in the snow that the boot and walker's weight can rely on, and will form a 'ladder' of steps directly up the slope as you progress. This technique can be used when ascending and descending and is brilliant for helping maintain balance and coordination.

Alternatively, diagonal slice steps are achieved by maintaining the cutting edge of your boot at a constant horizontal angle to the fall line of the slope, as you progress diagonally upwards. When you create a horizontal step your boot will not fall out. Always check your angles. If your toes are pointing uphill your foot could easily slip out of the step created, particularly if firm snow means the steps you are not very deep. When you have created your first step bring your downhill boot across and in front of your uphill boot, to make your second step a few inches uphill. Continue the procedure. The smaller the steps, the more balanced you will be. It is important to maintain a horizontal step to the slope.

Remember

The term 'slice step' means when you make the step you slice your uphill boot edge into the snow almost like a saw action.

Top Tips

- Always look ahead and visualise a line across the slope and follow it as you slice step. Stop deliberately and change direction when you need to.

- Before changing direction it is wise to create a single step big enough for your feet to comfortably balance on. This can be achieved by using your ice axe or your boots to cut the snow away.

Descent – The slice step in descent is very comfortable to use and is similar to the slash step with an ice axe, but achieved without using the axe.

Start by ensuring your boots are positioned horizontal to the slope fall line, keeping your feet directly above and below one another. Your feet do not cross. The uphill boot can reinforce the steps created by the downhill boot. Again, it is important to maintain an even stride by slice stepping only a few inches from the uphill boot with the downhill boot. Once you find a rhythm you will be able to balance and step your way down the slope, creating a series of steps that look like a ladder.

This technique is only advisable for small patches of snow. Should the slope be longer and more serious, crampons should be used.

Pigeon Hole Steps

These are very easy to achieve and comfortable on the calf muscles.

Begin by facing into the slope and take a small step first. Using your knee as the pivot or hinge, kick the nose of your boot into the snow, maintaining a constant right angle to the slope whether you are ascending or descending. It is also important to maintain your feet at least shoulder width apart as this will give good balance when stepping up or down.

This technique is excellent for descending, especially when the slope is steep and controlled balance is required.

Heel Plunge Steps

This is a very important technique, commonly used for descending in soft-to-medium snow density, and is very easy to achieve.

Position your feet at least shoulder width apart, then in small steps proceed to plunge your heels into the snow, ensuring that you take small steps to maintain balance. Your feet should remain at right angles to the snow pack – simply bend your knees and steady your balance by leaning forward slightly, then lift your knee and kick down into the snow, one step at a time.

Changing Direction: Turning on a Snow Slope

If you are zigzagging up a slope and need to turn to change direction, use your ice axe for support and security. Always stop, and either kick or cut a secure platform for both feet. If kicking, assist your balance by self-belaying with the axe in the snow slope in front of you held at the top with both hands. Turn on the platform, place your axe in the uphill hand, and continue.

Changing direction by cutting a platform big enough for both feet and holding the axe head for security while turning

Ascending a snow slope with an ice axe

Step Cutting with your Ice Axe

The most frequently asked question on a winter skills course is: 'When do I step cut?' The answer is always difficult because it depends on circumstances. When you are ascending steep terrain, for instance, you will probably have the sense to put your crampons on. But if you only have one small hard patch of snow, on a relatively easy angle, you may decide to step cut across it in either ascent or descent.

Good step cutting requires a lot of practice, but it is worthwhile putting in the time for when you need it, rather than just relying on a theoretical knowledge of how to go about it if you have to. Find a safe snow slope on which to practise.

Ensure your ice-axe leash fits correctly. The wrist loop should extend to the end of the axe only. Push your hand through the wrist loop and hold onto the bottom of the axe shaft, maintaining a firm grip on the axe and ensuring that the wrist loop is tight.

Cutting steps on a diagonal line up and across a snow slope

Slash Steps

Ascent – Cant the axe at 45° to the slope, which allows a square-cutting edge of the adze to cut through the surface of the snow in a smooth, slashing action, producing a step in the surface. Try and find a rhythm when swinging the axe. Slice step your feet into each new step as it is cut and you move forward. When travelling diagonal style visualise a line across the snow pack and using the axe cut a step in front but just above the uphill boot.

Continue until you need to change direction. Before doing so cut a large step so that both boots can stand firmly – then change direction and repeat the process.

Descent – A slash step in descent is again rarely used these days for long snow slopes, only for cutting across small isolated pockets. Again, if in doubt put your crampons on.

Hold your axe in the downhill hand, using the leash to secure it. Your uphill arm can hold on to the slope for support when descending.

Combining step cutting and slice steps to ascend a snow slope

To make progress simply swing the axe in a pendulum fashion with the axe at an angle of 45° to the slope. This will slice the snow away and create steps wide enough for your boot to step on to. Care must be taken when swinging the axe as you may lean out of balance by trying to cut steps out of reach. Always maintain your balance by cutting the steps a few inches away from your boot.

Once you cut the step simply place your downhill boot into it and then move your uphill boot into the existing step previously cut – continue the process to complete your line of descent.

Step cutting and slice steps to descend an easy-angled snow slope

Top Tip

- Remember to always maintain a horizontal boot placement to the fall line of the slope. This will prevent you from slipping out of your slash step.

Traverse Step Cutting

This technique is used when you intend traversing a slope, and involves maintaining your feet at shoulder width and horizontal to the slope fall line.

Holding the axe in the downhill arm, and using the axe leash to secure it, cut steps above and below one another across the slope just a few inches away from the boot. The uphill hand can either hold on to the slope for balance or hold on to the ice axe, so the axe is double handed.

Step cutting while traversing

Bucket Steps

Bucket steps are brilliant, but for uphill use only. They give you a great excuse to dispense with finesse. Buckets are steps wide enough for both boots to step into.

Hold on to your axe with both hands, one hand remaining through the axe leash. Using the adze, excavate the snow wide enough so that both boots will fit on to it length- and widthways. It is a good idea to cut two steps to begin with, especially when cutting on steeper angles, making the cutting and stepping combination more natural. Step into the first step, and start on the next one (that is, two steps up). Eventually you will have created a staircase of snow steps.

Bucket steps are very easy to achieve but can be tiring, so are useful when ascending a small slope. They provide first-class security for the ascending walker and anyone else following behind.

Bucket steps provide a secure way of ascending a snow slope... and releasing pent-up aggression

Avalanche!

After an avalanche

We are constantly negotiating with the forces of gravity in mountainous terrain, but these forces are rarely as lethal as when a huge volume of snow breaks away and relocates itself at speed down a mountainside. If you happen to be there at the time, you will not only know about it but you probably triggered it.

An awareness of the mechanics and causes of avalanches is absolutely essential when travelling in the British mountains in winter conditions, but more important still is to know how to avoid getting caught in one. The good news is that nearly all avalanche accidents can be avoided. Avalanches occur in the winter mountains much more frequently than we hear about; 90% of those people who get caught in an avalanche trigger it themselves (and, logically, these are the ones we do hear about). Most commonly these are 'slab' avalanches.

Avalanches have been the subject of a great deal of study, and the science of the snow-pack can be pretty baffling. Our aim here is to keep things simple and practical, providing strategies for safe travel and avalanche avoidance in snow-covered terrain.

Avalanche avoidance is largely about preparation, information and – finally – good judgement. Having put yourself in a position to avoid an avalanche, be sure never to let personal ambitions cloud your judgement when making vital route decisions.

Avalanche Awareness and Risk Assessment

Pre-Trip Planning Should Include:

- Weather and avalanche forecast for the area. In Scotland specialist information on avalanche risk can be obtained from the Scottish Avalanche Information Service www.sais.gov.co.uk.

- Avalanche equipment – transceiver, shovel and avalanche probe for trips into hazardous terrain

Terrain Warning Signs

- Slope angles between 30 and 45° are most prone to avalanche – although avalanches can occur on much lower angles

- Lee slopes and sheltered, steep-sided gullies are vulnerable. When the wind has transported snow from the windward side of the mountain to the lee side, slab avalanche commonly results.

- Slope shape – concave and convex angles can both be very serious, particularly the latter when loaded with fresh snow

- Previous avalanche debris – this indicates that avalanches have occurred; you should choose your route carefully and not take the same angle, aspect and altitude of the avalanche path. Signs of avalanche activity are nature's biggest clue.

Snowpack Warning Signs

- Obvious avalanche debris. Try to avoid slopes that face the same direction.

- Snow cracking, collapsing or blocking away from underfoot, often accompanied by 'whumping' noises. This indicates unstable snow conditions; note the angle and aspect of slope.

- Snow easily breaking from the snowpack during a Rutschblock or shear test (see below). Shear tests should be conducted at altitudes where problems are likely, taking into account angles and aspects of the test slope.

- A single shear test will give you good-quality information relating specifically to the shear test location and altitude of the slope, but it will not give an accurate picture of the whole slope. For instance, a couple of degrees increase in slope angle above the test site can make a difference to the instability of the snowpack.

- Look out for 'sunwheels' and 'roller balls' – when the snow is naturally rolling off the slopes, which may be associated with long periods of strong solar warming.

- Evidence of cornice collapse in the area may indicate that a sudden rise in temperature is occuring or has occured.

The snowpack is made up of layers. Most avalanches are the result of weaknesses where these layers meet. Depth hoar (brittle and very unstable snow crystals) are present in the obvious horizontal line.

Weather Warning Signs

- Heavy snowball activity down slopes.

- Wind loading on lee slopes – it doesn't need to be snowing, just windy enough to transfer snow from the windward side to the lee side of the mountain. An easterly wind, for example, may transfer snow to west-facing slopes.

- Rain and warm wind will cause a sudden rise in temperature – the layers of snow that make up the snow pack are constantly moving and changing, so such a change can make a big difference to the structure and stability of the overall pack of snow lying on the surface of the mountain.

- Sudden rise in temperature.

- Fresh snowfall.

Testing the Snowpack
Shear Tests

This is a way of assessing avalanche risk in a specific location. The test is easy to do and will provide you with lots of information on the current stability of the snowpack at the given altitude, aspect and angle. A walking Rutschblock test is the most common shear test for winter walkers.

A block of snow isolated during a Rutschblok shear test

Select a safe and undisturbed area of snow that is representative of the slope or route you wish to travel on. Remember the slope angle should be at least 30°.

Excavate a block of snow roughly 1 x 1m square and 1.5m deep, using a snow shovel (arguably an essential piece of kit in winter conditions) at the front and an ice-axe shaft for the side and back edges. Only go down as far as you can with the length of your axe or until you hit the first hard layer of snow when isolating the sides of the block.

As the photograph illustrates, the block has been excavated all around, but left intact and in position. The idea now is to see under what degree of stress it will fail – that is, fracture away from the rest of the snowpack (if it hasn't already done so). This will give you a good indication of the pack's stability. The following series of observational tests should be applied to the block:

- Fails whilst isolating the test block – extremely unstable – get out of there!
- Fails whilst approaching the block from an angle of 45°, walking from above it, then sitting just above it and shuffling feet, toe to heel, on the block – highly unstable – change your intended route
- From a sitting position, fails whilst rising up on to the block – very unstable – choose another route carefully

- Fails with a 'down sink' – that is, throwing your weight into your feet whilst standing on the top edge of the block toe to heel. Unstable snowpack – retest any other intended route chosen.
- Fails with a soft jump on the block – marginally unstable – be careful. Travelling with large groups is not advisable on this type of slope.

The back wall of the block (the interface) after it has 'failed' – time for a sharp exit?

- Fails with a hard jump – stable – good indicator that your travel on this slope will probably be problem free

You must bear in mind that conducting a single shear test is not enough when travelling around the mountains. Conditions can change rapidly so you need to constantly evaluate the snowpack, perhaps conducting several tests in the course of a single journey.

Avalanche Avoidance

When it comes to avoiding getting caught in an avalanche, there are therefore four key factors to consider:

A classic site for a likely windslab avalanche

- terrain
- weather
- snowpack
- people.

When all the information you have indicates an unstable snowpack, and therefore a high avalanche risk, only careful route selection will lead to safe travel.

Some Safe Route Travel Tips

If you feel you have no alternative but to cross terrain that could be avalanche prone:

- consider the likely consequences if caught in an avalanche – do you really have no alternative but to cross?
- traverse as high as possible across the slope.
- zip up clothing to prevent snow from entering. It also helps to reduce drag and even to create an air pocket if you get avalanched.

- Remove trekking-pole straps and ice-axe leashes – if avalanched you don't want either implement clattering around your head or vital organs.

- You may decide to travel one at a time – all eyes should watch that person. Consider a roped crossing one at a time.

- Travel in the same track as the other members of your team – don't assume other lines across the slope will be safe (and don't rely on tracks that may already be in the snow).

- Move quickly, using islands of rock for protection if possible.

- Have a rescue plan should someone get caught.

Some Survival Tips if you Get Caught in an Avalanche

- Shout out immediately – you have a much better chance of being found if someone watches you fall, so you need to draw their attention to the fact.

- Try to get out of one side of the avalanche.

- Get rid of gear – drop your axe or trekking pole.

- Try to stay on the surface by 'swimming'.

- As the avalanche stops, strain every sinew to get part of your body, such as your hand, to the surface. This can help to create an air supply once everything as stopped, and may give you a chance of being seen and dug out more quickly.

- As things slow down, but before the snow settles into its new position, try to make a breathing space around your face.

- When everything has stopped moving, try to relax your body.

Most victims who don't survive an avalanche tend to be found facing upwards, hence asphyxiation sets in rather fast as the airways become blocked with snow.

If you observe someone else being caught:

- watch them carefully and try to note where you last saw them – start looking for them in that spot, and just below it
- check for sources of continuing danger before approaching
- get the attention of others if possible
- if you have a mobile phone and have reception, call the emergency services
- immediately search the avalanche area – do not wait for other rescuers
- look for clues as to where the victims are. Do not remove them from the surface, but check in the snowpack beneath them.
- appoint a look-out if you have one – in case another avalanche comes down
- conduct an avalanche transceiver search if you have one

- mark where the person was the last time they were seen
- probe in likely burial spots using your trekking poles with baskets off, or an avalanche probe if you are carrying one
- if there is no communication with outside help, and if numbers of rescuers allow it, send someone for help
- the harsh reality is that you may be the victim's only chance of survival – avalanche victims have a 92% chance if dug out within the first 15 minutes; after two hours this drops to just 3%. Don't give up!
- most recovered victims will require first aid for injuries sustained during the avalanche
- generally, the job of avalanche rescue teams is to recover bodies.

Keep Practising

Mountaineering skills improve with practice. Climbing comes naturally to some, less so to others. The same can be said of navigation, ropework, even communication. But the level of ability required in these and other areas to fulfil ambitions of the sort outlined in Part 3 can only be achieved through learning and experience. To be a safe climber, everyone needs a mountain apprenticeship.

This is as true for the psychological aspects of the sport as for the physical and technical ones. Anyone who has been on a climbing course, or even a trek over challenging terrain, cannot fail to have noticed that over time – whether a weekend, a week or a month – their level of performance improves as they adapt to their surroundings, and become more practised in their knots, moves, compass readings or the way in which they are affected by exposure.

> **Remember**
>
> When it comes to mountaineering, familiarity breeds not contempt, but competence and confidence.

So what is the best way to train and practise the techniques you will need to master the step up from simple hillwalking to mountaineering? Where do you practise what, and how do you develop your skills when there are only limited opportunities to get out and practise on actual routes? You need to find an approach that suits you, your lifestyle and aspirations, but our intention here is to provide some food for thought, and to avoid you discovering – when it really matters – that your skills are not quite as honed as you would like.

Regular mountaineering – there's no substitute for the real thing, and for getting 'out there' as frequently as possible, in as many different settings and conditions as you can. Set yourself realistic objectives, and try to do a range of routes at each grade you want to tackle, to consolidate your techniques and build your confidence.

'Controlled practice' outings – most people find stopping to practise skills in the course of an enjoyable day out a real pain. Organising some dedicated practice sessions means that when you really need your new skills you won't struggle to remember them. You might be able to do an abseil, lower and belay sessions, for instance, for an hour after work, with reliable partners at a safe location, with plenty of bomb-proof anchor options and a forgiving gradient. Or go out in poor visibility – night-time is good – and set yourself measurable navigation tasks to really test your compass and map-reading skills.

Climbing walls – indoor walls are everywhere these days. They do not replicate the outdoor climbing experience and are probably best for building up the very specific kind of fitness – from fingers to toes – that aids climbing. But they are also fun, good for building confidence – say, when leading – practising certain types of move, practising belaying and team building. You need to be able to trust your belayer both indoors and out. For some scramblers, the experience of an indoor wall can provide a psychological boost when it comes to tackling a 'real' crux climbing move – if you can say to yourself you've already done something like it at the climbing wall, it's like telling yourself you know you can do it.

Climbing courses – outdoors – a climbing course out in the real world with a qualified and experienced instructor will bring to life some of the required skills and techniques in a realistic, but still reasonably controlled, environment. You can use it to kick-start your learning – making progress can be a slow and daunting task on your own – or to get some practice in, say, leading, and to build your confidence. The main advantage is that, when you then go out without an instructor, the skills and techniques gained will be directly applicable to the experience you are having on your own.

Guided climbing – going climbing with a qualified and experienced guide, individually or in a small group, will enable you to get 'routes' in that may be beyond your present experience and ability. You will almost certainly learn a great deal from observing – and simply from being on the mountain with – your guide. At the same time you will be able to gauge your own level of skill and technical competence, to build your confidence and assess your level and likely performance if you were on the same routes on your own. However, it will not replicate the experience of climbing unguided, for two reasons: firstly, the guide will take responsibility for all the important decisions and secondly, he or she is also likely to manage all the equipment. If you can afford it, guided climbing can be a great learning experience and an excellent way to fulfil mountaineering ambitions, but it is not generally a short-cut to the skill-set you need to acquire to be out there on your own.

Mountaincraft Courses

Safe and enjoyable mountaineering is about a fully rounded understanding and appreciation of the mountain environment – of the risks and rewards it holds, and how to minimise the one while maximising the other. Mountaincraft is the name given to the combination of skills and abilities that enable you to do that, and a course in mountaincraft – or aspects of it, such as navigation or survival – will help you acquire those things in ways that will be directly relevant to every outing.

Another good way of brushing up on the speed and accuracy of your basic navigation skills is to get involved in orienteering.

Winter Courses

The winter environment in Britain's mountains is completely different to other times of year, and the objective dangers far greater. No one should be tempted onto high ground in winter without having spent some time specifically practising winter skills in a safe and controlled situation first. One of the best ways is to book onto one of the many winter courses offered each year, the most consistent conditions for these being in Scotland. Depending on your level of ability and ambition you may choose a winter skills, winter mountaineering or winter climbing course. The experience of taking a course in the winter mountains will almost certainly boost your confidence and ability when you plan a trip of your own. Make sure you book with a reputable organisation that can guarantee you will be in the hands of an experienced, professional instructor, who is qualified to UK Mountain Instructor Certificate (MIC) or the international UIAGM level.

Mountain Leader Training

Mountain Leader Training UK has developed a range of mountaineering qualifications as the sport has become increasingly 'professional' in recent years, but these 'tickets' are not just of interest to someone who wants to make a living from being on the hill. The MLTUK Mountain Leader Award is a well-rounded mountain qualification that develops and tests knowledge and awareness of the mountain environment, and competence to operate in the British mountains in summer conditions (effectively in everything except winter conditions). Skills tested include route planning and navigation in poor visibility, basic ropework, river crossing and emergency procedures. Similarly the MLTUK's basic climbing qualification, the Single Pitch Award, will test a range of skills that are directly relevant to much of what is discussed in this book. Both awards are experience based, rather than for beginners, but they provide an excellent means of acquiring and testing important skills, even if your motivation is entirely personal.

Buy your Own Gear

If you don't have access to the basic tools of the mountaineer developing your skills is going to be hard. Equipment is rarely cheap, but investing in it – and in the best you can afford – is almost always worthwhile. Hiring equipment can be a useful introduction, and can help you decide what will be best for you when you do come to buy. But the sooner you can 'get your rack together', along with all the other gear you have decided you need, the sooner you will get familiar with it and use it to its full potential.

Accidents will Happen

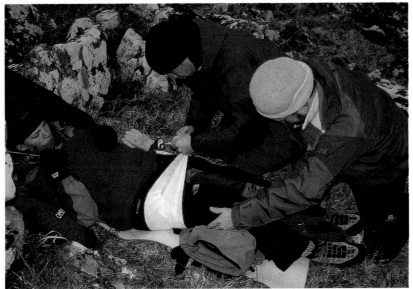

Casualty ... but can you help?

In the mountains, accidents happen – and not usually because the unfortunate victims are stupid or ill-prepared. Talk to any Mountain Rescue team and they will tell you that in most cases it's a question of 'There but for the grace of God go I'– and that's why they work in Mountain Rescue. The good news is that despite a huge increase in the number of people using the British hills for recreation, the number of accidents as a percentage of outings has fallen steadily in recent years. This suggests people can, and do, learn to look after themselves in the hills.

Nevertheless, a glance through the logbook of any UK rescue team will produce a litany of sobering tales of people who went out to enjoy themselves for the day and got into difficulties. Usually the reasons are predictable.

The best 'advice' that can be given about mountaineering accidents may sound patronising, but is no less true for that. It's simply that accidents in the mountains are best avoided! This observation encapsulates one important truth – while they can happen to anyone, the vast majority of mountaineering mishaps are 'man made' events that need never occur. It follows that if greater care is taken to avoid the circumstances where accidents most commonly occur, they are less likely to happen.

From peak-bagging to cragging, 'the simple slip' is the most common factor behind accidents. But what causes the slip? By the time it happens things have almost always been going wrong for a while – inappropriate footwear or a heavy pack causing delay; the threat of getting caught in the dark with no head torch, causing a rush to get down; overstretching technical abilities and gear; going off route on the descent and straying onto steep terrain; succumbing to the cold, which can cause loss of balance; poor clothing resulting in lowering of morale due to wet and cold; lack of concentration caused by dehydration, lack of food, or fatigue from the day's exertions. In all these cases the fateful slip would be the predictable and avoidable consequence.

But the biggest single cause behind these problems is navigational error, which can have a nasty habit of producing a knock-on effect. There will usually be an underlying reason to that, too, relating back to planning, preparation and approach. Focusing on these areas, first and foremost, is the best way to avoid a mountaineering accident. This is particularly significant when making the transition from hillwalking to mountaineering, because the likelihood is that you will, by definition, be operating at the outer limits of your comfort zone. In such circumstances *not to prepare thoroughly is to invite an accident*.

Planning and Preparation to Avoid Accidents

- Work out your route distance, ascent/descent and timings (allowing for delays and varying conditions)
- Study the guidebook description, but be prepared for the unexpected – remember: grades are opinion, not fact. Conditions can change everything.
- Consider the terrain you will be crossing and anticipate problems you may face
- Work out the technical requirements of the route – the gear and the skills
- Work out the navigational requirements in legs – identify useful features and potential pitfalls
- Your route may be challenging, but is it realistic for you and your team?
- Make sure you have the appropriate equipment – footwear, clothing, maps, technical gear – and relevant spares without over-burdening yourself
- Make sure you have enough food, and water (or knowledge of water sources)
- Make sure you have the skills needed for your chosen route
- Consider escape routes, and what you might do in an emergency
- Monitor the weather and assess its likely impact on your trip
- Tell someone where you are going and when you expect to be back

Planning should be done as a team, including cutting down on weight by avoiding unnecessary duplication of gear. It has been known for the team 'leader' to plan the whole thing as a surprise, only to find the rest of the team is ill-equipped and ill-prepared – this is just plain stupid.

A Cool Head

There's a great deal to be said for a steady and considered approach in the mountains. Whatever situation you are in, a cool head is essential. Don't dawdle on a route, but don't rush either. Get an early start and give yourself plenty of time. Enjoy the mountains, but don't just save your concentration for the bits you need to be 'psyched' for. You should be focused and in control the whole time, constantly monitoring all aspects of your situation from the moment you set off to the time you return. Try to keep a steady pace throughout the day, as the process of constantly overheating and cooling down can be debilitating. Look after your physical well-being, and make sure you consume enough calories and water. Take each obstacle as it comes, and don't over-stretch yourself. Don't climb up something that you are not confident you have the skills to get back down if necessary. Don't be afraid to alter your plans according to what conditions, the terrain and your party's responses dictate.

Above all, perhaps, don't relax into the feeling of having achieved your objective before your trip is over – it's true at all levels of mountaineering that more accidents happen on the way down than on the way up.

> **Remember**
> You always have choices, so make them carefully, taking into account all the available information: 'Nothing is more deadly in mountaineering than a determination to achieve a particular objective, whatever the conditions' (Ed Douglas and David Rose, *Regions of the Heart*).

When an Accident Becomes an Emergency

Not all accidents automatically lead to an emergency. Whether or not they do depends on a combination of factors:

- the nature of the incident
- prevailing conditions and location
- your team's ability to deal with the situation – it's probably fair to say that once your team loses that ability an emergency is likely.

The other relevant factor would be where an urgent medical condition has arisen or is imminent. In both cases there is a strong possibility that outside assistance will be needed, but almost always there will be things you can do to help on the spot.

Mountain First Aid

It's hard to think of an emergency in the mountains that would not involve a first aid dimension, and the hillwalker-mountaineer should be specifically practised in mountain first aid. This section of the book will look at aspects of first aid practice in the context of the mountain environment. We have chosen to cover a range of the most likely conditions the hill-goer will meet, but this is by no means an exhaustive list. Anyone active in the mountain environment should be familiar with the basics of first aid, should attend a relevant course to cover the necessary skills in detail, and should practise them. Any course taken should be with a provider familiar with the specific challenges of first aid in a mountain setting.

The primary aim of first aid is to *preserve life, to limit the worsening of the condition* and *to promote recovery*. Before looking at various ways of achieving this, depending on the nature of the problem, it is important to understand how to manage the relevant incident initially.

> **Managing First Aid**
> The first priority of first aid has to be to ensure that you don't add to the list of casualties. So when preserving life, make sure you include your own!

Managing the Scene

The mountains present specific risks that need to be appreciated and managed. Even if the reason someone needs medical assistance is not immediately linked to one of these, the fact that they are injured in a potentially hostile environment will have an impact on how we deliver first aid.

On approaching an accident scene, assess what seems to have happened and be alert to possible risks. Is there a continuing danger posed, say, by unstable rock? Is the casualty likely to fall further? What is the safest approach for both of you?

Taking a measured approach will bear dividends, but make sure that your companions behave likewise. There is nothing worse than people coming from all directions, kicking off rocks, dropping their rucksacks and shouting about what a mess the casualty is in. Someone needs to take control to ensure that everyone is safe.

Having established that risk factors around the casualty can be managed, keep it that way. Don't let people clamber about on loose scree above the injured party (and yourself) and try to keep movements immediately around the casualty to a minimum. It is amazing how easy it is to kick small stones or heather flecks into a casualty's eyes and just make them more uncomfortable. Whatever else happens don't let anyone lean on or step over a prone casualty – they will get kicked, invariably on the *bad* leg.

As your assessment of the casualty's condition is made, try to manage the scene for the next steps. Have you got everything you need? If you have to undertake some sort of procedure is there enough clear space? If you are going to move what is your route? Can a helicopter land? If you put the casualty in a bivi bag will he slip? If so, prepare a ledge beforehand. Can you create shelter? Can you go lower? Think a few steps ahead all the time.

Looking After Number One

If the immediate environment doesn't present a risk to you, your casualty certainly does! Sterile medical gloves should always be carried and must be worn if you are doing anything involving body fluids. As one paramedic said, 'If it's wet or sticky, and it's not yours, don't touch it without gloves on!' In the urgency of the moment it is easy to forget to look after yourself in other ways. Make sure you keep warm, dry and fed – it might be a long wait.

Managing the Team

If you are with companions, make sure they also look after themselves and each other. If you are attempting to act together – say to coordinate a lift of a casualty – make sure you manage the process. Agree who is doing what, when, why, on whose command, and what happens next. Clarity of direction isn't just about being bossy; the smoother you act, the kinder you are to your casualty, and the better the chance that everything will work out well.

Managing the Casualty

The more you communicate with and involve your casualty, the better he will feel and the more you will know about his status and condition. Being injured is frightening enough without feeling that you have lost all control. Talk to your casualty!

Communicating with the Emergency Services

In these days of mobile phones, you may well be able to communicate with the emergency services about an incident via the 999 service. Think what you are going to say before you phone. The more specific you are about who is involved, location, weather conditions and casualty assessment, the easier it will be for emergency personnel to assist. This is one reason why careful monitoring of your casualty's condition, and particularly their 'vital signs', can help others to help them.

And if you have no mobile phone or mobile signal? You may well face the dilemma of whether to stay with the casualty or leave to get assistance. Making this decision will depend upon their injuries, weather conditions, time of day and whether you can be sure that the alarm will be raised if your party is late back. If you decide to leave the casualty to get help you should ensure that they are packaged to stay as warm and comfortable as possible, protected from the elements and effects of the surrounding environment. You should reassure the casualty and leave food and drink if they are able to take it. You should also inform them of your intended plan and route. Take a detailed note of their condition and position using a 6-figure grid reference and a description of the surrounding terrain. Mark the casualty's location if possible using a trekking pole or a brightly coloured item of clothing, especially in winter conditions. This will allow the search and rescue teams to locate them much more easily.

Leaving a casualty is one of the hardest decisions to make in an emergency situation and in most cases people rightly choose to stay put, especially where breathing difficulties, or severe blood loss, have occurred, or where the casualty is lying in an awkward position and cannot be moved due to possible spinal injury. Another reason to stay is if the casualty appears to be distressed at the prospect of being left. Your bottom line should be whether the casualty's condition will worsen as a result of you not being there – if it will, don't leave.

Remember
Whichever method you use to get a message to the emergency services, you must inform them immediately and accurately of the casualty's location, situation and apparent condition.

Initial Casualty Assessment – the ABC Priorities

In this section of the book we will return to the priorities of **A**irway, **B**reathing and **C**irculation repeatedly. Without oxygen we die. The airway is the route by which we take it in; the process of breathing transfers it to the blood; the circulation of blood takes it to all the organs of the body. If any of these functions are missing we have a problem so, no matter what else may grab the attention, these are our priorities.

The easiest way to assess a casualty in this respect is to check for a set of 'vital signs'. If you can count the number of respirations per minute, taking a pulse at the wrist and a pulse at the neck, you can provide vital information about your casualty's condition – such as: are they breathing? do they have circulation?

Initial Casualty Assessment and the Resuscitation Sequence
Airway

On approaching the casualty his level of response should be gauged. Is he conscious? Is he alert? Put simply, if he is talking to you, you don't have an airway problem.

If the casualty is breathing, but unconscious, he should be quickly, but carefully, checked for other injuries, before being placed in the 'recovery' position which will stop the tongue or vomit blocking the throat.

It may be that on approach the casualty's airway is simply blocked – by his tongue for example – or he may be breathing but making the 'snoring' sound typical of a partially blocked airway. A simple chin lift or jaw thrust may resolve the problem, but keep monitoring and don't assume that's it sorted. It may be that you are dealing with an unconscious casualty who has choked on vomit. When dealing with an avalanche situation, an airway can be blocked by snow; or there may be facial trauma, such as a broken jaw, where teeth and bits of bone can compromise the airway. Clear it out, *wearing gloves.*

Opening the airway

Checking for airway obstructions

Checking an unconscious casualty for breathing and chest movement

First Priority
The first priority in caring for the casualty is *to check for, open and maintain* an airway.

Jaw thrust – a straightforward technique to prevent the tongue from obstructing the airway

Before moving an unconscious casualty into the recovery position you should quickly but carefully check them for circulation and further injury

A common query is, 'What if I suspect a neck or spine injury?' The answer is that the airway must always take priority, but that any movement of the casualty should be made with the utmost care to avoid any articulation of the spine, and a chin lift should be used whilst keeping the spine in line.

The casualty may be suffering from spinal trauma or injuries you cannot see without examining them fully

By checking the underside of the casualty fluids may appear on your gloved fingers, indicating other injuries are present

Breathing

Breathing should be unlaboured, with both sides of the chest moving evenly; if this isn't the case you may have an injury to the chest wall or lungs. If your casualty is not breathing, you may have to breathe for them (it is wise to have a face shield in your first aid kit, an item specially designed to protect you from blood and saliva contamination while performing mouth-to-mouth to breathe for the casualty).

Step 1 – Placing the casualty in the recovery position will ultimately stop the tongue or vomit from blocking the airway.

Step 2 – Remember to protect the casualty's head.

Step 3 – When rolling the casualty into the recovery position maintain eye contact.

Step 4 – Protect the casualty's head and airway.

If you have an **A**irway, and you have **B**reathing, you can now check for...

Circulation

Minor cuts are not a big problem at this stage, but you must look for major bleeding. This can reduce the amount of blood in the system and lead to the condition of *shock*, where a lack of blood leads to reduced 'perfusion' of tissue that will stop organs, critically the heart, functioning properly. Shock can be fatal.

Symptoms of shock are a rapid pulse, pale/grey/waxy complexion and poor circulation at the extremities. (Try pinching a fingernail for five seconds; it will go white, but colour should normally return in two seconds.) As the condition becomes more serious, dizziness and nausea become apparent, the pulse at the wrist weakens and the casualty will become restless, even aggressive.

Treatment of shock is to staunch any major bleeds and keep the feet higher than the body core and head, whilst monitoring progress and watching for the all-important airway and breathing. Shock must be treated.

If your casualty does not have a pulse (**C**irculation) then you may have to commence Cardio-pulmonary Resuscitation (CPR). This technique should be learnt and practised through a first-aid training course, but the essence of the sequence is:

- check response
- open airway
- check breathing. If this is OK then place casualty in the recovery position
- if you have no breathing, provide 2 'rescue breaths'
- check for circulation: if this is not present for over one minute consider commencing CPR at 15 chest compressions to 2 breaths until definitive care arrives or is reached.

Whilst a number of conditions or illnesses can be linked to breathing and circulation, two are worthy of specific mention:

Heart attacks occur when the blood supply to the heart is interrupted by, for example, a blood clot. The main risk is the chance the heart will stop. The essence of treatment is to make the patient as comfortable as possible and minimise the work the heart is doing.

The casualty will complain of a persistent, vice-like pain which radiates down the left arm and does not ease with rest. Complexion will be ashen, pulse may be rapid, weak and irregular, and the casualty will complain of giddiness.

The casualty will probably favour a supported, half-sitting position. If the pain persists, and the casualty is conscious and alert, 300mg of aspirin can be offered to chew or dissolve on the tongue.

Although there are differences between heart attacks and other chest pain, such as angina, any condition involving chest pain should be treated as serious, and as a potential heart attack, until medical advice dictates otherwise.

Asthma is evidenced by wheezing, an inability to speak and a pallor to the skin. A serious asthma attack can be frightening for both casualty and observer.

The key to managing an attack is to remain calm, and to reassure the casualty. If he has a relieving inhaler, usually coloured blue, he should be encouraged to use this, but you should be aware that a higher dose than normal may cause some palpitation, and be prepared to reassure the casualty. Encouraging slow, deep breaths will aid relief and the episode will usually pass. It should usually be possible to walk the casualty off, but be aware of unsteadiness and the need for a gentle, cautious pace.

Injuries to Head, Neck and Back

Head and spinal injuries probably cause the greatest concern to the hill-going first aider. All such injuries are potentially serious, yet treatment you can offer as a first aider is again relatively simple.

Head Injury

The key to dealing with head injuries is the quality of your assessment.

As with other injuries, the cause, or way the injury was sustained, may give significant clues. A scalp wound may bleed profusely and look very dramatic, but may simply require dressing if caused by a minor force such as walking into a sharp, low, rock overhang. Conversely, a more serious skull fracture linked to a long fall may show no obvious external bleeding (and you may get distracted by other more obvious trauma).

The big clue will often be found in the casualty's presentation and the assessment of their level of consciousness. Think of the acronym **AVPU**:

- **A**lert. Is the casualty alert?
- **V**oice. Does he only react to a voice?
- **P**ain. Does he only react to pain?
- **U**nconscious or not?

Rather than cover the pathology of the head injury itself, it is worth considering what you can see and do. Was the casualty alert when you arrived, but is now a bit 'out of it' and only reacts when you shout at him? It's important to take note of this sort of trend and, if possible, keep a record (remember that it is worth checking whether a casualty has taken drugs or alcohol which can affect these observations).

On the hill, the treatment of a head injury is really confined to two primary areas. The priority is to maintain the provision of oxygen to the brain, so watch the patient's consciousness level and *ensure that an airway is maintained* if he is unconscious. The second priority is to staunch any bleeding to reduce the level of shock.

Spinal Injuries

As above, the assessment of the casualty is the key to dealing with this possibly serious problem. The events leading to the injury will again provide clues. In the case of a long fall, or a tumbling fall, you may suspect spinal injury. If a casualty is complaining of spinal or neck pain, unusual sensations in extremities or says he thinks he's broken his neck… listen to him!

Treatment is again simple, but requires to be rigorously managed. The priorities of Airway, Breathing and Circulation must be monitored, as must the level of consciousness, and immediate and sustained immobilisation must be applied until appropriate assistance arrives to evacuate. The casualty should be moved as little as possible – and then only if the injured part is kept immobilised using improvised splints – by at least four people and in a properly coordinated lift or 'log roll'. To find out more about these and other specialist techniques for moving a casualty the value of a first aid course cannot be overestimated.

Bruises, Breaks and Dislocations

The majority of injuries on the hill will fall into this category, with most occurring to the extremities. Most of us will have encountered a foot, ankle or leg injury (either personally or happening to others). A lot can be done to improve both the casualty's comfort and condition, so a good knowledge of the basics is important for the hillwalker or mountaineer. With the right intervention, it may even be possible for an unassisted evacuation, which will invariably be less complex, and possibly less risky, than a drawn-out rescue.

Injuries fall into two broad categories: soft tissue injuries, and fractures and dislocations.

Soft-Tissue Injuries

Blisters must be the most frequently encountered soft-tissue injury in the mountain environment. Often dismissed as a minor ailment; they can be acutely uncomfortable, are prone to infection and can be very debilitating. Blisters form on skin which has been damaged by friction or heat (as in sunburn) and are caused by a leakage of fluid, or serum, into the affected area below the skin's surface. The affected area eventually grows new skin from the base of the blister within a sterile environment before the old skin whitens and peels off.

Whilst in general blisters should not be broken due to the risk of infection, continued hobbling along will often result in this happening and lead to the exposure of an angry, red (and very tender!) layer of skin. The area should be totally covered in a dry, lint-free, non-adhesive dressing, well secured with adhesive tape. It is always worth spending time to do this properly, as a dressing which comes adrift in a sock will only aggravate matters.

As ever, the best treatment is prevention. Getting the right boot and sock combination is the first line of defence (see 'Hands and feet' page 23). If you know a boot is prone to rub in a specific area, preparatory use of adhesive gaff tape on the known 'hot spot' can avoid a lot of pain later. A Compeed-type dressing is probably the best blister-prevention plaster available, but must be applied in good time – as soon as the rubbing and tenderness is noticed.

A blistering pace!   *Gaffed up blisters – treat the symptoms early*

Cuts, lacerations and abrasions occur when tissue is damaged. They can range in size, depth and seriousness, but treatment for all is largely the same: pressure, elevation and immobilisation of the wound. Prompt action to reduce bleeding is always beneficial, but in serious cases can be essential to avoid the patient developing shock and its attendant complications.

In the first instance pressure can be applied using a gloved (repeat *gloved*) hand before a suitable dressing can be put on. Pressure should be maintained for a minimum of ten minutes with additional dressings being applied on top of the first. The injured limb should then be immobilised and elevated using a sling or splint as necessary. Remember, there are two big 'no no's' here:

- don't keep peeking at a wound to see if the bleeding has stopped – you will probably start it again
- don't bind or splint the wound so tightly that you form a tourniquet which stops blood circulating to the unaffected parts of the limb below the injury. The wound may stop bleeding but the limb may not recover. You can monitor blood flow to the uninjured parts of the limb ('perfusion') by checking for a pulse or capillary refill below the site of the injury and dressing. The best example of capillary refill is when you squeeze a fingertip until it turns white and then release it. As the blood flows back in it turns red or a healthy flesh colour again. If you do this to the casualty, and the finger stays white, there may be a circulation problem as a result of the pressure applied to stop the wound above bleeding

Bruises are caused when small blood vessels just under the skin are damaged and leak, causing discoloration and swelling around the affected area. Treatment is simple: rest; application of ice or a cold pack to the area; compression using a crêpe-type bandage; and elevation. Deeper bruises (or haematoma) in a big muscle such as the thigh can be dangerous and difficult to identify; but in this case your casualty may well be in significant pain and unable to use the limb.

Fractures and Dislocations
These are not infrequent injuries on the hill. Bones may be broken (fractured) or displaced from their normal position at a joint (dislocated). With any break, bleeding will occur, with the likelihood that the bigger the bone the greater the bleeding. In view of this fractures of the femur (thigh bone) or pelvis need to be viewed as particularly serious.

Fractures can be simple or complex. They may be contained within the skin (closed fracture), or a section of bone may be seen to have punctured the skin (open fracture).

The history of the patient and clarity about the 'mechanism of injury' are useful clues in diagnosing fractures. A major force such as a long fall will suggest possible fractures and the risk of damage to large bones; a smaller force such as a trip may suggest that a wrist or collarbone has been fractured.

The Signs and Symptoms of a Fracture are:

- pain, which may range from a dull ache to excruciating agony. Pain may also be centred on soft-tissue damage as well as the actual break, and will usually increase with movement

- loss of function or mobility, including the ability to bear weight

- apparent deformity (try comparing the casualty's limbs)

- swelling (often very pronounced)

- a very nasty crunching sound when the affected area is moved and the bone ends grate together

In the case of a dislocation, deformity and loss of function will also be present, and the pain can again be excruciating. History will also be important: if someone tells you they've dislocated their shoulder and they know this because they've done it three times before, they might well be right!

The management of a fracture is relatively simple: immobilise the joint above and below the fracture, and then splint, applying support to as much of the affected limb as possible. The deformity may need to be reduced, by applying gentle traction until the pain reduces. The bone can then be aligned and splinted. On the hill, creativity can be exercised in making splints by using ski poles, axes and, of course, the casualty's other leg. In the case of a femur fracture, the traction should be maintained to reduce both pain and blood loss. In the case of a pelvic fracture, splinting is critical to stabilise an injury that may cause major blood loss.

Applying traction to a femur normally takes two people: one comforting and supporting the casualty at the head, the other holding the lower leg and applying steady but firm traction (pulling)

At least four triangular bandages will be required, or you may improvise with equipment such as dyneema or tape slings

Stabilising the femur after traction

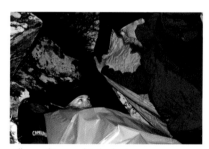

All casualties need to be kept warm or hypothermia will quickly set in

Sprains

These, and the phrase 'He went over on his ankle' often seem synonymous with the end of a long day on the hill (which had been happy up until then!). These injuries are not fractures, but damage to tendons or ligaments. What is the difference between a sprain and a fracture? Is it a ligament or is it a tendon? Most of us can't tell the difference, and the truth is it doesn't really matter. A sprained wrist can be strapped and supported in a sling. In the case of an ankle – if your

Trekking poles are very useful for splinting lower limb fractures

casualty can't bear weight – you should treat the injury as a fracture and splint it (see *Fractures and Dislocations*). If this is the case, you and your casualty may be in for a long wait. Make them comfortable, make yourself comfortable and *watch out for hypothermia*.

Hypothermia, Heat Illness and Dehydration
Despite their apparent positions at opposite ends of the spectrum, these issues are the most common conditions that hill-goers are likely to come across. Hypothermia is the condition that is most likely to have an effect on people who have stopped, whether through injury, darkness, being lost or exhausted, in a hostile environment. The impact of weather and temperature should not be underestimated as these two conditions really do have the ability to turn a drama into a crisis.

Hypothermia
Our bodies operate at around 37°C, but we are all different and all likely to respond differently to a drop in this core temperature. Generally speaking, however, the descent into hypothermia is incremental as the functions of the body shut down. As such, loss of coordination and strength, and a developing level of confusion or 'absence', can accompany apparent shivering and exhaustion. The absence of shivering, combined with a reduced level of consciousness, should be a cause for concern. The odd behaviour of 'paradoxical undressing' may even be observed as a clearly cold and confused casualty starts to take his clothes off.

Hypothermia can be categorised as mild (where the casualty is still conscious and shivering) or severe (for stages beyond this). Once a casualty reaches temperatures of 35° to 31°C, shivering, increased respirations and pulse, along with disorientation and reduced consciousness, can be expected. Below this, an irregular pulse and unconsciousness can be expected with the heart shutting down somewhere around 27° to 25°C. None of these are strict rules however, as very cold people with temperatures below 25°C – who were apparently dead – have been rewarmed and resuscitated in hospital. This has lead to the view that a low temperature is not necessarily incompatible with life. You should act on the basis that the casualty is 'not dead until he is warm and dead', and strict attention should still be given to maintaining an airway, even in a very cold, unconscious casualty, where there are no signs of life. Until you know otherwise there is always the possibility that once warmed the hypothermic casualty will prove to be alive. This is not as uncommon as you might think.

Treatment of Hypothermia is Relatively Simple:
- reduce further heat loss, which means sheltering from the elements and getting extra layers on. Don't forget to put a hat on the casualty if he isn't wearing one, and insulate him from the cold ground

- maintain an airway

- monitor breathing and circulation

- monitor the casualty's presentation and consciousness level

- watch out for any companions (his and yours); it's easy not to notice that everyone else is getting cold while hanging around and concentrating on the casualty.

Your casualty will be cold, hungry and thirsty. Where hypothermia is mild you should feed him and provide fluids. You may well be able to walk him out; if you do, monitor his presentation and consciousness levels.

Dehydration and Heat Exhaustion

The body is not meant to get either too cold or too hot. Anyone who has been to Skye on a flaming May weekend will have discovered that, even in Scotland, it is possible to experience heat-related problems. Dehydration is one of the main reasons even experienced parties fail to complete the traverse of the Cuillin Ridge, although hot weather is not an essential ingredient for the condition. Lack of bodily hydration at the start, lack of fluids on the hill and a heavy, sustained 'work rate' are quite enough. But hot conditions make dehydration and overheating that much more likely.

Heat exhaustion can develop gradually as the climber sweats away fluids leading to dizziness, loss of strength and coordination, headaches, cramps and rapid pulse and breathing. Heatstroke is a more severe extension of the condition where the body temperature will have exceeded 40°C.

The treatment is to place the casualty in the shade, raise the feet and provide rehydrating fluids in quantity. Hopefully 'two pints of water and a packet of crisps' and some rest will do the job. As ever, the best treatment is prevention. It really is worth doing 'buddy checks' with your colleagues. In hot weather check when folk last had a pee (and whether or not it was the colour of creosote). This will keep you mindful of the need to maintain fluid levels and provide an early warning of potential problems. Don't forget: the casualty may be dehydrated and sunburnt, but once the clouds appear or the wind gets up, look out for the dangers of hypothermia!

Mountain First Aid Kits

There is nothing quite so useless as a large, comprehensive first aid kit left at home. You should design a first aid kit that meets your needs and which you will carry with you. This means light and flexible, with a tendency towards improvisation.

Suggested Items

- Bothy bag and rucksack for insulation
- Disposable gloves – at least two pairs and always handy in a pocket
- Gaff tape (carried on a trek pole) – it repairs gear and bodies
- 10 large plasters
- 2 large sterile dressings
- 2 triangular bandages
- Compeed
- Face shield
- Tweezers
- Scissors
- One 4in/10cm crepe bandage
- Midge cream and sting relief
- Vaseline

Anti-inflammatories are good for personal use once your knees have gone!

Getting Help

You may decide that you need to get help. Nowadays, many emergency calls are made via mobile phones. Dial 999, but try to have good information to hand about the circumstances and location of the incident. Also, remember that an uncharged mobile will only be of use in attracting a rescuer's attention if you throw it at them.

Contacting friends and asking them to make calls on your behalf can lead to confusion about who the caller is, and Chinese whispers about the nature of injuries. If you must do this, try to use 'hill folk' who understand the context and make sure they know your number to pass it on.

In a cold environment, batteries run down fast so don't get caught out part way through your call. Planning ahead will make the best use of limited battery life and ensure that you get maximum information over.

Calling for help – have all the information to hand

However you Establish Contact, Make Sure you are Clear About:

- where you are (6-figure grid reference, aspect of slope and description of nearby landmarks)

- who you are

- who the casualty(s) is (are)

- what has happened. Keep it relevant – nobody needs to know immediately that 'Jim was moving up off a sidepull when it snapped, the friend ripped', and so on. Mechanism of injury is good and the name of the route may help: 'He fell about 40ft off Stuart's Rake, incurred head and back injuries and is now on the scree at the bottom of the cliff'.

- details about any risks such as crags

- weather and environment

- what your party looks like (colours of jackets helps)

- casualty's name, age, and any relevant/serious previous medical conditions

- details of your casualty's current condition (describe vital signs)

- any trends (use vital signs)

- what you have done for the casualty and how he or she responded

- any plans you now have.

If you are in direct contact with a rescue team, don't waste your batteries telephoning to ask if they have set off yet. They will move as fast as they can, but you will usually be in for a long wait and constant asking will only deplete your phone and make it hard to pass on really useful details. Save the battery to tell them when you see their lights and flares and so on.

Keep shouting and using whistles – the international distress signal – but listen in between, and think of using your camera flash.

If the rescue team have advised you to walk on a bearing towards safety, don't hold the phone and compass together. Not surprisingly the magnetic field may mess up the compass... yes, it really has happened!

Helicopter Evacuation

In the event of a serious incident, few things can be as welcome as the sound of an inbound helicopter. You can do a lot to assist its safe arrival.

Ensure that in communications with emergency services you give an accurate location, a clear idea of weather at the scene (with particular attention to wind strength and direction, and visibility) and any warnings such as snow instability, or a nearby crag. It is also worth describing your clothing to ensure that the wrong people don't get your taxi!

Recognised Signals for Communicating with a Rescue Helicopter

Yes, I need help

No, I do not need help

It is helpful to find as clear and level a spot as possible and identify this for the crew. Standing well back and holding a shirt aloft may also assist in identifying wind direction.

When a helicopter approaches, it will cause a minor hurricane. Ensure that all gear is well secured down and try to protect your casualty from flying grit or snow. Do not approach the aircraft until the winchman signals to you or comes out to meet you.

If the winchman is being lowered, he will be preceded by a thin line called a 'stinger', designed to discharge static electricity. Don't grab it – it will sting! Stay back until the winchman has landed. Basically, *always* do what you are told, and *don't* do it until you are told to.

When preparing your casualty for evacuation, brief the winchman with as much information as possible about the history of the incident and the casualty's progress since. Not only can an aircraft take your casualty to definitive care rapidly, but they also carry technical medical equipment, and the crew are skilled in its use. The winchman may well ask you to accompany the casualty.

Key Points to Remember on Mountain First Aid

Monitoring a casualty's vital signs will allow you to gauge *trends* that can indicate if they are improving, deteriorating, or stable.

Appearance, Consciousness and Awareness

- First impressions are important. When you first set eyes on the casualty you will pick up numerous clues. Do they notice you? Are they grey? Do they 'look sick'? If they say hello, they have an airway!
- Assess temperature. Is it 'normal', given the situation? All casualties should be treated as potentially suffering from hypothermia, hypoglycaemia (needing sugar or food) and dehydration *if* they are conscious.
- Assessing level of consciousness is important. It informs your opinion on the casualty's ability to maintain a safe airway and overall state of health. Although the Glasgow Coma Scale (or GCS) can give a very accurate scoring to define a person's level of consciousness, the AVPU acronym (see below) is simpler.
- Remember: when ascertaining level of consciousness, you are also picking up vital information about your patient's awareness, breathing, the history of the incident and so on.

Alert?

Can the casualty engage with you? Are they aware of surroundings?

Voice?

Do they respond to voice? Are they distant, or 'out of it'? Do you have to shout to get eye contact?

Pain?

Do they only respond to pain? Eg a pinch? If so, how hard? Do they mumble or speak in response?

Unconscious?

Are they completely disengaged from their surroundings? If so check the **Airway**

Airway!

If you don't get this right, nothing else will work properly. Learn to do it right, and practise it, and it could be a life-saver. Check the airway in an unconscious casualty... then check it again... then keep checking.

- A simple chin lift may be all that is required to maintain a safe airway
- A jaw thrust may provide an alternative method, and is very useful if a person has some facial injuries
- The recovery position may allow the unconscious *but breathing* casualty to be left in position while you wait for assistance. Learn to do this and practise it, including for a casualty who you suspect may have a spinal injury.
- 'Not the recovery position...' Sometimes you may have an unconscious, breathing casualty who is lying in an awkward position. If so, think through why you might move them: what are the benefits? Do you have enough people? Will you worsen their condition? It may be safer to keep them as they are *but* monitor their condition constantly.

Finally, **record everything**. It may not mean a lot to you, but the trends you record could help others to save your casualty's life.

PART THREE
MOUNTAINEERING IN BRITAIN

...to be a classic it must be not only of excellent quality, but it must have withstood the test of time.

Richard Gilbert, *Classic Walks*

A classic British mountain landscape: looking west from the summit of Sgurr nan Gillean to Am Basteir (nearest), Sgurr à Fionn, Bruach na Frithe and Sgurr Thuilm

In their own way the mountains of Britain are as good as any in the world, offering superb opportunities for adventure on a scale to suit whatever time, level of commitment or experience you may have. What they lack in height they more than make up for in the quality of terrain, scenery, atmosphere and the sheer experience of 'being there'.

The classic mountaineering objectives featured in this chapter are typical of the terrain and challenges the ambitious hillwalker will encounter should he or she aspire to take up the most inspiring challenges thrown down by the mountains of Britain. They form, in our opinion, the most exciting passages of great mountaineering outings that can often be varied to suit. The selection is in no way definitive, although most of them are likely to have figured – in principle at least – on your 'radar' of possible future objectives.

The mountains featured are geographically spread around the British mainland, making it possible to practise skills in different locations on different trips. We could have covered routes just in one location – most obviously Scotland – but with the idea of gradual learning and a mountain 'apprenticeship' at the heart of our suggested approach, this would not have been very convenient. We have tried to make the selection of routes as accessible as possible for the widest number of people.

We believe that each of the routes, or locations, merits the description 'classic', although you may well substitute your own choice to cover ground of the same grade, or to practise similar skills. You will probably be able to propose your own list of ideal routes at each grade to consolidate skills and experience.

Britain's alpine ridge: perfect spring conditions on the technical and demanding
Black Cuillin traverse

ROUTE	GRADE	NOTES
Twelve British classics		
Tryfan North Ridge (direct)	grade 2	
Forcan Ridge (direct)	grade 2	
Fiacaill Ridge/Buttress	grade 2	
Wistow Crags	grade 2 to 3	
Scafell Pike – Scafell traverse	grade 3	(Difficult section)
Pinnacle Ridge	grade 3	(Difficult pitch)
Curved Ridge	grade 3	Moderate
Aonach Eagach	grade 3(S)	Moderate
Cneifion Arête	grade 3(S)	Difficult
Clach Glas–Blaven	grade 3(S)	Difficult
Coire Lagan Round	grade 3(S)	Moderate (with Difficult option)
Tower Ridge	Difficult	Harder than a top-end scramble

The routes are described in approximate order of difficulty, but we are not suggesting that you automatically move from one directly to the next. The last route, Tower Ridge, for instance, is a long-term goal and, in terms of the commitment required, in a different league to the others. To tackle it you will need to be confident and well practised in virtually all the mountaineering techniques outlined in this book, and have the temperament to deal with sustained periods of exposure, over a long day, with very limited prospects of escape.

Grade Explanation

Essentially the routes are ordered according to the level of commitment likely to be required to fulfil them in the context of your overall mountaineering objective, rather than necessarily according to the grade of the hardest passage. The Coire Lagan Round, for instance, makes for a bigger overall commitment than the Cneifion Arête, although the hardest section of the Cneifion Arête is graded 'Difficult' rather than the Coire Lagan Round's 'Moderate'.

Each level of commitment should be practised on a number of routes of a similar grade before you attempt to 'move up' a level. You would be ill-advised, for example, to attempt a route with sustained sections of grade 3 scrambling if you are still struggling with any aspect of a grade 2 route.

Most of the routes featured are, in our opinion, best climbed as a pair, because it is faster and less complicated. However, if you are confident it will not delay you too much, climbing as a three is perfectly feasible. If there are four in the party it is generally best to climb in two pairs, assuming each pair has the requisite skills.

Finally, we believe most hillwalkers aspire, above all, to traverse the great ridges of the British mountains on their classic days out and we focus here on ridge lines as the 'crux' of challenging outings. But this is not primarily a 'routes' book and while we suggest options we do not, in most cases, prescribe the complete mountaineering journeys of which these ridges form part. That is for each party to decide for themselves and clearly – as well as the technical, climbing-related skills required on the ridge sections – a wide range of the mountaincraft skills and approaches discussed here will be needed.

With this in mind it should be noted that while you may well find 'summer conditions' at any time on the English and Welsh routes (depending on varying winter conditions year to year), the effects of winter on the Scottish routes is far more predictable, with snow and/or ice a real possibility at any time from October to June, and a virtual certainty from December to April. Winter conditions will turn any of the scrambling passages featured here into graded winter mountaineering terrain, requiring an additional and often distinct set of skills to those discussed. Any technical routes encountered in winter conditions are beyond the scope of this book (although not out of reach for the ambitious hillwalker who works towards the right skills and attempts the routes in the right company).

Climbing in Pairs

The best way to plan to tackle the scrambling parts of these routes is to climb in pairs. This will give you a number of advantages:

- communication is straightforward

- rope management is simplified

- moving together on a rope is likely to be faster and even safer

- belaying one person is easier than belaying two or three

- two (rather than three) scramblers will allow more room at a small belay stance

- route planning, mountaineering tactics, acquiring necessary skills and equipment is all much easier with two people rather than three or four

- you avoid the situation where the rest of the team are climbing above you, possibly precipitating loose rock and other flying debris in your direction.

Responsible Access

The question of access to land is an important issue for practical, environmental, and – as far as local communities are concerned – social reasons. Before setting out on any mountaineering expedition you should make yourself aware of your responsibilities and rights relating to the land you are planning to visit.

On many of the routes described here there are, in practice, no major questions over access, due largely to the excellent stewardship and hill-user-friendly policies of landowners and managers such as the National Trust (NT), National Trust for Scotland (NTS) and Scottish Natural Heritage (SNH). Much of central Lakeland is in NT hands; the Glen Shiel area is managed by NTS; the Cairngorms are managed by SNH. Such organisations, as a policy, don't just maintain the land but actually want you to enjoy it – something we should all give not just thanks for, but also money when we get the opportunity. Paths are built and maintained, facilities provided, landscape, flora and fauna protected. The British mountains are necessarily among the most managed of all 'wilderness' environments, and any mountain-goer owes it him- or herself to support such work. Of course some land is privately owned. The answer is to do your homework before setting out.

Giving our support also includes cooperating with any restrictions or notices that may be in place, such as footpath diversions, temporary closures or avoiding areas because of, say, nesting. All the usual codes of practice and etiquette should automatically be respected, and in parts of Scotland the Scottish Hillphones system should be used for up-to-date information on how deer stalking might affect your plans in late summer and early autumn (see page 19 for more details).

Responsible access is about being aware and taking care. As ever, sticking to simple rules is the key: when walking in to any climb through cultivated land and forests, for example, stick to a path or track, and help avoid harm to deer forests or grouse moors. The bottom line – and the guiding force behind excellent initiatives such as the Scottish Outdoor Access Code – is that the freedom to enjoy our countryside combines rights of access with the obligation of responsibility. The most obvious expression of this is to observe the Country Code:

- enjoy the countryside and respect its life and work
- guard against all risk of fire
- fasten all gates
- keep dogs under close control
- keep to public paths across farmland
- use gates and stiles to cross fences, hedges and walls
- leave livestock, crops and machinery alone
- help to keep all water clean
- take your litter home

Talking Rubbish

The world's popular mountain environments, from Ben Nevis to Everest, are under intense pressure, and walkers and climbers are part of the problem. While most UK mountaineers would consider themselves to be environmentally concerned, it's what you actually *do* about it that counts. It's crucially important to follow the codes and conventions that are there to protect the mountains and their environs, for the benefit of everyone who loves and lives with them. Respect for property, paths, people, buildings, livestock, fauna and flora should be a given for anyone using the hills for recreation.

'Leave nothing but footprints, take nothing but pictures' is a good philosophy, although even the impact of footprints should be minimised by treading carefully and knowing what you are walking on. And always be aware of the ways in which you can cause pollution. It's not just about material litter, totally unacceptable though that is. One team crossing the Cuillin found human faeces on almost every summit. This is just ignorance; even biodegradable junk can degrade the environment. At best it is an eyesore. Does anyone go to the mountains wanting to see more banana skins and apple cores in a wilderness setting? What is it that makes someone carry an orange up a mountain, but prevents him from carrying the peel back down again? At peak times some British mountain summits are visited by hundreds of people a day, and with the accumulation of litter and 'leftovers' our natural wonders can end up feeling like urban waste ground, or a food market after the stallholders have gone home.

At some access points to our most popular summits it's now possible to pick up a plastic bag, not just for your own rubbish, but also for gathering any other detritus seen on the route. The 'Keep the Cuillin Clean' campaign is one example, and it's an initiative that should be applauded. Only if we love the mountains enough to clear up after ourselves – and the unfortunate minority who don't – will they remain special and life-enhancing spaces.

Tryfan North Ridge (direct)

Location	The Glyderau, Snowdonia
Grade	2***
Maps	OS Explorer OL17 1:25 000 Snowdonia: Snowdon/Yr Wyddfa and Conwy Valley/Dyffryn Conwy
	OS Landranger 115 1:50 000 Snowdon and Caernarfon
	Harveys Superwalker 1:25 000 Snowdonia: The Glyderau and the Carneddau (Cwm Cneifion is indicated by name on OS Explorer, but not on Harveys Superwalker)

Making a successful transition from hillwalking to what can more accurately be described as mountaineering involves the acquisition of practical skills in incremental steps, and the steady accumulation of mountain experience. The distinction between hillwalking and mountaineering is not always black and white, and some of the most important learning will take place in the grey areas between the two. That is why we start our route suggestions with Tryfan's famous North Ridge.

Having indicated that the routes featured in this guide take for granted a level of competence and comfort on all the popular grade 1 scrambles, the question is how does Tryfan – possibly the most popular mountain in Britain – fit in? The answer is – at this point – perfectly. Around 70% of the Ogwen Valley Mountain Rescue team's call-outs are on Tryfan, the majority on the North Ridge. That suggests this is ground where hillwalkers commonly overreach themselves for want of some basic mountaineering skills.

As John Hunt's team knew when they were preparing for the first successful ascent of Everest back in 1953, Tryfan is the perfect training mountain, containing just about every grade of walking and climbing that Britain has to offer. Not only is its spiny profile very inspiring, but on the practical front its

Glyder Fach · Bristly Ridge · Far South Peak · Bwlch Tryfan · Heather Terrace · Tryfan · North Gully · Nor' Nor' Gully · North Ridge · Heather Terrace · Cwm Tryfan · Ogwen Valley

north buttress drops conveniently down to the road-side, offering possibly the most accessible passage of scrambling on a mountaineering route in the country.

No matter where you travel, you may never see a mountain with a more appealing profile than Tryfan, and its North Ridge and the continuation options offer an entry point for the aspiring mountaineer, and an excellent way to test your level. Tryfan by the North Ridge is a very solid grade 1 scramble in good conditions – but testing enough to merit a grade 2 in some opinions if the most direct line is adhered too. Wet, windy or winter conditions can in moments change the grade to something even more serious. Precisely how serious can also be down to you: this is a route that gives you options and varying degrees of difficulty at just about every turn. In including it here we assume the most direct line will be the goal, in good conditions, but there is an easier alternative almost every step of the way. Tryfan's North Ridge is where the activities of hillwalking, mountaineering and rock climbing both meet and diverge.

If you already know Tryfan and think you might feel conspicuous gearing up and placing protection on such a popular route, change your mindset. It may not always feel that way, but Tryfan's potential seriousness makes it a genuine test and some simple security measures on the most exposed sections can be common sense, especially if the weather is less than kind. What matters is that you practise and develop your skills, and get round safely. There is no need to feel self-conscious about doing the safe thing for you and your party. Pride comes before a fall. However, if you can choose a quiet day you may find it gives you more time and space to concentrate on your own agenda.

Approach

Park just off the A5 below Tryfan or nearby, and take the path that leads directly south from the road. This brings you almost immediately to what is effectively the toe end of Tryfan's North Ridge, the climbers' playground of the Milestone Buttress.

Route

The angle of the path from the A5 is very soon 'in your face', as it bears left over boulders, heather and mud-covered rock steps, skirting the Milestone Buttress. The best line can become a bit vague and ill-defined, and in many ways this is a good introduction to the range of possibilities that lie ahead. The idea is to emerge onto the crest (a broad ridge really) by striking right up the mountain, then follow the crest as best you can. The best place to do this is above 'Piccadilly Circus', a small but obvious grass-and-rock-terrace below the path to the left (more or less in line, as you look down, with Gwern Gof Uchaf, on the valley floor). If you continue round the mountain from this point you will end up on the Heather Terrace that traverses its eastern flank. An alternative, easier – and for some preferable – way to reach this point is via the path that leads south west past Tryfan Bach.

Above Piccadilly Circus head directly up towards the crest, via a small notch where slabby steps trend left onto sloping scree and a heathery terrace with a rocky skyline

Tryfan's North Ridge. The precipitous west face, seen here, should be avoided by scramblers

above. Trend rightwards to pick up the crest via a big jumble of rock steps, providing a number of entertaining options. From a flat, wide, north-facing terrace, continue up via more terraces, ledges and rock bands to the obvious landmark of The Cannon and its distinctive quartz terrace.

The upper section of Tryfan's North Ridge (Photo: Tom Bailey, Courtesy of Trail *magazine)*

A Good Test

Tryfan's North Ridge can be a confusing objective because there are so many options for both attaining and then traversing the length of its broad bulk. It provides an excellent route-finding test, as there's a large element of being guided by the contours and features of the terrain.

Although there are many possible routes, as a general rule problems are best avoided on the ascent of Tryfan's North Ridge by going left, usually onto easier ground. (On descent, trending right is the rule, to avoid the considerable danger of getting drawn onto the precipitous West Face.) Passing The Cannon to the left you come almost immediately to a steep groove of knobbly rock on your right, which provides the first bit of potentially awkward scrambling (this is our route, but it can be avoided by continuing past it). Surmounting this brings you onto the sloping table of the Quartz Pavement, with an excellent view of Tryfan's jagged summits ahead.

The pyramidal bulk of the North Wall directly ahead is very impressive, with the West Face plunging away to the right. To continue the scramble, approach the wall by trending left to a large, square rock at its base. Now comes the crux where, depending on conditions and ability levels, some security may be advisable. Head up blocky steps and angled slabs – on a winter's day this ground can be transformed by the merest smattering of ice and snow – in the obvious direction, with significant exposure to the right. Take great care in inclement conditions, but enjoy the good – if sometimes over-smooth – rock, and superb situation.

Eventually you reach a significant notch and drop down – a move or two that might make you think – to meet the top of Nor' Nor' Gully coming in from the left (a path that skirts the main ridge line avoiding the grade 2 terrain rejoins the main ridge at this point, via a scramble over blocks jammed in the gully).

Exit the notch rightwards and ascend a gully, continuing with steepish scrambling that brings you onto the North Summit and subsequently to the Main Summit, via scrambling as easy or as difficult as you like, where the option of the leap between the prominent stones known as Adam and Eve awaits you.

What Next

Having ascended to the summit the option of continuing down Tryfan's South Ridge and then up onto the Glyder plateau via the equally (perhaps more) challenging Bristly Ridge – another testing and exhilarating grade 1 scramble – on your way to Glyder Fach, can make for a fantastic day out. Descend from Glyder Fach down Gribin Ridge, and you've got a full day's route where you will probably have spent as much time scrambling as you have walking. Not a bad outing for a self-assessment.

Forcan Ridge (direct)

Location	The Saddle, Glen Shiel, North West Highlands
Grade	2***
Maps	OS Explorer 414 1:25 000 Glen Shiel and Kintail Forest
	OS Landranger 33 1:50 000 Loch Alsh, Glen Shiel and Loch Hourn
	Harveys Superwalker 1:25 000 Kintail (Glen Shiel)

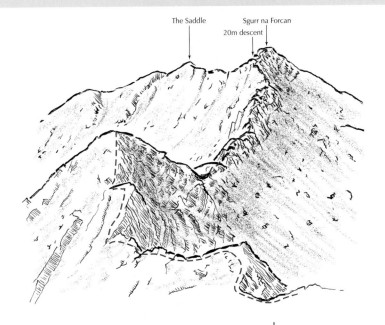

The Saddle   Sgurr na Forcan
20m descent

Few locations stir the interest of the British hillwalker more than south Glen Shiel and its famous seven-in-a-day Munro-bagging opportunity. But once you've had your big day out – and probably succumbed to the temptations of the Five Sisters on the north side of the glen too – there's just one problem: you still haven't tackled the best mountaineering ridge outing in the glen.

The Forcan Ridge is a sharp spine that snakes pleasingly up en route to the summit of south Glen Shiel's best-known Munro top, The Saddle. It offers that most comforting of options to anyone uncertain of their abilities on a grade 2 scramble – a grade 1 alternative, with little real reduction in the quality of the overall day out. This fact, combined with its truly magnificent situation and generally excellent rock, make it something of an essential route for the budding mountaineer.

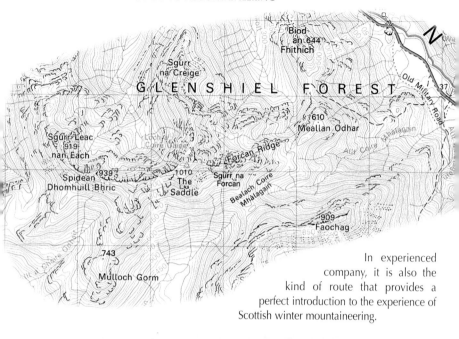

In experienced company, it is also the kind of route that provides a perfect introduction to the experience of Scottish winter mountaineering.

Approach

The Forcan Ridge is actually the east ridge of Sgurr na Forcan (the summit of which, in the context of the route to the top of The Saddle, is little more than a brief pause, immediately followed by the trickiest part of the route). To find the ridge leave the A87 about 350m north of the road bridge that crosses the Allt Mhalagain.

Route

Initially follow the path south, then south west, before heading west uphill via the stalker's path that rises in a series of zigzags up the shoulder that heads towards Meallan Odhar. This path steepens as it carries on to the bottom of the Forcan Ridge proper.

The early scrambling is straightforward before you arrive at the first potentially mettle-testing passage, a rocky corner that, while not big, can be tricky in the wet. It's one of the grade 2 bits that can, if necessary, be bypassed via a slightly easier option to the left-hand side of the ridge.

It is obvious you are heading up towards the interesting sections of scrambling, which begins after around 800m, although first you have to negotiate some slabs that combine the not-always-complementary qualities of smoothness and exposure. After this the ridge is made up of smaller, broken ledges. The most sustained challenge lies directly on the crest, negotiating two blocky sections in particular, with the easiest ground found to the right. Either way will soon bring you to the top of Sgurr na Forcan.

The top of Sgurr na Forcan is a superb position, but also marks the start of 20m or so of descent directly to a gap – without question the most difficult and technical bit of the whole traverse, if you choose to tackle it directly.

*On the atmospheric
Forcan Ridge
(Photo: John Cleare)*

The drop is on steep, worn slabs – again grade 2 scrambling – and is certainly worth protecting with a rope for anyone who is not entirely comfortable on this ground.

The traverse continues along the narrow crest, over the east and west tops to the trig point (not, incidentally, the high point – which you have already passed).

What Next

The terrain of South Glen Shiel is big, committing country and there are plenty of continuation options from this point, giving mountaineering outings of varied character and length. They include Sgurr na Sgine to the south east (the best ascent option for quality being its north-east ridge) or, to the north west, following a number of route possibilities that take the rim of Coire nan Uaine and descend in the area of Sgurr a Gharg Gharaidh (the latter is likely to involve more road walking at the end of a long day). Whichever way you head you will already be assured of a day that involves the best the area has to offer.

Top Tips

- In early spring snow can be present throughout Glen Shiel, turning the Forcan Ridge into a technical winter mountaineering trip requiring appropriate skills and equipment.

- Secondly – and most importantly – given a good forecast try to get an early start. One or two parties disturbing your traverse is fine, but making way for a stream of others can get tedious. You want to get the most out of the crux of your route, and if you do deploy your rope you don't want to be hassled. Plan to start the route while others are still having breakfast, and you will reap the rewards.

Fiacaill Ridge/Buttress

Location	Coire an t-Sneachda, Cairngorms
Grade	2***
Maps	OS Explorer 403 1:25 000 Cairn Gorm and Aviemore
	OS Landranger 36 1:50 000 Grantown and Aviemore: Cairngorm Mountains
	Harveys Superwalker Cairn Gorm 1:25 000

The Cairngorms National Park encompasses a unique range of mountains, whose barren, wind-blasted plateau form one of the most atmospheric landscapes you will ever come across. Being the highest and most exposed tract of land in the country means this is always a testing environment. Cairngorms winds, in particular, are extreme. They can pick you up in an instant and transport you just where you didn't want to go! Winter is arctic in its severity. This is a land as wild and dangerous as it is beautiful and – for those lucky enough to enjoy the privilege of journeying through it – as challenging as it is breathtaking.

The regular gradients produced by the area's geology have created a hillwalker's paradise in summer or winter (and, in the right conditions, great ski-touring country too). But while those same rock formations also offer an abundance of winter and summer climbing – notably on the huge headwalls of the Northern Corries – there is far less opportunity for the kind of scrambling associated with many of Britain's other mountain ranges. One superb exception to this, however, that literally splits the Corries in two, is the Fiacaill Coire an t-Sneachda.

Taking in the traverse of the Fiacaill Coire an t-Sneachda – the 'toothed ridge of the snowy corrie' (there is another

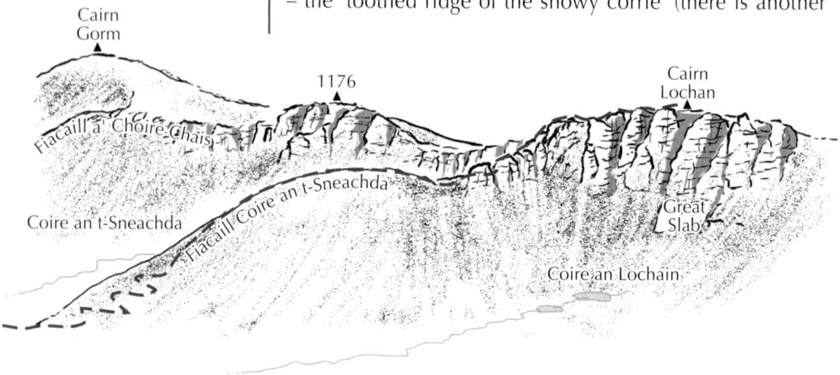

Cairn Gorm

1176

Cairn Lochan

Fiacaill a' Choire Chais

Fiacaill Coire an t-Sneachda

Coire an t-Sneachda

Fiacaill Coire an t-Sneachda

Great Slab

Coire an Lochain

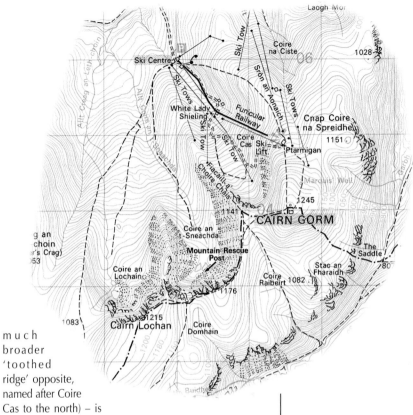

much broader 'toothed ridge' opposite, named after Coire Cas to the north) – is an unbeatable way to scramble onto the Cairngorm plateau, and provides an outstanding focus for a day's mountaineering that feels extremely remote, but is actually very accessible.

The Fiacaill Ridge offers the challenge of exposed grade 2 scrambling, but with the option of much easier ground. The walk in and continuation routes can not only carry you into some of the Cairngorms' most stunning locations, but also provide a real test of your mountaincraft skills – not least because, if you are ever going to experience four seasons in as many hours, there is every chance it will be on a day here.

Approach

Skiing developments have scarred the north-west Cairngorms, but they do bring the advantage of a car park at an altitude of almost 2,000ft (610m). Take the road from Aviemore that winds up via Colyumbridge, through the forest, and aim for the most southerly of the huge car parks near the ski centre alongside the Allt a' Choire Chais.

The business end of the Fiacaill Ridge in winter makes a superb introduction to Scottish winter mountaineering. This book however, assumes summer condtions.

Route

From the main Coire Cas car park take the path that follows Allt Coire an t-Sneachda up into Coire an Sneachda (see map). As you walk into the corrie, Fiacaill Buttress – the business end of Fiacaill Ridge – will appear on your right, rising up towards the plateau in blocky profile from the obvious notch in the ridge. Head east up the rocky slopes to the notch, the best place to gear up. An alternative approach (illustrated) from the car park is to cross the Allt Coire an t-Sneachda and steadily ascend the Fiacaill Coire an t-Sneachda from its base, in which case you will drop down to the notch that marks the beginning of the ascent of Fiacaill Buttress.

Good descriptions of the ascent of the Fiacaill Buttress are hard to come by, no doubt largely because the direction from this point is obvious and straightforward, on big granite blocks – a bit like a giant's staircase. However, the usual inference that this is just easy scrambling should be qualified. There is some gaping exposure of the very vertical kind on the left and the crest narrows enough to make you feel it, with one or two moves that, while not difficult, can bring you very close to the drops. The views down into the corrie and across to the nearby headwall are awesome, and could even be unnerving for some.

What is more, the ridge steepens noticeably about halfway up, and there is a passage of crest scrambling that is at least grade 2, assuming your route finding is good. This is the best line, and there is plenty of scope for natural protection, best taken advantage of by draping slings over boulders, with good belay stances available if required. On the right side, below the crest to the west, there is much easier (or rather, less technical) ground in the form of the steep scree slopes that make their way down into Coire an Lochain. They offer a walking option, particularly if the main ridge is busy. This sloping ground can be easily accessed at various points along the ridge and leads to the same spot on the plateau north east of Cairn Lochan – but ascent by this means does lack the grandeur, position and aesthetic allure of the crest line.

Avoid the Crowds

Under snow the Fiacaill Coire an t-Sneachda, like the Forcan Ridge, makes for a fantastic introduction to Scottish winter mountaineering, assuming you have the skills and the right company. However, because of its accessibility, quality and the absence of nearby alternatives, it can get very busy at any time of year. Making the effort to get an early start, or to be there on a quiet day, will be well rewarded.

What Next

From Cairn Lochan you can continue your mountaineering itinerary in numerous ways depending on time, conditions, gear and provisions, and fitness levels. Cairn Gorm itself is to the north east, the magnificent crags around the Shelter Stone at the head of Loch Avon to the south east. Ben Macdui, second only to Ben Nevis in height among Scotland's mountains, lies directly south, from where you can descend into the long high pass of the Lairig Ghru... and so it goes on.

Whatever your plans, good mountaincraft dictates two immediate concerns once you land on the plateau after ascending the Fiacaill Buttress: firstly, an adjustment to your clothing will almost certainly be necessary. Conditions on top of the Cairngorms are frequently very different to those found in the shelter of the corries, and you should assess this quickly in the context of your onward plans. Secondly, having followed a reasonably straightforward route to get where you are, you should now pay great attention to navigation, and to your location at all times. On this confusing, apparently featureless, terrain it can be hard enough to pinpoint your position at the best of times; if the weather comes in – which can happen fast and frequently – and you don't know where you are, finding your way out again will not be easy.

Top Tips

- Try to be on the Fiacaill Buttress section of your route at a quiet time – and try to stick to the crest for the best fun.

- Don't make do with a general weather forecast – when planning to be on the Cairngorm plateau you need to pay great attention to predicted temperatures and wind speed/direction, and the likelihood of heavy rain and low cloud/poor visibility.

- On the plateau be certain of your precise location at all times.

- Give corrie edges a wide berth when they are affected by snow, as cornice collapse is a danger that can last until well into spring.

Wistow Crags

Location	Pillar, The Lake District
Grade	2/3***
Maps	OS Explorer OL4 1:25 000 The English Lakes: North Western area (the area of Wistow Crags is indicated by name)
	OS Landranger 89 1:50 000 West Cumbria, Cockermouth and Wast Water
	Harveys Superwalker 1:25 000 Lakeland West

The name 'Wistow Crags' may not set your pulse racing in the way some other classic UK routes do, but this dramatic two-tiered buttress, thrusting up high on the remote-feeling southern slopes of Pillar in the Lake District, is something of a forgotten classic. A superb ascent on scrambling terrain ranging from grade 2 to 3, it tops out just 200m from the broad summit plateau of a mountain with a genuine claim to be one of the cradles of British rock climbing. All of which makes it even more surprising that so few people have heard of Wistow Crags, and gives you all the more reason to go and explore.

Pillar (892m) forms one of a cluster of mountains defining the Wasdale watershed, and marks roughly the midway point of the Wasdale Circuit, a horseshoe walk that offers a long but memorable day on some of the highest fells in England,

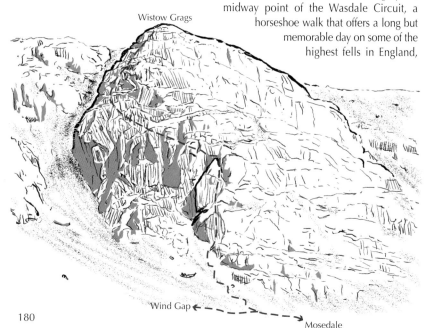

Wistow Grags

Wind Gap

Mosedale

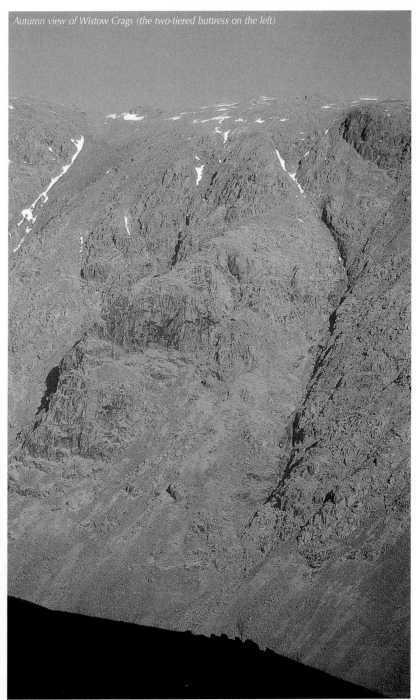

Autumn view of Wistow Crags (the two-tiered buttress on the left)

Wistow Crags is a perfect place to practise and develop the more advanced scrambling skills required by the mountaineering hillwalker

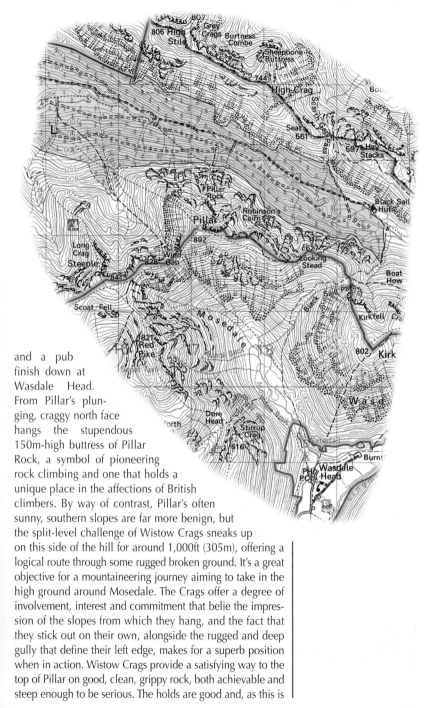

and a pub finish down at Wasdale Head. From Pillar's plunging, craggy north face hangs the stupendous 150m-high buttress of Pillar Rock, a symbol of pioneering rock climbing and one that holds a unique place in the affections of British climbers. By way of contrast, Pillar's often sunny, southern slopes are far more benign, but the split-level challenge of Wistow Crags sneaks up on this side of the hill for around 1,000ft (305m), offering a logical route through some rugged broken ground. It's a great objective for a mountaineering journey aiming to take in the high ground around Mosedale. The Crags offer a degree of involvement, interest and commitment that belie the impression of the slopes from which they hang, and the fact that they stick out on their own, alongside the rugged and deep gully that define their left edge, makes for a superb position when in action. Wistow Crags provide a satisfying way to the top of Pillar on good, clean, grippy rock, both achievable and steep enough to be serious. The holds are good and, as this is generally a quiet area, you can take your time. We understand the early pioneers took this route to the summit of Pillar long before the challenges of the Ennerdale side of the mountain became popular – truly classic credentials.

Climbing Through History

The Wasdale area is England's biggest mountain country and holds a number of scrambles that hark back to the pioneering days of British climbing. It's a great place for some challenging mountaineering circuits on a scale hard to find in Britain outside Scotland.

Approach

Park on the green/parking area at Wasdale Head, 200m back down the road from the Wasdale Head Inn. All the high ground around Wasdale Head is in the hands of The National Trust, so there are few access problems. On the path just north of Wasdale Head there is a collection box, with a notice explaining that the management of these fells is funded entirely through donations. Take some cash and give generously – this is a sensational landscape, and no matter how much you give, there's probably no better-value day out to be had. If you park at Wasdale Head you can, on a good day, see Wistow Crags to the north west, clinging high to Pillar's southern slopes to the left of an obvious, long gully which runs down the mountain.

Route

Leave Wasdale Head and to make your way up into the valley of Mosedale, following the trail for Wind Gap. The most direct way to arrive at the start of the Wistow Crags scramble is to veer right after 2km, up steepening slopes, until you arrive at grassy terraces at the base of the crag. However, if you have time and reasonable visibility on your side it can be interesting to continue up the path towards Wind Gap until you are roughly level in height with the base of the Wistow Crags buttress, and then traverse back across the slopes in an easterly direction – doing so gives a much clearer perspective of the situation of the crags, in particular in relation to the deep scree gully defining their western edge. This gully runs directly up the edge of the buttress, and is the source of some of the exposure that you will experience on the route as some of the best scrambling keeps close to its edge. However, although you can get into some great situations on the ascent of Wistow Crags, the exposure is entertaining rather than mind-blowing, and the fact that rock is interspersed with grassy terraces allows a comfortable and steady progress. In many ways, when you're ready for it, it's a perfect training ground.

Wistow Crags from the path to Wind Gap, clearly defined by the broad gully on the left

Once you have arrived at the grassy platforms at the base of Wistow Crags the scrambling begins almost straightaway, up clean rock on the left-hand side. The main problems come early on and although, in certain conditions, it can be tempting to think that you can scramble up unprotected – the rock is not vertical – this is ill-advised except for competent rock climbers. Scramblers should 'pitch' this section, setting up a solid belay with the leader placing protection before belaying the second.

From the grassy terraces a nice introductory section leads to the crux, a steep slabby wall, deceptively exposed. It can be avoided by a gully on the left-hand side – but hey, that's not why we're here, is it! There are two ways to tackle it: a crack on the right – with an exposed move about 6m up; or on the left – a steep start followed by widely spaced moves. It's the harder option, but one of the beauties of Wistow Crags is that it provides such alternatives at a number of points, which you might choose to tackle depending on how confident you are feeling. Here both options, if successfully negotiated, bring you to the base of a beautiful rib, to the right of the gully.

Follow the rib up, either by a delicate start, or initially via a large block on the left of the gully – the nature of the climbing changing as you go – to arrive at more broken ground with an easier angle about 100m further up, where you can walk to the foot of the second tier of the buttress. Ascend an obvious rib to the left of the slab (again, a harder alternative is to climb the slab direct, which goes at a climbing grade of around Difficult), walk along the ledge above to the left edge of the buttress, and tackle the narrow slabs above you. On an easier angle again, mixed walking and scrambling now leads across the top of the gullies. Trend left to rocks above, bypassing a thin flake, keeping to the right at the next bouldery flakes (those on the left are best avoided). Scrambling becomes walking as the grassy ridge merges with the side of the mountain. You've gained 300m or so in height, and a short walk up the slope will bring you to the summit of Pillar.

From the north-eastern edge of Pillar's broad summit plateau you can peer down onto rocks that have a place in Lakeland climbing history. You may even have in mind to explore by way of the High Level track that traverses the Ennerdale side of the mountain. The grade 3*** Slab and Notch scramble to the top of Pillar Rock is a true classic, but a very serious proposition and one that also requires you to descend the same way before completing your trip to the top of Pillar. A fine grade 1 route leads to the top of Pillar's smaller neighbour, Pisgah. The setting in both cases is magnificent.

What Next

For a big day out, having gained the high ground, head south east in the direction of Kirk Fell, and the delights of Great Gable and the Scafells; or continue on the Wasdale Circuit in an anti-clockwise direction if you prefer. As with many of the crux passages featured in this book, the ascent of Wistow Crags lands you in the heart of exquisite terrain, in which you can plan a comprehensive mountaineering journey of either a technical or non-technical nature.

Top Tips

- Don't rush Wistow Crags. It's perfect ground for honing your climbing skills, including the management and placement of gear, and there's a good chance that you'll have the place to yourself.

Scafell Pike – Scafell Traverse via Broad Stand

Location	Lake District
Grade	3*** (due to one short Difficult section)
Maps	OS Explorer OL6 1:25 000 The English Lakes: South Western area
	OS Landranger 89 1:50 000 West Cumbria, Cockermouth and Wast Water
	Harveys Superwalker 1:25 000 Lakeland West

Thousands of hill-goers each year gaze from England's highest point, Scafell Pike, across the linking col of Mickledore to the appealing bulk of Scafell, a few hundred metres away, and covet the direct route between the two. Far fewer make the journey successfully, due to one small but serious problem: Broad Stand. It would be interesting to know how many walkers have dropped down to the col and squeezed through what is literally the entrance to this route – a cleft in the rock known as Fat Man's Agony – only to be

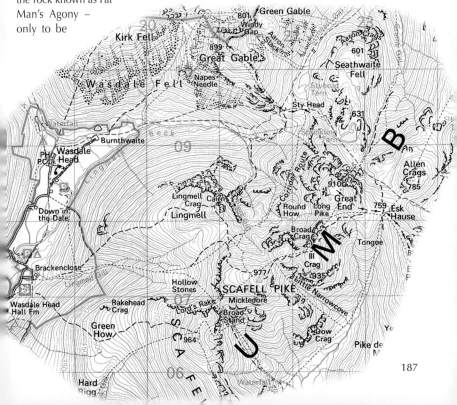

The view from the top. Looking across to Scafell Pike from Symonds Knott, above Broad Stand.

surprised to find that tackling this seemingly obvious line is not something they were prepared for. In terms of ability and equipment it requires a bit more than the average hillwalker has in his armoury.

There are various ways of crossing the divide between Scafell Pike and Scafell, but for those without the requisite skills the direct route via the infamous slabs of Broad Stand

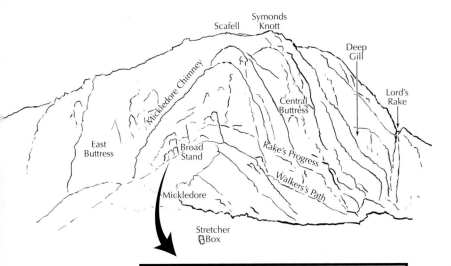

is not one of them. Yet for the sake of a handful of moves (one admittedly awkward for the less agile) and the ability to protect each person at a couple of critical moments, this great traverse is yours for the taking.

The actual scrambling on Broad Stand may be too short to be referred to as a classic scramble, but a classic crux it certainly is, in terms of terrain, objective, notoriety and history. Broad Stand was almost certainly first descended (and later described) by the poet Samuel Taylor Coleridge in 1803, in a manner that goes refreshingly against all the advice you will ever see in an instructional book on mountaineering – including, according to some reports, being under the influence of opium.

Nowadays it is common to hear of walkers getting into trouble on the crux of Broad Stand, usually whilst ascending, and we aim to help prevent this. While being defeated by this short section is understandable (particularly in poor conditions) there is no reason why, given the right skills and equipment, a safe retreat cannot be made and an alternative route taken. Equally there is no reason why, given good conditions, a careful approach and the right equipment and technique, walkers who have failed to ascend Broad Stand (they include Alfred Wainwright, so you'll be in good company!) may still not enjoy this traverse in reverse, abseiling down or past all the difficulties to the col on the way to Scafell Pike.

Best of all though, without a doubt, is to have a go at the ascent of Broad Stand, giving yourself the best possible chance of success, but secure in the knowledge that you can deal safely and efficiently with whatever the challenge throws at you and your team.

Approach

Broad Stand is situated at the west end of the ridge between the north and east face of Scafell, just above Mickledore, the col that connects Scafell Pike with Scafell. It can be reached from any number of start points in virtually all directions

There are so many ways to incorporate Mickledore and the ascent of Broad Stand into a Lakeland circuit that we will not prescribe one here. However, the shortest way up to Mickledore is to park in Wasdale at GR181076 and head directly east, initially alongside Lingmell Gill, up to the col. A circuit giving you the greater satisfaction of the direct crossing from Scafell Pike to Scafell would involve arriving at the summit of Scafell Pike via one of the several routes that approach it from the north east and north west, although inevitably you will not arrive at the crux quite as fresh, with Scafell possibly being your last summit before making a descent.

Route

Here we concentrate on the crux of this route, the ability to ascend and descend Broad Stand safely, allowing you to link Scafell Pike and Scafell in either direction, or simply traverse Scafell without missing out one of the best bits of the mountain.

The crux of Broad Stand may be very short, but it goes at 'Diff' standard, and is seriously exposed, so is definitely a place where you will want to take as much time as is necessary to get it right. It's well worth it. The bouldery terrain above the crux 'bad step' has a wild feel to it, and offers interesting if not intricate scrambling, and some great positions if you care to seek them out – including fantastic views from the edge of Scafell Crag – with a little route finding thrown in (the rock marks are not that obvious). In poor visibility the blocky terrain is potentially confusing,

and certainly best avoided as a descent if you have not already gone up it.

Mickledore, the col linking Scafell Pike and Scafell, from Great Moss

Ascent

This description assumes generally good conditions, because in the wet it is best avoided, certainly for first-timers. Begin at

191

Fat Man's Agony, the narrow cleft in the rock at the bottom of Broad Stand, found on the left of the ridge. Opening out onto Mickledore at one end it literally forms the entrance to this route. Squeeze yourself through the short, open-top tunnel to emerge onto the first of a series of compact, sloping rock shelves. The move up to the next shelf is via a slanting step on the left, which brings you out onto a short, exposed scramble up smooth rock slabs, angling upwards from left to right. Steady yourself for a couple of moves, because the exposure is very significant – it's not a place to fall, and leader-placed protection is encouraged. Once the lead has reached the next horizontal ledge at the top of the slab, there are good belays above for protecting the second up onto the ledge.

The Crux

The 2.5m slightly overhanging corner wall at the back of this ledge is the make or break of your attempt on Broad Stand. It's a classic 'bad step'. Again, leader and second protection is essential for all but very competent rock climbers, given the sloping aspect of the small platform you are now on, and the potentially very tricky moves ahead. Again, the exposure is deceptively serious.

The most obvious way over the steep wall is either up the vertical corner (the best handholds are at the top of the corner) or head on, although the footholds are smooth, spread out, usually greasy, and awkward for the inexperienced. Some of the handholds above are not much better. A groove in the wall over on the left-hand side offers an alternative, but this is more seriously exposed still (particularly for the lead). Handholds are a bit better in the groove and the crucial move involves getting a foot up into it – possibly easier for a second with rope assistance!

Don't Take Short Cuts

The situation on this section of Broad Stand is one where you might be tempted to get by with a classic leg-up for the lead (!), but this is not a great idea. It's not good climbing practice but, far more importantly, it would not be easy to secure the second (the one giving the assistance) during the manoeuvre, bearing in mind that a secure belay involves having your hips below the height of the anchor, and the rope to the climber tight and stable. Climb it properly, or go and get some more practice.

Depending on the ability of both lead and second a 'one step at a time' approach may be advisable. Rather than the lead running out a rope length and then inviting the second to follow, a better approach would be to set up a 'bombproof' belay for the second on the shelf directly above the crux.

Once you do surmount the 'bad step' you are literally over the main problem – and still only about 10–15m above Mickledore. A slabby, stepped corner now requires care, and is still exposed, but a flattening (and a flattened cairn) mark the top of the steps, where the terrain broadens out into an atmospheric bowl. The way ahead is directly upwards and trends slightly leftwards over pleasing, bouldered terrain, heading for a small notch in a rib on the left-hand side. Continue up towards the plateau via Mickledore Chimney, taking care not to dislodge any stones onto climbers on the path below the East Buttress. As you pick your way though the rock scenery, exiting at the impressive sight of Scafell Pinnacle at the top, you will enjoy a sense of satisfaction at having achieved one of the most coveted and enigmatic mountaineering traverses in Britain.

Descent

If you struggle with the crucial moves on the ascent of Broad Stand but still want to make the traverse, it may be enjoyed perfectly well as a descent. Coleridge, it seems, took the direct route down the slabs unroped, and definitely did not enjoy the experience. Nevertheless it is feasible for the competent mountaineer with abseiling skills and equipment to find a safe way down, and it can be satisfying in its own right, not just as an alternative to going up for those who can't make it over the 'bad step'. Good conditions are important, especially if you have not ascended the route and are unfamiliar with the terrain.

Assuming you have made your way down to the top of the 'crux' steps (a large flattened cairn marks the spot where they descend off in a series trending rightwards) you may choose to follow them down in a series of small abseils and lowers. Alternatively you can nip round to the left (as you descend) from the top of the steps, until you are almost directly above (but not far above) the line of Mickledore. A large boulder here provides a perfect abseil point, enabling you to complete the crux of this famous traverse.

Top Tips

- Don't tackle Broad Stand if it's wet or if you're in a hurry.

- Before you embark on this notoriously awkward little route, make sure you have the ability to retreat safely if you need to.

Pinnacle Ridge

Location	St Sunday Crag, Lake District
Grade	3***
Maps	OS Explorer OL5 1:25 000 The English Lakes: North Eastern area
	OS Landranger 90 1:50 000 Penrith and Keswick, Ambleside
	Harveys Superwalker 1:25 000 Lakeland Central

Most hillwalkers asked to name two classic Lakeland ridges would almost certainly come up with Striding Edge on Helvellyn and Sharp Edge on Blencathra. Both are fine grade 1 routes – the former longer, the latter more of a scramble – but neither requires technical skills nor equipment. Striding Edge owes its grade to its situation and one 'bad step', but is not a sustained scramble. Sharp Edge is a superb short scramble but, while capable of producing the odd leg wobble, it is neither too difficult nor scary for most hillwalkers with a decent head for heights. You may have done both already, and if you have its odds on you didn't need a rope. Now you fancy something a bit more serious. Welcome to Pinnacle Ridge on St Sunday Crag.

You'll find Pinnacle Ridge – if you look carefully – on the craggy, broken, north-western face of St Sunday Crag, that drops down into Grisedale, the flat-bottomed valley that runs south west from Patterdale on the A592. Exposed situations, good holds, manageable moves, plenty of protection, a

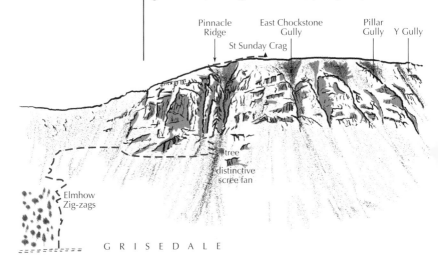

Pinnacle Ridge   East Chockstone Gully   Pillar Gully   Y Gully

St Sunday Crag

tree

distinctive scree fan

Elmhow Zig-zags

G R I S E D A L E

pleasant walk in, good access without crowds, and a peak at the top of the route – Pinnacle Ridge has everything you look for in a classic grade 3 scramble, and to climb it on a good day could well be the most fun you'll have in the Lake District without your rock shoes on. True, it involves one rock pitch at Difficult level, but in the context of the route this is manageable and, along with a couple of other challenging situations, is what makes Pinnacle Ridge a perfect scrambling experience.

The famously photogenic pinnacles of Pinnacle Ridge in the Lake District

The other beauty of Pinnacle Ridge is its location. One of the greatest attractions of the Lake District

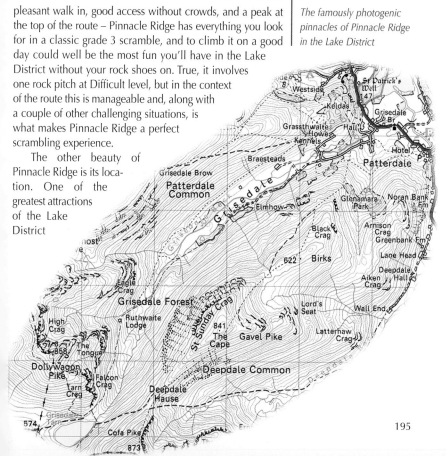

195

mountains is the number of 'horseshoe' walks that fit neatly into a satisfying day. Ascending Pinnacle Ridge, after starting in Patterdale, brings you up almost directly onto the top of St Sunday Crag (841m) in an ideal location to continue up and over Fairfield, just along the ridge to the south east, and complete any number of circuits, including the option of descending Helvellyn via Striding Edge. Having just climbed Pinnacle Ridge it would make an interesting comparison.

Approach

The walk in to Pinnacle Ridge is one of the many pleasures of this route. The best place to park is along the lane just off the Patterdale road at Grisedale Bridge. After a few hundred metres of tarmac, the path continues up the floor of Grisedale on its southern edge until you reach the buildings at Elmhow, and a pine plantation to the left of the track.

Route

Immediately after Elmhow Plantation, bear left directly up the grassy slope along its edge, and left again at its top corner to follow the grassy Elmhow Zigzags, which gradually become more defined as you ascend.

The zigzags lead up to a large, horizontal, grassy terrace, with the path marked on the OS map continuing up the slope towards the skyline of St Sunday Crag straight ahead. The faint path for Pinnacle Ridge, however (which is not marked on the OS Explorer map – although Pinnacle Ridge is) heads right at this point, traversing the terrace in a south-westerly direction, very soon crossing an obvious beck which forks very close to this point. Continue the flattish traverse on about the same contour, although the path, less distinct in places, descends slightly as you pass through a grassy boulder field. Do not attempt a rising traverse towards the crags that you see ahead. The path is much more straightforward and will bring you to the easiest point from which to locate Pinnacle Ridge. The obvious ridge that you can see ahead on the skyline is not Pinnacle Ridge – the first challenge that St Sunday Crag throws down is how to locate and identify it.

There are plenty of good landmarks, the best of which is an obvious scree fan. The path soon crosses this directly and comes to a full stop at its far edge. This point can also be identified by a rowan tree and a large boulder. Pinnacle Ridge is now directly above you, with an obvious deep gully directly on its right-hand side. Around 50m above you there is also a small rowan in the gully on the right-hand side.

Belaying the first awkward slabs on Pinnacle Ridge

Even in good visibility this bouldery and jagged landscape can be a bit confusing, and to identify the start of the scramble precisely it is useful to retrace your steps back 30m or so to the other edge of the scree slope. Directly below you in the valley base you will see (again, assuming good visibility) a sheepfold and a footbridge. Looking up from here you will see a prominent cannon-shaped block leaning at an angle of about 45° from right to left – it is about halfway up Pinnacle Ridge. Walk directly up, with the scree slope on your right, and you will find a small cairn right at the base of the rocks directly above the scree. This is the start of Pinnacle Ridge, and the gully you could see from below runs directly up its right-hand side. It should be noted, before you begin in earnest, that the difficulties of Pinnacle Ridge can generally be avoided by a gully path on the left-hand side. But if you do take this option you will miss out on the special experience of the ridge, so keep it as a last resort.

Start just to the left of the obvious gully, scrambling easily up the crest of blocks and keeping towards the right-hand edge of the buttress you are now ascending, for around 100m. The edge becomes exposed down into the gully as you progress, creating some excellent situations, but while care is required this section is exhilarating rather than scary. In bad weather, though, or if conditions are slippery underfoot you may consider using a rope.

Soon you arrive at the base of 5m or so of smooth, right-to left-angled slabs that herald The Cannon. Now things are getting more serious and there is plenty of scope, and real justification, for leader-placed protection, particularly in wet conditions. The final smooth slab can be avoided by moving right, round behind an obvious block.

The ridge continues to a prominent pinnacle that is strictly the preserve of rock climbers. Skirt it on the left, and round the back you will find a steep grooved wall with an obvious corner crack. This is the crux, and should be pitched for the purposes of the ascent, with a great belay stance on the small platform at the foot of the wall, secured by a threaded anchor in the back of the groove a few feet up. The wall offers about 15m or so of climbing up to Difficult standard, and can be slippery, but the opportunities for protection are good. Ascend the wall steadily, using leader-placed protection. Climb and place your gear with care and concentration and you should surmount the problem without too much difficulty.

At the top trend slightly left, to a good belay stance. Next work your way along the narrow and exposed crest to the final pinnacle, a grippy, steeply angled slab that provides all the best pictures of endeavour on Pinnacle Ridge! All along the way there are good holds on great rock, with excellent possibilities for protection. Pull yourself directly over the angled slab, and down its highly exposed edge on the other side to a mini col. Alternatively step through the obvious gap, face in, and step directly down a couple of moves before trending across towards the obvious gap a little lower down. Either way, all but competent rock climbers should protect this section. (If absolutely necessary moving left from an earlier belay stance offers the option of avoiding this pinnacle altogether.)

The continuation of the ridge pulls up the slopes on the other side of the gap and is relatively straightforward after what you have just done (take a moment to admire the position you have just experienced), although you may wish to stay roped up for now. A little way up a move left followed by the ascent of a few steep blocks leads you to the top of the route, emerging onto the wide ridge of St Sunday Crag. A few hundred metres along the main ridge to your right is the top of one of Lakeland's best-situated peaks.

What Next

Whether you head straight back down the north-east ridge of St Sunday Crag to Patterdale, or strike off south west for Fairfield and beyond, you are already guaranteed a day – combining walking, navigation, route finding, scrambling and ropework – that will enhance your mountaineering experience in an exceptional location.

Top Tips

- Go early and try to get the route to yourself. Give yourself plenty of time on the route to practise your skills and techniques, get to know your equipment, and complete the route successfully.

- If you're still working on your lead-climbing skills, Pinnacle Ridge is a great route to consolidate on. If you've done it once, think about doing it again. Practice on familiar ground is a great confidence builder.

- A dry day without too much wind will, as ever, make things easier and more enjoyable.

Curved Ridge

Location	Buachaille Etive Mor, Glen Coe
Grade	3*** moderate
Maps	OS Explorer 384 1:25 000 Glen Coe
	OS Landranger 41 1:50 000 Ben Nevis, Fort William and Glen Coe
	Harveys Superwalker Glen Coe 1:25 000

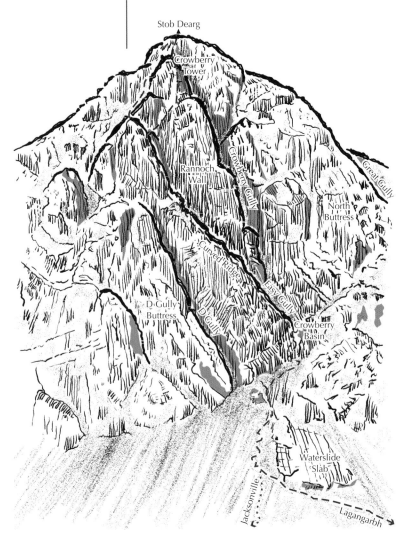

The Aonach Eagach may grab the headlines in Glen Coe as the finest ridge traverse on mainland Britain, but on your way west on the A82 it's quite impossible to miss the elegant lines of Buachaille Etive Mor taking up a pose that, for sheer mountaineering allure, competes with anything anywhere. The pyramidal bulk of the Buachaille – the Great Shepherd of the Glen – guarding the head of Glen Coe, throws down an irresistible gauntlet to any hillwalker. It's a picture-perfect mountain, and one which demands you do it justice. The answer is a day on Curved Ridge.

You only have to drive through Glen Coe on a moody day to conclude that the 'Glen of Weeping' is one of the most stirring places in the British Isles. Most who do so cross the wild and water-jewelled expanse of Rannoch Moor before Glen Coe's most defining image strikes an unforgettable blow on their psyche. Buachaille Etive Mor is a towering volcanic monolith that shouts 'Climb me!' every time you look at it. Curved Ridge ascends in a gentle arc that is among the more subtle of the striking lines – including famous names like Crowberry Ridge – that draw the eye from below. In terms of its situation alone, and not least its sensational views of Rannoch Wall and Rannoch Moor, Curved Ridge is a British mountaineering classic.

The 'business' end of the long Buachaille Etive Mor massif is Stob Dearg, the Munro peak at its north-eastern extremity. The name means

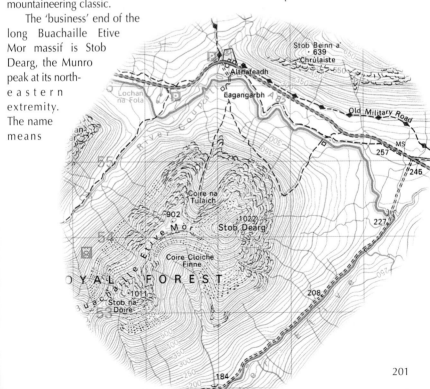

'Red Peak', after its appearance in certain spring, summer and autumn light. At the other end, 3km to the south west, lies 956m Stob na Broige (Peak of the Shoe), which you might want to include in your itinerary, easily taken in by a straightforward traverse along the ridge – the more relaxing leg of the day that lies ahead if you choose that option.

Rising almost vertically from the valley floor, Stob Dearg (1,021m) is one of Scotland's most-visited Munros, and home to some of the best mountaineering routes found in Glen Coe, offering high-quality and solid rock. Virtually surrounded by rugged steep to vertical ground, it can nevertheless be reached by the walker via the corridor of Coria na Tulaich. If you choose to ignore the easy option, though, you will be in good company – because when G.B.Gibbs made the first recorded ascent of the mountain in July 1886, it was via Curved Ridge.

Approach

To access Curved Ridge, park at Altnafeadh on the A82. There are usually spaces but arrive early at busy periods, just to be sure. Follow the path down to the bridge and over the River Coupall. Continue past the Lagangarbh hut and then fork left to contour round the end of the massif towards the eastern side of Stob Dearg.

Route

Before the scrambling begins you have to find the start of Curved Ridge. As you progress round and steadily up the mountainside, Broad Buttress and then Great Gully will appear on your right-hand side, with North Buttress dominating the skyline ahead. Once past North Buttress continue past the waterslide – a small waterfall with a massive slab and a stream below. Cross the stream, and continue on the path for 150m or so, when it rises suddenly up the mountain in a westerly direction. The left-to-right line of Curved Ridge, with Easy Gully and a steep rock face to its right, is above you.

Continue following the path up the steep terrain with a stream to your right-hand side. The path will veer right, then scramble through some rock shelves.

Continue ascending with Easy Gully on the right-hand side as you look up the mountain until you come to a buttress, the right-hand edge of which leads into Easy Gully itself. If you are in the right place you have reached an altitude of 630m, and the start of Curved Ridge. The route is well worn and the way ahead at this point is obvious.

Continue up the rib of rock that runs alongside Easy Gully. If you are fit and feeling confident you will probably make good early progress, with a nice combination of solid

*Elegant lines of rock arch-
itecture on 'the Buachaille'.
Curved Ridge is marked by
the light erosion patch on a
terrace half way up.*

holds and a steady angle. You might also be aware of the significant exposure of Easy Gully on the right-hand side. It's a taste of things to come, and a good indicator of why specific mountaineering skills are essential to enjoy the ascent of Curved Ridge in safety.

Sections of steep scrambling are interspersed with walking sections – although not, it should be stressed, with escape routes. You can use the easier bits to relax and check out the views across Rannoch Moor, but stay focused as you need to stay 'in the zone' for the harder stuff to come. As the ridge steepens with the increase in height, it may be time to assess your performance and that of your party – and don't hesitate to place protection if you feel it is necessary. Not that a fall is likely. The holds are excellent, but if a rope makes anyone feel more comfortable it is important to use one – enjoying scrambling on this kind of terrain is largely a mind game.

About 50m of scrambling brings you to a large wide flattening, from where the breathtaking Rannoch Wall can be

The sensational position of Curved Ridge, with Rannoch Moor behind
(Photo: Gary Latter)

viewed well on the right-hand side. Curved Ridge continues to snake its way through impressive rock scenery, and more easy scrambling leads to the upper section of the ridge. Here two 50m sections of exposed climbing are encountered, and it is certainly a good place to employ your rope skills, especially if the rock is wet.

Easy but enjoyable scrambling then leads to a narrowing and small flattening at the ridge end, where a small cairn can be seen opposite the top of Easy Gully. From this point – which is the top of Curved Ridge – there are two options to take you to the summit of Stob Dearg.

- **Option 1** – traverse the top of Easy Gully on the right with care, leading you onto the upper section of Crowberry Ridge – this involves 'moderate' climbing. Now follow the ridge to where Crowberry Tower is reached. On the right Crowberry Gully extends to a small col, Crowberry Gap. Descend Crowberry Tower via your ascent route for 20m, veering continually left to reach the top of an awkward step. Descend this step 5m to the narrow col below (Crowberry Gap) at the top of Crowberry Gully. A short scramble out of the gap up a narrow gully leads to the summit slopes.

- **Option 2** – from the top of Curved Ridge continue to traverse diagonally left under Crowberry Tower. This then turns right under the tower and up to the col (Crowberry Gap) from where you also take the short scramble out of the gap and up the narrow gully to the summit slopes.

Option 1 is the highest quality finish, option 2 more straightforward and shorter if you are pushed for time. If snow is present – as it often is in early spring – option 2 is very strongly recommended. Whichever way you choose, the views from the summit of Stob Dearg, notably across Rannoch Moor, are hard earned and well worth the effort.

What Next

The obvious continuation from the summit of Stob Dearg – and particularly if you favour a bit of 'bagging' with your scrambling – is to head for Stob na Broige, another Munro summit. If you're feeling energetic you might even do a round taking in the more diminutive Buachaille Etive Beag across the glen.

The best way to get directly off the mountain from Stob Dearg summit is to follow a well-marked path to the top of, and then into, Coire na Tulaich. When descending northwards stay left of the Allt Coire na Tulaich. Take care in poor visibility as this path can be less than obvious, and it's common to hear of parties getting disorientated (OK... lost!) between Stob Dearg and Corie na Tulaich. All being well, the Coire na Tulaich descent is reasonably straightforward after an initially loose 200m, and ultimately brings you right back to the car.

Descent via Curved Ridge

Some rock climbers will use Curved Ridge as a descent route, although we do not recommend that for readers of this book. In fact, most rock climbers prefer to ascend it, not least because it is a useful approach for climbing routes on Crowberry Ridge and the Rannoch Wall area.

Top Tips

- Plan to be at the start of the route by 9am, allowing two hours for the walk in.

- Choose a dry day – in wet conditions the rock can be quite slippy, and the route very serious in places, especially the steeper bits.

- Get your rope out and use it – on the first 50m pitch you will need a rope if following the crest proper, and the middle section holds two short pitches that are also very exposed. The rock is sound and the anchors are plentiful.

- If the route is very busy you can escape into Easy Gully from the middle sections of the ridge. The climbing does not get easier but you can escape from any build up of unnecessary queuing – not that Curved Ridge generally gets clogged up like some routes.

- Don't hang around. This route is deceptively long, and full of challenges – you need to keep moving on.

- Take plenty of body fuel – once you start scrambling there are no water supplies until you reach the descent path in Corie na Tulaich, and if you are staying high you will have to wait even longer.

- In early spring there is often snow at the top of Easy Gully, Crowberry Tower Gap and on the summit slopes. A rope should definitely be used, as the run outs in the event of a snow slide would be terminal.

Aonach Eagach

Location	Glen Coe
Grade	3(S)*** Moderate
Maps	OS Explorer 384 1:25 000 Glen Coe
	OS Landranger 41 1:50 000 Ben Nevis, Fort William and Glen Coe
	Harveys Superwalker 1:25000 Glen Coe

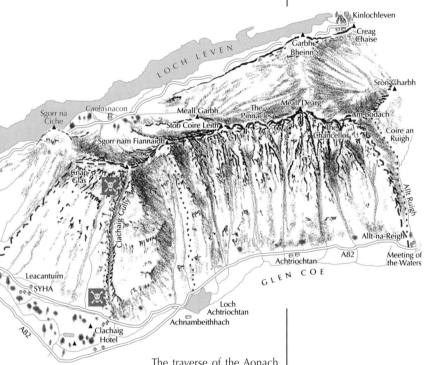

The traverse of the Aonach Eagach – the 'notched ridge' that forms Glen Coe's massive and menacing northern rampart – is rightly rated as not just one of the most popular, but also one the most testing scrambles on the British mainland. But the technical difficulties involved in traversing this stupendous line safely are often underestimated. The Aonach Eagach can, on its day, provide a serious challenge for an accomplished climber, and yet is one of those outings that pops up all the time in guidebooks aimed at hillwalkers. This is completely understandable for a route that is right at the top of many a walker's list of objectives. But 'walk' is a dubious description

What lies ahead? Contemplating the challenge of Aonach Eagach, Glen Coe

for a ridge that is sustained, frequently technical, highly exposed, slippery when wet, and pretty much 'out there' if you hit problems. The Aonach Eagach is a 'must do', but should be handled with care for maximum enjoyment.

The full ridge stretches from the Devil's Staircase in the east to the Pap of Glen Coe on its western end, but the main technical section is between Am Bodach (to the east of the Munro top of Meall Dearg) and the second and most westerly Munro summit of Sgorr nam Fiannaidh. Between these two points a long section of 'crazy pinnacles' provides a scrambling challenge to compete with anything in Britain. The first complete traverse was achieved in August 1895 by pioneering climbers A.R. Wilson, A.W. Russell and A. Fraser, around the beginning of the 'golden age' of climbing. Between then and around 1910 there were many first ascents of Scotland's classic ridges and rock routes, and the Aonach Eagach was up there with the best of them.

The fact that nowadays thousands attempt the traverse every year is no guarantee of success. For hillwalking mountaineers it's a major tick in the book, and offers a full-on day that, if all goes well, will not disappoint. Under wet or difficult conditions, though, Britain's premier mainland ridge traverse notches up a few more degrees of difficulty.

Planning and Preparation

The Aonach Eagach traverse is a big mountain day, so you should plan your tactics. Familiarise yourself with the route descriptions and start early

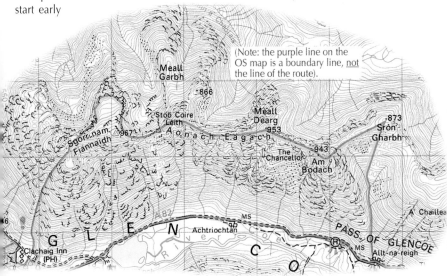

so you can finish in good time. The route can easily take around eight hours – longer in wet conditions. The slowest section is the pinnacles, where you will encounter full-on scrambling and, on good weather weekends, lots of traffic.

Like most routes in this book the best way to tackle the Aonach Eagach is to climb in pairs. You should plan to have the ropework skills for ascending, traversing and descending. Given a dry forecast a fit party moving well will take from six to eight hours. Allow up to two hours to the summit of Am Bodach, around four hours for the traverse and two for descent.

There are no water supplies on the crest, so drink plenty in advance and carry fluids too. The Aonach Eagach is no place to suffer dehydration. The ridge is long, committing and, in many ways, remote. It's a classic mountain day in all ways.

Approach

The Aonach Eagach is best traversed from east to west. Not only does that give 120m less ascent but, more importantly, better views. Start from the car park about 300m west of the white cottage of Allt-na-reigh. Either climb the broad south ridge directly to Am Bodach following a well-defined path for most of the way, or alternatively ascend to the right of the ridge along a branch path into the corrie east of Am Bodach, from where easy slopes ascend left to the high point.

Route

From the summit of Am Bodach continue along the ridge in a westerly direction. The first problem – the descent from Am Bodach – is well known and arrives immediately. This is essentially a big 'bad step' involving some down climbing, for which you should face into the rock. It can feel a bit dodgy in places, especially if it's wet. There is an awkward step on the north side, before moving back left where a short pitch descent is made. The holds are good and plentiful, and the next move is generally obvious. Nevertheless a fall would be very serious in places, and some people will find a rope distinctly reassuring. The difficulties should not be exaggerated, however – the bigger problems on the Aonach Eagach are yet to come – and there is plenty of scope for protecting the descent of Am Bodach.

Once past the difficulty, continue along the ridge very easily to the summit of Meall Dearg. The most interesting part of the ridge lies between Meall Dearg and Stob Coire Leith. The sustained and narrow pinnacled section begins

The many awkward steps of the Aonach Eagach are even trickier in the wet, when a rope makes a lot of sense

on the west side of the summit of Meall Dearg, with many awkward slabby descents and short but exciting pinnacles to climb. It's exhilarating scrambling, but requires great care and good technique. You'll want to keep moving but you should also reckon to use a rope on some sections. There is plenty of scope for direct belays to protect weaker members of the party without losing momentum.

The pinnacles are too complex to describe in detail, but work your way along the crest, using your route-finding skills to select the best line. In places the main path drops down below the crest, so don't lose concentration, particularly in poor weather. There are several points that present tricky, challenging and even surprising problems, but eventually the ridge widens and the terrain becomes easier to walk on, emerging at Stob Coire Leith, where the difficulties are behind you – provided you choose your descent with care.

The pinnacled section of the Aonach Eagach is very long – approximately 1,400 horizontal metres of up and downs. In good weather a traverse of the ridge provides a magnificent outing in superb surroundings, but wet weather and poor visibility will slow you down. Under these conditions you'll need to plan more time to safely complete the traverse. Remember that escape options are limited, to say the least.

Crux

In wet conditions the crux section (The Pinnacles) are potentially lethal as the rock is mostly mica schist, which can get very slippery. The rock tends to be very good when dry, and is sound in most places. The crest is very exposed with steep terrain on all sides, the only 'escape' routes available being the descents highlighted. There are plenty of good anchors for those using a rope on the more serious and awkward down climbs and ascents through the pinnacles.

Descent

The Aonach Eagach is a committing route in many different ways. One of these is escape. Remember that there are no safe descent routes on the Glen Coe side of the ridge between Am Bodach and Stob Coire Leith. Although climbers have been known to descend by abseiling down some of the south-facing gullies, this cannot be recommended. If a party has run out of daylight then it is best to either complete or reverse the ridge or, if you are prepared, stay put until it is light enough to complete your journey safely.

Once past Meall Dearg the first safe descent into Glen Coe encountered on an east–west traverse is the long slope leading down to Loch Achtriochtan from Sgorr nam Fiannaidh. A descent due south from this peak is safe (except in winter, when avalanches can pose a huge danger). Do not travel too far west, as you will find yourself in a rocky gully with a steep stream.

The safest way off the Aonach Eagach, especially in poor visibility and darkness, is to continue to follow the ridge west, then north from Sgorr nam Fiannaidh to the col before the Pap of Glen Coe. From the col descend south west and reach the old road between Bridge of Coe and Leacantuim Farm. When descending from the west end of the Aonach Eagach by this route avoid the fenced-off area above the youth hostel, which is private land used for livestock grazing.

Danger!

One descent option that **should be avoided under any circumstances** is the path on the west side of the gorge of Clachaig Gully. It is very steep, badly eroded and the scene of a depressing number of fatalities. The line of descent can be difficult to follow and conditions underfoot are treacherous. It may lead directly to your pint at the Clachaig Hotel, but there's a good chance you'll never get to drink it!

Top Tips

- On all the Scottish routes you must be careful in spring conditions as there can be much snow around at 2,500ft (763m) and above, especially in gullies and on open slopes. In spring the Aonach Eagach can be snowed up on many sections of the crest.

- Get a dry forecast.

- Do not attempt if covered in snow unless you have winter climbing skills.

- Leave early in the morning.

- Climb in twos or threes.

- Ensure you have the right skills for the traverse.

Cneifion Arête

Location	The Glyderau, Snowdonia
Grade	3(S)*** Difficult
Maps	OS Explorer OL17 1: 25 000 Snowdonia: Snowdon/Yr Wyddfa and Conwy Valley/Dyffryn Conwy
	OS Landranger 115 1:50 000 Snowdon and Caernarfon
	Harveys Superwalker 1:25 000 Snowdonia: The Glyderau and the Carneddau (Cwm Cneifion is indicated by name on OS Explorer, but not on Harveys Superwalker)

The Cneifion Arête is a sharp, alpine-style crest tucked away in an atmospheric cwm of the same name – Cwm Cneifion, the 'nameless' cwm – in the remote heart of the Glyderau, Snowdonia. When it comes to Welsh scrambling Crib Goch and Tryfan's North Ridge may grab all the headlines, but the Cneifion Arête is a different prospect altogether. It's technically far more challenging, and a British mountaineering classic in every sense of the word. You may see it given a grade 2/3, but we would call it serious 3s scramble or moderate

Glyder Fawr

Cneifion Arête

Cwm Cneifion

On the Cneifion Arete

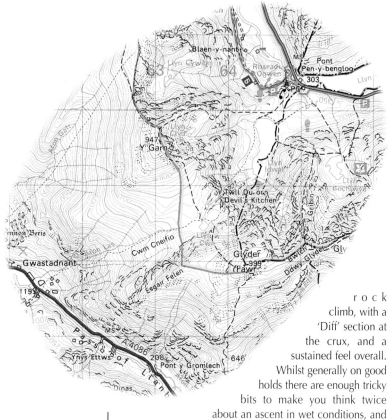

rock climb, with a 'Diff' section at the crux, and a sustained feel overall. Whilst generally on good holds there are enough tricky bits to make you think twice about an ascent in wet conditions, and the sheer drops to the north from the genuinely knife-edged crest means sensible folk will avoid it in strong winds.

Cneifion Arête is an arête in the true sense, a classic, jagged line of pinnacled rock rising directly from the floor in the north-eastern corner of Cwm Cneifion. It surmounts the western flank of Gribin Ridge, which provides a natural continuation route (at a much easier grade) to the summit plateau of the Glyderau, between the high points of Glyder Fawr or Glyder Fach. As such the arête is not only techni-cally and physically demanding but also slots neatly into any number of wider itineraries, making it a perfect 'crux' for a great day's mountaineering.

The setting and situation make for a memorable objec-tive, with variety and sustained interest that will push any thoughts of the daily grind far from your mind. You are forced to pay serious attention to your mountaineering. The Cneifion Arête is a 'must do' route, but not one that should be taken lightly.

Approach

There's plenty of parking off the A5 in the Ogwen Valley, but the prime spot is certainly Ogwen Cottage where space is limited. Starting early, walk steadily up on the constructed path to Llyn Idwal until you arrive at the outflow, then continue along its eastern side, taking account all the time of the ground rising up to your left.

Route

There are no paths up the hillside but after 500m or so, about 400m before you reach the Idwal Slabs, you come to a very distinctive free-standing rock next to the path that looks like a miniature Matterhorn. At this point break left up the slope, keeping to the left of the waterfalls that descend here, and make your way up into Cwm Cneifion. As you enter the cwm the Cneifion Arête forms the obvious wall on the left-hand side. An alternative, and more gentle, way to arrive at the base of the arête is to skirt along the western flank of the Gribin Ridge, below the crags on a path (not marked on OS maps) that runs high up on the Sub-Cneifion Rib, best accessed from the path that bears south up the Gribin Ridge from between Llyn Idwal and Llyn Bochlwyd. The arête appears on your left as you enter the obvious cwm. However you get here it's an atmospheric and lonely amphitheatre in the middle of one of the most popular mountain landscapes in Britain.

From some angles the Cneifion Arête can appear as a razor-sharp crest, and it does fall severely away down the right-hand side along its length. But inspection at the foot of the crag reveals that before you gain the crest a steep rock section has to be negotiated. It's a hard start, involving climbing to 'Diff' standard, and should be pitched. Walk up towards a grassy area to begin climbing towards the right of the base of the crag, heading initially back left on good holds, employing leader-placed protection. Only a rock climber would call this scrambling: it's exposed climbing in a serious situation. After 30m or so of ascent you arrive at an obvious ledge, beyond which a move left (that could prove awkward for the leader) brings you into the short groove of a chimney. The ascent of this leads to the crest itself, and a true appreciation of your position. The sweep of the arête angles perfectly and evenly upward, in a series of sharp fins. The moves get technically easier, but there is still plenty to concentrate on; the exposure alone justifies the continued use of the rope. Depending on the ability level of your team, continued pitching of the route or moving together are both options – the answer must be whichever feels safest and gives

The sharp line of the Cneifion Arete from the 'football pitch' on the Gribin Ridge, Glyderau. The route of ascent is on the other side of the arête.

most confidence and enjoyment. Use good technique – three points of contact at all times, take it steady and enjoy the situation. Follow the crest steadily up on great scrambling terrain to a point where there are some big flakes on the left-hand side. The holds are always good, as are the opportunities for placing protection, primarily by using the natural features of the rock. Soon the rock merges into the grass as you reach the plateau section of the Gribin Ridge, having gained less than 140m in height, but feeling like a great deal more.

For a continuation, a short walk south across a distinctive flat grassy area known as the football pitch brings you to the start of the Gribin Ridge's high-quality grade 1 scramble up onto the Glyder Plateau. You shouldn't need your gear for this, but you will still need your concentration and energy so it's a good time to take on some food and water. The direct line of the crest offers some adventurous scrambling with a degree of exposure on the left, but no real problems. You'll top out on the Glyder plateau, a bit less than 1km from Glyder Fawr, the highest point in the range.

What Next

There are numerous routes off the Glyder Plateau. Whichever one you select, apply your basic route-planning principles, according to weather, time and your overall objectives. Continuing your circuit via the Devil's Kitchen and Y Garn is perhaps the best option, giving you a chance to stay high while practising navigational skills in a classic mountain setting. It will also, by dropping down off the ridge to the north of Y Garn's summit, bring you back to Ogwen Cottage. The weather can change fast on the Glyderau, as anywhere in our mountains, so have in mind some escape routes, and tick them off as you go, whether you need them or not.

Clach Glas – Blaven Traverse

Location	Cuillin, Isle of Skye
Grade	3(S)*** Difficult (extremely exposed in parts)
Map	The best map for Blaven/the Cuillin Ridge is Harveys Superwalker 1:25 000 Skye: The Cuillin, aimed at the mountain walker (Cuillin Ridge enlarged to 1:12 500 on the reverse side)
	OS Explorer 411 1:25 000 Cuillin Hills
	OS Landranger 32 1: 50 000 South Skye and Cuillin Hills

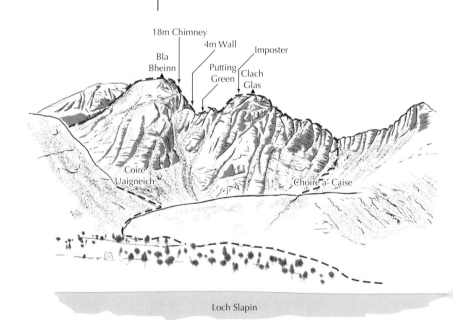

Loch Slapin

Blaven – or Bla Bheinn (928m) – stands alone, not just physically but also in terms of its reputation, and its spectacular situation at the head of Loch Slapin. 'The Blue Mountain' is the sole Munro on Skye that does not form part of the Black Cuillin Ridge, although it does link with the westernmost Red Cuillin. It was held by the great Skye pioneer Alexander Nicolson to be the finest hill on Skye, and not only does Blaven offer two summits for the price of one, and spectacular views across to the main Cuillin

Ridge, it also lies at one end of what is arguably the scariest ridge traverse in Britain. At the other end stands the Corbett of Clach-Glas, once dubbed 'the Matterhorn of Skye'.

Sometimes treated as a warm-up for the main course of the Cuillin Ridge traverse, the Clach Glas–Blaven traverse has sections of knife-edge exposure that make parts of the main Cuillin Ridge traverse look like an energetic picnic. It is not for the faint-hearted. It poses serious questions of skill and ability, with route finding, rope handling and the ability of at least one member of the party to lead to a 'Diff' climbing standard all required. But in good conditions accomplished climbers manage it unroped with no trouble, and while that is not something we would recommend in the context of this book, it does suggest that – with the right skills and mind-set – the Clach Glas–Blaven traverse is a reasonable objective for the ambitious hillwalking mountaineer, albeit a testing one.

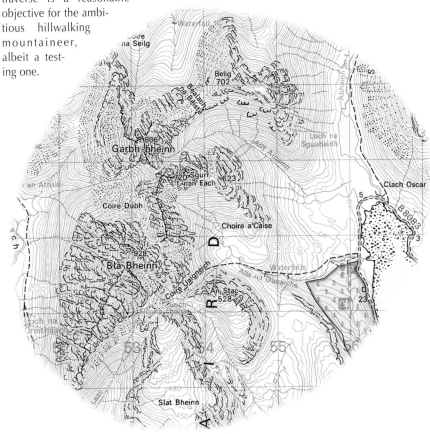

Access to the Isle of Skye

These days car is the best and most popular way of getting to Skye, via the toll bridge at Kyle of Lochalsh. From April to October you can also still get the ferry from Glenelg to Kylerhea. The other option is by ferry from Mallaig to Armadale in the south of the island, which operates from March to October. If you have no car and plenty of time you can get a train to Kyle of Lochalsh and then a bus on to the island.

Approach

Take the road from Broadford round the head of Loch Slapin, with the line of the traverse clearly visible on the high horizon to the west, and sometimes reflected in the waters of the loch as you drive along the eastern rim (weather permitting). Park in a good car park on the right just south of where the road crosses Allt na Dunaiche about 1km down from the loch head on the west side.

Route

Start a steady walking ascent over heathery and, at times, swampy terrain on the path that runs alongside Allt na Dunaiche. Follow the path for about a mile with the Blaven massif – and the horizon line of the traverse – looming directly ahead, before striking north west over rising ground through Choire a Caise. This eventually leads to scree slopes rising alongside a glowering rock buttress on your left. Eventually you arrive at a bealach (or col) with the summit ridge of Sgurr nan Each leading off to your right, and Clach Glas, Blaven and the line of the traverse now hidden away to your left (south). This is a good place to gear up, take some fluids and focus on what lies ahead.

To leave the bealach and begin the traverse, ascend a steep little wall to the south, up and out it. Alternatively, a rising gully leading to the left of the wall offers pleasant scrambling up onto slabs and an obvious crest. Gain and follow the crest, which will lead to a gap on the Loch Slapin side. Then continue to scramble along a short arête (very exposed). Continue to traverse on easier ground below the main crest of the ridge. Rejoin the ridge by pulling up through a small notch, and from here continue to follow the crest proper, where another exposed narrow neck of rock will be encountered. Care should be taken in wet conditions. A steep and exposed descent leads down the main crest of the ridge. Continue along until a steep drop appears. If you have not already employed one, a rope is certainly preferable at this point. If down climbing, go down left and then back to the right to reach a narrow col. From the bed of a gully continue

Mist eases the mind-boggling feeling of exposure on The Imposter, Clach Glas summit

*The Clach Glas – Blaven traverse saves one of its many tricky
bits for the end: climbers in the 18-metre chimney*

to follow the crest until another wide scree-filled gully is reached. Look out for a slanting V-shaped groove and continue bridging past some awkward chockstones with a slabby wall on the right-hand side. This wall can also be climbed from halfway up the groove, which leads to a short, sharp arête. At the end of the arête, turn a small ledge on the left. The next pitch is direct, 50m, and a sustained and spectacular position. Turn right along the ridge to gain an excellent patio that forms the summit of Clach Glas.

Descent from Clach Glas

Continue along the crest with care. Where it suddenly steepens, a sharp edge appears with a vertical drop on the right, and the slabs you are standing on drop away eerily to the left. This section is known as The Imposter, and is at the heart of one of the most adventurous sections of the traverse. Continue along a well-defined arête, with exposure on all sides. The route now leads to a fine breast of rock; turn this on the left at its top. Continue down exposed slabs, to where a small path is gained. Follow this path to the right and continue to follow the ridge. Where the slabs steepen, veer left to the second breast of rock. Descend a long, slanting slab on the Loch Slapin side. Follow a faint path veering to the right which leads to a gully with a chockstone in it. Continue on a traverse on ground which inclines steeply

Mountaineers contemplating the tricky descent of the Imposter, Clach Glas summit

from left to right. A steep drop will appear. This is the top of Bealach Tower, and an awkward and exposed descent is required. This can be descended directly, or traversed from right to left. Gain a faint path on the Loch Slapin side and continue into a gully. From the gully climb out, following the crest. This now leads to an area known as the Putting Green, a large flattening between Clach Glas and Blaven. You can escape from the putting green by descending the screes on the Loch Slapin side (the route is obvious). In wet and windy weather this section is extremely serious.

From this point there are great views of the Prow, Blaven's spectacular buttress, rightly famed for its rock climbing.

Continue to Blaven

From the Putting Green follow an obvious path which veers to the left and then back to the right. At the top of a gully The 4-metre Wall is encountered. Climb this wall – horrible when wet, and worth protecting with a rope in any conditions. This leads to a loose, slanting scree slope. Follow a faint scree path leading right. This leads to an obvious left-slanting groove, which in turn leads to a leaning terrace. Look out for an 18m-high, grooved chimney, which is sustained at 'Diff' grade, with excellent situations for the final climb.

From the top of the chimney, step over a right-slanting rib of rock into a broad gully. Turn left and climb to the col. Half-crown Pinnacle is on the left-hand side. Follow the tourist path to the summit of Blaven and – on a good day – enjoy the vista of the whole Cuillin Ridge spread out before you to the west.

Descent from Blaven

The descent from the summit is a straightforward affair, heading down into Coire Uaigneich on a well-worn tourist path, although you may wish to take in the south summit first, staying high for as long as possible and enjoying the well-earned situation. Whatever you choose to do from this point, the Clach Glas–Blaven traverse will have guaranteed you a no-holds barred mountaineering outing to savour.

Top Tip
- Avoid the traverse on wet or windy days.
- Be prepared! – physically, technically and psychologically.

Coire Lagan Round

Location	Black Cuillin, Isle of Skye
Grade	3 (S)*** Moderate (with Difficult option)
Map	The best map for the Cuillin Ridge is Harveys Superwalker 1:25 000 Skye: The Cuillin, aimed at the mountain walker (Cuillin Ridge enlarged to 1:12 500 on the reverse side)
	OS Explorer 411 1:25 000 Cuillin Hills
	OS Landranger 32 1: 50 000 South Skye and Cuillin Hills

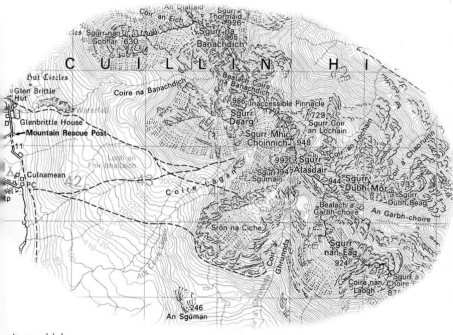

It would be easy to say that the Black Cuillin of Skye – Britain's finest mountain range – needs no introduction. In terms of its reputation that may be true. But for anyone with ambitions to experience this spectacularly twisted and vertical landscape for themselves, there is nowhere in the land that requires more planning, preparation, competence – or effort! – than the Cuillin Ridge.

A Distinguished Record

Skye has a history of pioneering mountain climbs, and also the only recorded tradition of mountain guiding in Britain, dating back to 1874 when local man John MacKenzie guided the first ascent on Sgurr Dubh with Alexander Nicolson. MacKenzie went on to be involved in practically every major ascent over the next 50 years.

The alpine nature of the Cuillin offers some of the very best mountaineering to be found in the UK, along a jagged ridge that stretches chaotically for more than 11km (7 miles) on rock types that comprise some of the grippiest and (when wet) 'slippiest' anywhere. It's most famous for its gabbro, a flesh-eating monster that will tear at gloveless hands, but that provides superb friction. After a light shower in places such as the basalt Thearlaich Slabs, you may wish for the whole ridge to be made of gabbro. The Cuillin is famous for other features, of course, such as the Inaccessible Pinnacle – the only Munro top that necessitates rock climbing – and also for giving unreliable compass readings. This problem can be overcome by good methodical compass work: if you take several bearings they will, on the whole, be accurate, and the rogue ones will stand out. But you should never believe (and act on the fact) that, as you are on a ridge, the correct route can only be one way or the other – that is simply not true here.

The complete traverse of the main ridge, taking in all 11 Munro summits, is a huge undertaking at any time. It may have been done in a record time of around 3 hours 30 minutes, but two to three days is far more common, and even more so is failure to complete it. To do so successfully is to undertake what is probably the finest mountaineering trip anywhere in Britain, one that perhaps requires a degree of rock-climbing ability (if nothing else) that put it a little beyond the immediate scope of this book.

Nevertheless, it's perfectly realistic for any fit and active hillwalking mountaineer to have the Cuillin traverse in their sights as an ultimate goal, whether assisted or independently, and the best chance of achieving it is to play the 'long game': it's most important to get solid experience on sections of the Cuillin Ridge before attempting 'the big one'. The Cuillin is not like other British mountain ridges – in purely navigational and route-finding terms it is often easier to go wrong than right, with serious consequences a distinct possibility – so an approach that helps you to establish a level of familiarity with this extraordinarily committing and disorientating

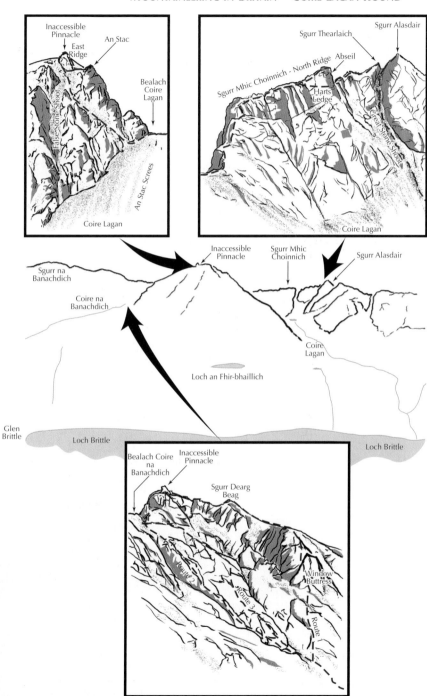

Typical Cuillin scrambling (grade 2/3) on the west ridge of Sgurr à Mhadaidh – not on the Coire Lagan round, but a classic way to access the main Cuillin ridge

terrain is a must. With the requisite skills and equipment, the Coire Lagan round is an excellent objective with which to begin your Cuillin quest.

So, how do you start to tackle the Cuillin? The ridge has numerous exciting and challenging sections, but the Coire Lagan round also combines some of the best-known peaks – the Inaccessible Pinnacle, Sgurr Mhic Choinnich, Sgurr Thearlaich and Skye's highest peak, Sgurr Alasdair – with some of the finest situations. In good weather, with fitness, determination, and the right approach and skills, there is every chance of tackling it successfully.

Whatever your ambitions on the Cuillin, you should never underestimate it. This is serious mountain country in any conditions, and the utmost care should be taken, including in planning and preparing your visit. Tackling the Cuillin is a markedly different experience from anything else in Britain. It demands sound scrambling and route-finding skills and, very importantly, the ability to decide when to turn around, and how to escape, if the weather is closing in.

If you enjoy the Coire Lagan round there are many other classic routes too numerous to mention here, but the SMC's *Skye Scrambles* guide will point you in the right direction.

Approach to Glen Brittle

Most visitors need to spend at least two days on Skye for it to be worthwhile. Devoting a week to it will increase your options and your chances of success, whatever your objective, not least because you are more likely to get the all-important weather window.

Getting to Skye is relatively straightforward (see page 222) particularly now that the bridge links the mainland at Kyle of Lochalsh to Kyleakin on the island. From there follow the A87 (T) to the Sligachan Hotel, then take the A863 Dunvegan road, before turning left onto the B8009 towards Carbost, finally turning left at Merkadale onto the single-track road leading down to Glen Brittle. Follow this road for 7 miles and park at the telephone box just beside the farm and the BMC memorial hut. There is enough space on the verge for a few cars.

The Coire Lagan Round

The Coire Lagan circuit is a big commitment and we will deal with it in sections. For the first of these there is also a range of degrees of 'difficulty', hence some options are given. We have tried not to be prescriptive about timings in this book, partly because calculating these is one of the skills of planning a mountaineering outing. Nevertheless, we believe the overall time you should allow in this case is around 10 hours, if all goes well.

Approach

From the Glen Brittle Memorial Hut follow the well-trodden footpath leading eastwards towards Coire na Banachdich, which travels alongside the Allt Coire na Banachdich, the stream that pours from this spectacular amphitheatre. Cross the stream on a footbridge and head up the hillside to the edge of Eas Mor, then head left around its eastern end – avoid following the path into Coire Lagan. A path south of Allt Coire na Banachdich leads to the lower corrie. Continue walking in on stonier ground. You will see Banachdich Gully, a deep chasm high up to the left of the coire. From the lower corrie there are three routes you can choose to the top of Sgurr Dearg (978m).

Route 1
Window Buttress Difficult** 90m

You will find Window Buttress about 600m up on the southern side of Coire na Banachdich. These days it is often used as a route on the way up to the Inaccessible Pinnacle, but was first climbed in 1906 by Norman Collie. Its history and situation make it a Skye classic in its own right.

The demands of the Cuillin also bring rewards: the view south from Sgurr na Banachdich

Having identified where you need to be on your walk in, a scramble up slabs brings you to the base of the

Window Buttress, where the climbing begins on good holds, taking you initially a little rightwards, before trending left. Then go right into a groove which shortly brings you to a ledge. Ascending a second groove takes you past some large blocks, before facing the crux, which comes in the form of a steep corner above a ledge. Carry on up the obvious slabs to arrive at the window-shaped stack of blocks from which this route derives its name. Routes on the window itself are problematic and best avoided. This can be done by going left and climbing another obvious groove to a large ledge, and continuing to the crest ridge of Window Buttress. Over the other side of it you will see a gully that leads to a neck of rock, but instead of dropping down at this point remain on the crest and ascend steeply to the high point of a pinnacle, from where access into the neck is simple. Descend into it and continue up good rocks on the other side, scrambling at grade 3. Route finding is straightforward, first trending right and then left, before continuing up corners, slabs and finally a long pull up a bouldery ridge to emerge on screes beneath Sgurr Dearg Beag. Continue easily to the summit of Sgurr Dearg where the Inaccessible Pinnacle dominates the skyline (and, almost immediately, your thoughts).

Route 2
Banachdich Slab Grade 3**
This is perhaps a more interesting approach, which brings you out at Bealach Coire na Banachdich (851m) at the head of the corrie. It is a 'top-end' grade 3 scramble with little relief, and far more difficult (and best avoided) when wet.

Just to the right of Banachdich Gully ascend the rocks that mark the start of this route, then continue up a corner before trending rightwards across slabs. It's very enjoyable climbing and a move-by-move description is not necessary as long as you are well prepared and concentrate on picking the best line at each point. Essentially you follow your nose as the route progresses, encountering broad ledges and steep faces, which can be negotiated or avoided by moving to the left and right as you work your way up. Finish at the bealach proper and then continue up the broad ridge to the summit of Sgurr Dearg.

Note
Do not be tempted to go into Banachdich Gully, a serious undertaking that, even in dry conditions, is graded Very Difficult.

Route 3
Easy Path Route Grade 1

This is the easiest route by far at this stage, but nevertheless a perfectly reasonable option at the start of what will be a committing day's mountaineering. If you're all psyched up for the In Pin as the first big challenge of the day, don't feel that you're bottling out by taking the path here (it's hardly a stroll!) bearing in mind what lies ahead, and how you and your team have planned the day. The well-defined path follows the stream on the right side of Coire na Banachdich, eventually contouring the hillside back to the left and up to Bealach Coire na Banachdich proper. From the bealach, continue south and follow a broad ridge up to the summit of Sgurr Dearg.

From the summit of Sgurr Dearg carry on scrambling to the base of the east ridge of the Innaccessible Pinnacle, dropping down the slabs on the south side.

The Inaccessible Pinnacle (In Pin) 986m
East Ridge Moderate*** 70m

Every aspiring Munroist knows the Inaccessible Pinnacle – the real summit of Sgurr Dearg – as the one Munro you can't have without rock climbing (and perhaps a little help from your friends). But nothing can adequately prepare you for the awesome sensation of scaling this extraordinary blade of gabbro. It's an amazing climb with mind-boggling 'double' exposure but, contrary to its reputation, not actually too hard. The holds throughout are excellent and make the route feel very secure but, given its situation, if you do it independently you will have a justifiable sense of achievement.

Start Early

The Inaccessible Pinnacle was first climbed by the Pilkington brothers and John MacKenzie in 1880. Presumably that was on a quiet day but now, if you want to avoid queuing for the route, you should try to be at the base of the East Ridge well before 10am, especially at weekends and on Bank Holidays.

Walk down the huge sloping slabs to the south of the In Pin to reach a wide platform, with a small stone bivi circle at the bottom. Climb up the side of the 'fin' and continue on up to the crest via big holds, in the obvious direction until you arrive at a not particularly good belay stance. The ridge steepens for a while – really this is the crux section – and it's hard not to be aware of the adrenaline-pumping exposure. If you climb carefully, however, there is plenty of

A climber on the East Ridge of the In Pin – spectacularly exposed, although only graded 'Moderate' in rock climbing terms

natural protection and on a good day, the views – if you care to take them in – are sensational. Soon the angle eases (along with the heart rate) and you find yourself pulling up onto the flattening summit ridge. Continue on to the top, and descend a step to the summit blocks perched on a sloping ledge. Some people can't resist climbing onto the summit blocks to complete the experience – others have no problem not doing so.

Descent from In Pin

Descent is usually made by way of a 20m abseil down the steeper western end from a piece of steel cable at the foot of the big Bolster Stone boulder. When you get to the bottom, scramble back down the slab on the south side to the platform where you started the route.

Top Tips for the In Pin

- Leave your rucksack on the platform for the climb, and pick it up on the way back as you continue to travel south.

- The ascent should be protected at all times, the leader running out the full 50m of rope, before setting up a belay at the ledge by the summit blocks. The second should then begin to ascend, protected by the leader belaying from the top of the route.

- You can easily protect this ridge with slings and a small set of rocks on wires.

- The alternative is to take the ridge in two pitches with one intermediate stance.

- However you tackle the In Pin try not to hang around – while not rushing it – as you may find holding up or being passed by another group very unsettling.

An Stac 954m

An Stac is the next top, just a short distance away on the East Ridge of Sgurr Dearg. A trip to the top rewards the effort put in with great views. Follow your nose in a snaking ascent, staying mostly in the centre of the buttress. One word of warning: *descending An Stac's south face should not be attempted.*

To continue south after your ascent of An Stac, return to the obvious descending slab, passing the start of the East Ridge route of the In Pin on the way, and follow a brown-coloured slab down with a steep drop on your right-hand side – at the bottom an obvious traverse right is required, and you are now on scree. Follow this scree down for about 25m and scramble on to a neck of rock with a boulder. Do not follow the obvious scree descent at this point, as it leads to a nasty cliff.

Once through the neck of rock continue descending a brown-coloured slab with the An Stac buttress on your left-hand side. This leads down to a scree path that follows the An Stac buttress; then go straight up to rejoin the crest of the ridge to the Bealach Coire Lagan.

Follow the ridge proper until you need to descend 25m on the Coire Lagan side, remaining on the crest. You will arrive at a small col. On the east side is Rotten Gully.

Sgurr Mhic Choinnich 948m
North Ridge Grade 2**

Continue to Sgurr Mhic Choinnich via its excellent North Ridge. This is a superb undertaking and was understandably the first route used to climb the mountain by Charles Pilkington. Go down to the low point of the corrie edge, with the ridge rising obviously above, offering scrambling that is more involving than hard. Make your way up on small paths, then climb up grooves and blocks. Most of the route is on the west side of the ridge. Follow it until it levels out, and then on to a narrow crest, looking out for a slanting V-groove with a large boulder at the top. At the start of this groove, on the Coire Lagan side, is Hart's Ledge, and you may wish to return to this ledge once you have taken in the summit of Sgurr Mhic Choinnich. The crest now rises a little. Continue along it. On the east side it is noticeably slabby, so stick to the exposed knife-edge crest and follow it to the summit.

About 20m from the summit of Sgurr Mhic Choinnich is the top of King's Chimney, and a skilful and confident abseil down it is one way to join Hart's Ledge and Bealach Mhic Choinnich. If you are not entirely comfortable with that option, reverse the North Ridge to the start of Hart's Ledge.

Hart's Ledge
Grade 2

Hart's Ledge follows a very narrow and mind-bogglingly exposed path across the west face of Mhic Choinnich, creating a way from the North Ridge round to Bealach Mhic Choinnich. It is an extraordinary place for what is largely a footpath, and it feels like it. It is sometimes known as Collie's Ledge... but actually Henry Hart got there a year earlier in 1887!

The route on Hart's Ledge is obvious, and on the scrambling sections where the ledge merges into the face good holds are plentiful. But great care should be taken, especially in wet conditions when the basalt rock gets very slippery. At the end of Hart's Ledge descend a steep groove, and traverse a steep slab to the Bealach Mhic Choinnich proper. You might consider using a rope for all of this section.

Sgurr Thearlaich 978m
North Ridge Moderate

This is one of the best parts of the Cuillin Ridge, and undoubtedly one of the most exciting. From Bealach Mhic Choinnich descend slightly on to the west side of the Coire Lagan, and traverse to steep-looking rocks on the left. There's a narrow gully located 4m away with more steep rocks above it. Follow the rocks up beside the narrow gully and continue until a large prominent sloping slab can be seen on the right. Scramble across this slab to an exposed position on a crest, then trend left up this small crest to rejoin a broad section of the main ridge.

Follow the ridge and descend slightly to the top of a gully, which drops directly down to the Great Stone Shoot.

On the summit of Sgurr Alasdair, Coire Lagan Round

Cross the gap and follow the main crest of Sgurr Thearlaich, at times on the left-hand side. After a second gap the crest is very straightforward and pleasant to the summit of Sgurr Thearlaich. Descend the summit crest southwards until the crest ends and you can easily traverse right on to scree and walk back north for a short distance to the top of the Great Stone Shoot.

Sgurr Alasdair 992m

Sgurr Alasdair is the highest peak on the Cuillin Ridge, and slightly to the west of the main line of peaks, including Sgurr Thearlaich. It was first climbed in 1873 by Sheriff Alexander Nicolson, and is named after him. From the stony col at the top of the Great Stone Shoot a straightforward scramble brings you to the summit, and is something of a formality after everything else. Follow the short rocky ridge up, and return to the top of the Great Stone Shoot. Care should be taken in wet conditions.

Descent

Descend the Great Stone Shoot in the shadow of its great overbearing rock walls. It is quite wide, and underfoot is unstable scree. It can be a fast way down but particular care is needed where bedrock is exposed, and try not to knock loose stones and rocks into the path of parties lower down (ascending the shoot is painful enough, without that!).

Down in Coire Lagan pick up the main path that goes all the way down to the Glen Brittle campsite and beach. From the edge of the campsite follow a path north past some cottages and rejoin the main road through the farm to arrive at the car.

Tower Ridge

Location	Ben Nevis
Grade	Difficult***
Maps	OS Explorer 392 1:25 000 Ben Nevis
	OS Landranger 41 1:50 000 Ben Nevis, Fort William and Glen Coe
	Harveys Superwalker 1:25 000 Ben Nevis (Tower Ridge enlarged to 1:12 500 on the reverse side)

Tower Ridge is the biggest ridge on Ben Nevis – not just Britain's highest mountain, but also its most challenging. That there are very good reasons for the possible translation of its name as 'evil mountain' would, of course, be news to most of the trainer-clad day trippers who sweat up the rather dull tourist track on its western side on a summer's day. The name may owe something to the fact that the mainland's most complete mountain has many moods and, it's true, it can turn nasty. But 'The Ben' is by far Britain's most popular Munro. The 1,344m summit is visited by thousands every year and, of far more interest for our purposes, the various approaches to it include many of the UK's finest mountaineering routes. If

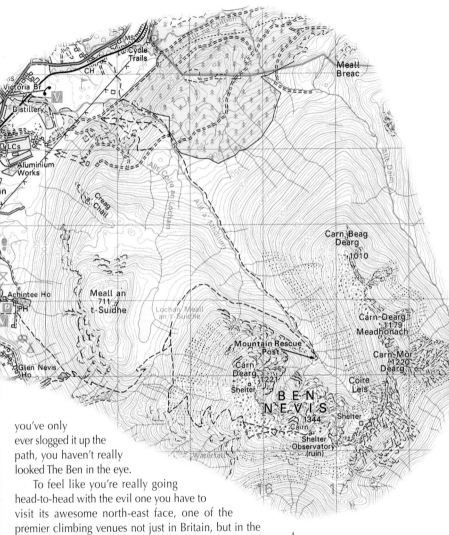

you've only
ever slogged it up the
path, you haven't really
looked The Ben in the eye.

To feel like you're really going
head-to-head with the evil one you have to
visit its awesome north-east face, one of the
premier climbing venues not just in Britain, but in the
whole of Europe. Over 1km high, it can be both a fearsome
and an exhilarating sight, and one that many hillwalkers are
happy to leave as just that. But for the aspiring mountaineer,
knowing you can take a classic route through this theatre of
rock is stirring stuff, for it contains some of the UK's longest
scrambling and climbing lines, including many 3-star clas-
sics through a wide variety of grades.

There's no question The Ben poses fine challenges for
any mountaineer, at any level, and the route we are aiming
for is one with impeccable 'classic' credentials: Tower Ridge.
Some indication of its seriousness, however, is indicated by

The famous North Face of Ben Nevis. Tower Ridge is the obvious central ridge line, with Tower Gap sunlit towards the top. (Photo: Gary Latter)

Noel Williams' decision not to include it in his excellent and essential guide *Scrambles in Lochaber*, because: 'An ascent of the entire ridge is, unfortunately, just a little bit too hard to be regarded as a scramble. It can be thoroughly recommended to those with climbing experience and it should serve as a goal for ambitious scramblers.'

Tower Ridge is one of the longest and most popular routes on Ben Nevis. If you're up for it, you'll love it. If not, wait until you are! The situation, exposure and route length of 1.5km makes Tower Ridge physically demanding and technically challenging too.

The First Descent

As for that little bit of climbing history that always adds something to a classic route, Tower Ridge has the unlikely distinction of having been negotiated downwards – on 3 September 1892, by the famous Hopkinson family – even before it was climbed. The ridge was not ascended until two years later by J.N.Collie, G.A.Sollat and J. Collier. Not to be outdone, however, this trio did it in winter.

To keep things simple, this book concentrates on a straightforward summer ascent. It's quite enough to be going on with. Given the right technical and physical preparation and a good weather forecast for your attempt on Tower Ridge, you can't fail to experience a comprehensive mountain adventure, combining hillwalking, navigation, the highest level of scrambling in some seriously exposed situations and, consequently, some ropework to see you safely through the crux sections.

When you combine all its elements, the ascent of Tower Ridge is a comprehensive and uncompromising mountaineering experience. Gain plenty of experience on a wide range of less committing top-end scrambles before you try it, including at least one other on the north-east face of Ben Nevis. One of the golden rules about making a safe transition from straightforward hillwalking to mountaineering of this sort is to know your limits and to operate within them.

The Tower Gap on Tower Ridge offers awesome exposure (Photo: Kirk Watson)

243

Other Ben Nevis north-face options before you attempt Tower Ridge could include:

Grade 1* –** *Ledge Route* This is an excellent line for getting a feel for the terrain on Britain's mightiest mountain face, though the early section of the route will cause serious problems for the scrambler until midsummer due to the accumulations of snow in Number 5 gully. For this reason it is best tackled later in the season.

Grade 3* –** *Castle Ridge* Not as steep as it looks from the Allt à Mhuilinn, this is a serious but a slightly easier alternative to Tower Ridge, although several steep sections still make rock-climbing experience (more importantly, ability!) advantageous and advisable.

Approach

There are generally no access restrictions in place when following the marked route from the North Face car park. However, the footpath following the Allt à Mhuilinn burn is in desperate need of repair, so expect to get muddy in the driest of weather. When walking in to any climb through cultivated land and forests always try to stick to a path or track, and follow the accepted practices and codes during the stalking season. Walkers who don't take care can do a great deal of harm to deer forests and grouse moors.

To get to Tower Ridge head for the North Face car park by turning off the A82(T) at Torlundy, and following the road over the old railway line before turning right. Follow the track until you reach the car park. From the car park follow the waymarked path which eventually meets the Allt a' Mhuilinn burn, then follow the path alongside the burn to the CIC hut.

The closer you get to the CIC hut, the more impressive is the looming presence of The Ben's imposing northerly aspect. It's a spectacular mountain setting on a grand scale that can make you feel quite insignificant. But don't be intimidated. Taking up a challenge in places like this is the very essence of mountaineering.

CIC Hut

The famous landmark of the CIC hut is part of the history of Ben Nevis. Located directly below the 2,000ft (610m) cliffs of the North Face, it was opened in 1929 in memory of Charles Inglis Clark, one of many young climbers to die in World War I. The hut made the North Face of The Ben really accessible to the early pioneers. Nowadays it can sleep up to 18, and also has a Mountain Rescue post.

Descending from the Summit Plateau of Ben Nevis

It's timely, in the case of this route, to look at the descent first. As ever, while your 'objective' will almost inevitably concentrate on the route up, planning the way down, round or wherever else you happen to be going, is equally important. Perhaps even more so, bearing in mind that descent is when most accidents take place.

On Ben Nevis planning your route down – and off the top, above all – is critically important. With the summit virtually surrounded by cliffs it's a very serious place to get lost, with at least three accident black spots. The only safe way back down for those unfamiliar with the area is the tourist track, and first you have to find it. People regularly get lost on The Ben's vast, featureless summit plateau, and in anything other than perfect summer conditions (rare) this can be disastrous.

No – the summit of Ben Nevis is definitely no place for your first lesson in navigation. You and your team should have map and compass ready and be able to use them with confidence, in any conditions. After a long climb – which Tower Ridge certainly is – you may be not only tired, but also running later than you anticipated. You will not be in a position to choose your conditions at the top. Be well prepared for getting off The Ben in any weather – study your descent plan in theory; write it down and take it with you; mark it on your map; stick to it in practice.

From the summit trig point, near the observatory ruins, follow a bearing for 231° grid for 150m – this will see you safely past the precipice of Gardyloo Gully, which drops directly down the north face. Once clear of Gardyloo, change bearing to 281° grid, and follow this from Gardyloo down to the middle of the zigzags of the main tourist path. This also avoids the infamous Five-Finger Gully on your left. Remember to map read, and aim to pick up the top end of Red Burn, now on your right-hand side. Follow the stony zigzag path down beside the Red Burn to where it traverses north across towards, and then above, the Lochan meall an t-Suidhe, below the little visited high point of Meall an t-Suidhe. From this point continue on the path to where it begins to double back to the CIC hut. Then head in a northerly direction until you reach the Allt a' Mhuilinn burn and continue down the footpath back to the car park.

Route

From the CIC hut look for the famous shape of the Douglas Boulder. If you miss it you're probably thinking too small, because this boulder is a spectacular dome of rock some 300m high. Tackling it head-on is a full-on rock-climbing proposition with grades at V Diff and above, so walk round the east side to the bottom of Observatory Gully. Once round the foot of the boulder scramble through the rocks above, to arrive at a grassy bay in the East Gully and on to the Douglas Gap, behind the boulder.

The first obstacle to negotiate from the Douglas Gap is a well-polished chimney that can be slippery when wet, but is essentially a moderate rock climb of about 20m leading to the crest of the ridge. Hitting the ridge is a moment of realisation of the seriousness of the commitment, as the scale of the massif becomes truly apparent. Continue until you soon meet a short overhanging wall. This is avoided by heading right and following a ledge which takes you onto a scrambling route at moderate climbing grade, leading to a level section.

Continue across two depressions, the second of which leads to the top of the Great Chimney, beyond which lies the Little Tower, a prominent rock feature blocking the line of the ridge. Climb this easily on the left edge – the situation is both exposed and spectacular – and follow a narrow and awkward ledge, where caution is required. The ledge leads to a right-hand corner, from where you climb easily to the top of the Little Tower. From here follow a rough, rocky, level section, before scrambling up easy ground to the base of the vertical rocks of the massive dome of the Great Tower. Continue on left round its north-east corner, known as the Eastern Traverse. Cross an exposed groove and enter the foot of a tunnel of rock. Climb through this and, at the top of the through route, exposed but obvious and easy climbing leads to the top of the Great Tower. In an extreme situation, it is also possible at this point to continue the Eastern Traverse to the foot of Tower Gully should you wish to escape off the ridge – but this is not a recommendation to do so!

Continue from the top of the Great Tower, making a slight descent, and traverse the narrow and highly exposed crest leading to Tower Gap. In windy conditions this is unlikely to be your favourite moment of the day, with an immediate 200m drop down the right-hand side.

The descent down into Tower Gap is awkward, especially in wet conditions, and requires great care. Moving out the other side is straightforward. Easy scrambling beyond the gap leads on to the final section of the ridge. At a steepening go to the right, via a ledge and groove, and reach the plateau.

Crux Moments

Tower Ridge has several crux sections, especially if the rock is wet:

- the chimney in the Douglas Gap – 20m of polished rock
- from the top of Great Chimney and on through the Little Tower

- the Great Tower section
- descending Tower Gap – a popular spot for winter benightment!

Summary

You'll need to know how to use your gear and what gear to take with you, along with well-practised ropework skills, including how to belay and abseil quickly and safely – check out the relevant pages for a skills update and revision and, before tackling Tower Ridge, get lots of practice in a less committing situation.

Top Tips

- Be aware and prepared for the scale and commitment of what you are taking on. To be fair, no one has ever described *this* route as a walk! For the hillwalker-mountaineer, Tower Ridge is a super-committing outing, and escaping off it in difficulties is a very serious proposition. Study the route in detail before you set off, and plan and prepare for the crux sections in particular. Tower Ridge is not a place to get confused, but neither is it a place to move slowly. You should know where you are at all times, anticipate what type of ground lies ahead of you and what will be required.

- It is well worth investing in the SMC's *Guide to Ben Nevis*, and using it in conjunction with your map to give a detailed Tower Ridge diagram. Use all this information to get to grips with Tower Ridge before you get out there. It will help you prepare mentally and technically and will greatly increase your chances of success.

- On a route such as this you should consider carefully which climbing partner will suit you best. Tower Ridge is long, arduous and should not be underestimated. Moving light and fast without compromising your safety is the key.

- This is no place to discover that your partner doesn't like exposure and doesn't know how to belay. Trying new skills here for the first time is only likely to result in panic, and possibly benightment if it causes delay.

- The best time to attempt Tower Ridge is from mid May to autumn, ideally in good, dry weather. High winds, poor visibility and heavy rain can make the route too treacherous. Snow can be present until mid June, so avoid any snow-covered terrain, especially snow gullies, if you go early to mid season.

- Finally, as ever, start early and plan to finish the route in good time. If you have poor visibility route finding, even though you are on a ridge, will prove problematic. Moving light and fast on Tower Ridge is the key to success.

APPENDIX

Further Reading

Inevitably we have referred to many sources in the preparation of *The Hillwalker's Guide to Mountaineering*, primarily to assist with route descriptions. Of course, ours is not a 'routes' book as such. The mountaineering passages we have featured are included not simply because they form part of great outings, but also because they provide a context (and a goal) for developing the specific mountaineering skills and knowledge discussed. There are many other routes that could have been included. While we have, between us, done all the routes covered, we are indebted to the authors of a number of guides whose work has been of great assistance when it came to drafting descriptions. If there are occasional echoes of their own words this may not simply be because we were passing over the same ground, but also because it would be very difficult to improve some of their descriptions: there seemed little point in trying to invent completely new ways of saying the same thing. That said, our view of some of the routes does vary significantly from that of other guidebook writers. Before embarking on any mountaineering outing it is always worth reading a number of descriptions of your objective, and that goes for those described in this book too. The following books – in no particular order – have been of most use to us, in some cases not merely as a source of practical information but also to give different perspectives, and even inspiration.

Allen, Bob.
On Foot in Snowdonia
(Michael Joseph, 1993)

Allen, Bob.
On High Lakeland Fells
(Pic, 1987)

Ashcroft, Jeremy.
Britain's Highest Peaks
(David and Charles, 1997)

Ashton, Steve.
Scrambles in Snowdonia
(Cicerone, 1992)

Birkett, Bill.
Great British Ridge Walks
(David and Charles, 1999)

Crumley, Jim.
Among Mountains
(Mainstream, 1993)

Drummond, Peter.
Scottish Hill and Mountain Names
(SMC, 1991)

Evans, Brian.
Scrambles in the Lake District
(Cicerone, 1996)

Hill, Pete and Johnston, Stuart.
The Mountain Skills Training Handbook
(David and Charles, 2000)

Williams, Noel.
Scrambles in Lochaber
(Cicerone, 1997)

Williams, Noel.
Skye Scrambles
(SMC, 2000)

Wilson Parker, J.
Scrambles in Skye
(Cicerone, 1995)

Wilson, Ken.
Classic Rock
(Diadem, 1979)

Other Useful Sources:

Heading for the Scottish Hills
(SMT, 1996)

Barton, Bob and Wright, Blyth.
A Chance in a Million?
(SMT, 2000)

Cliff, Peter.
Mountain Navigation
(Peter Cliff, 1991)

Long, Steve.
Hillwalking – The Official Handbook
(MLTUK, 2003)

Pedgley, David.
Mountain Weather
(Cicerone, 1997)

Phillips, Roger.
Wild Flowers of Mountain and Moorland
(Elm Tree Books, 1988)

INDEX

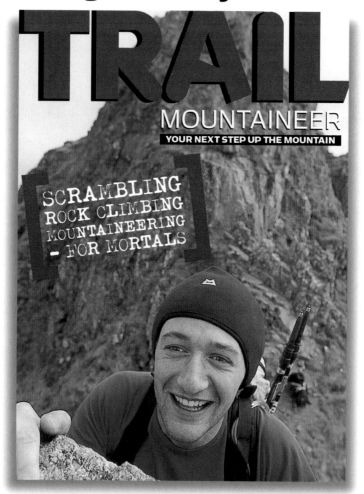

LISTING OF CICERONE GUIDES

Cicerone's mission is to inform and inspire by providing the best guides to exploring the world

Since its foundation over 30 years ago, Cicerone has specialised in publishing guidebooks and has built a reputation for quality and reliability. It now publishes nearly 300 guides to the major destinations for outdoor enthusiasts, including Europe, UK and the rest of the world.

Written by leading and committed specialists, Cicerone guides are recognised as the most authoritative. They are full of information, maps and illustrations so that the user can plan and complete a successful and safe trip or expedition – be it a long face climb, a walk over Lakeland fells, an alpine traverse, a Himalayan trek or a ramble in the countryside.

With a thorough introduction to assist planning, clear diagrams, maps and colour photographs to illustrate the terrain and route, and accurate and detailed text, Cicerone guides are designed for ease of use and access to the information.

If the facts on the ground change, or there is any aspect of a guide that you think we can improve, we are always delighted to hear from you.

Cicerone Press
2 Police Square Milnthorpe Cumbria LA7 7PY
Tel:01539 562 069   Fax:01539 563 417
e-mail:info@cicerone.co.uk   web:www.cicerone.co.uk

CICERONE